Praise for *The Business of Healthcare*

"The editors and writers of *The Business of Healthcare* have created a compelling and highly informative set of books that merge various disciplines and perspectives to create a comprehensive look at the challenges facing the healthcare industry. These books should prompt valuable discussion and, hopefully, action that will strengthen and advance the U.S. health system."

Craig E. Holm, FACHE, CHE
Health Strategies & Solutions Inc. Philadelphia

"Thoughtful and provocative, *The Business of Healthcare* is a clearly articulated exploration of critical issues facing healthcare leaders today."

C. Duane Dauner
President, California Hospital Association

"Just when the pressures and challenges on healthcare practitioners and organizations seem unbearable, Cohn and Hough have skillfully assembled this work which offers advice and comfort, not only on how to cope with today's climate, but how also to take advantage of the opportunities that abound while not abandoning the call to serve humanity."

Robert A. Reid, M.D.
Director of Medical Affairs, Cottage Health System,
Santa Barbara, California
Past president, California Medical Association

"Now, more than ever, this three-volume set is necessary and important. The format and breadth of content is impressive; rather than a prescriptive set of how-tos, I come away with an expanded vision of 'want to' and 'able to.'"

Leonard H. Friedman, Ph.D., MPH
Professor and Coordinator Department of Public Health,
Oregon State University

The Business
of Healthcare

Volume 3: Improving Systems of Care

EDITED BY
KENNETH H. COHN, MD
DOUGLAS E. HOUGH, PhD

PRAEGER PERSPECTIVES

Westport, Connecticut
London

Library of Congress Cataloging-in-Publication Data

The business of healthcare / edited by Kenneth H. Cohn, Douglas E. Hough.
    p. cm. — (Praeger perspectives)
  Includes bibliographical references and index.
  ISBN 978–0–275–99235–4 (set : alk. paper)
  ISBN 978–0–275–99236–1 (v. 1 : alk. paper)
  ISBN 978–0–275–99237–8 (v. 2 : alk. paper)
  ISBN 978–0–275–99238–5 (v. 3 : alk. paper)
  1. Medical care—United States. 2. Medical offices—United States—
Management. 3. Medical care—United States—Quality control. 4. Health
services administration—United States. 5. Health care reform—United
States. I. Cohn, Kenneth H. II. Hough, Douglas E. III. Series.
  [DNLM: 1. Delivery of Health Care—organization & administration—
United States. 2. Leadership—United States. 3. Practice Management,
Medical—United States. 4. Quality of Health Care—United States.
W 84 AA1 B969 2007]
RA395.A3B875   2008
362.1068—dc22   2007031135

British Library Cataloguing in Publication Data is available.

Library of Congress Catalog Card Number: 2007031135
ISBN: 978–0–275–99235–4 (Set)
       978–0–275–99236–1 (Vol. 1)
       978–0–275–99237–8 (Vol. 2)
       978–0–275–99238–5 (Vol. 3)

First published in 2008

Praeger Publishers, 88 Post Road West, Westport, CT 06881
An imprint of Greenwood Publishing Group, Inc.
www.praeger.com

Printed in the United States of America

The paper used in this book complies with the
Permanent Paper Standard issued by the National
Information Standards Organization (Z39.48–1984).

10 9 8 7 6 5 4 3 2 1

Contents

Preface

The healthcare system in the United States is a mass of paradoxes. We lead the world in the creation and application of technology for the clinical practice of medicine; yet the United States lags behind the rest of the developed world in basic health indicators (e.g., infant mortality rate, life expectancy). We provide some of the highest quality care in some of the premier health institutions that are the envy of the world; yet 45 million Americans cannot take advantage of these benefits because they lack health insurance. We outspend every other country on healthcare; yet almost no one is satisfied with the results: patients may get unparalleled quality care, but they pay a lot for that care and access can be erratic; payers are frustrated that they (and their customers) are not receiving good value for their growing outlays; and providers are feeling harassed by payers and regulators and unappreciated by patients.

Some claim that healthcare is being ruined by the intrusion of business interests, which put the bottom line ahead of the appropriate care of patients and denigrate the professionalism of those sworn to care for the sick. They worry that these interests are making healthcare no different than any other "industry" in this country. Others argue that the problems of inconsistent quality, sporadic access, and high and rising costs can only be solved by imposing the discipline of the market. To these observers it is business thinking and processes that can transform the current system.

The editors of *The Business of Healthcare* believe that the issue is not professionalism *or* business in healthcare, but professionalism *and* business. We believe that the healthcare system in the United States needs the perspectives and expertise of physicians and economists, nurses and accountants, technicians and strategists. We have organized this three-volume set for Praeger Perspectives to demonstrate how these mutual viewpoints can yield innovative solutions to our healthcare co-nundrum.

In designing *The Business of Healthcare,* the editors recognized that the solutions to the challenges facing the U.S. healthcare system will not come from one source. Rather, the solutions must address both the micro and the macro aspects of the system. Individual medical practices, as the foundation of healthcare delivery, must be operated as efficiently as possible. Healthcare organizations of all types must be led in ways to maximize the effectiveness of both human and financial resources. Finally, attention must be paid to the systems currently in place that affect all aspects of the healthcare sector.

To that end, we have organized *The Business of Healthcare* into three volumes that address each of these levels of the healthcare system in the United States. Volume 1 *(Practice Management)* focuses on those areas critical to the successful operation of physician practices: the process of joining and leaving a practice; promoting a practice; and managing the human and financial resources of a practice. It addresses the current structure of physician practices (including the continuing viability of solo practice) as well as the very future of the physician practice itself.

Volume 2 *(Leading Healthcare Organizations)* shifts the focus to the complex tasks of leading in healthcare. The chapters in this volume illustrate that leadership involves the integration of relationship management (such as the appropriate involvement of physicians in healthcare organizations), new modes of care (including such disparate areas as biotechnology, complementary and alternative medicine, and pastoral care), and operations (informatics, clinical supplies, liability risk management).

Volume 3 *(Improving Systems of Care)* widens the lens to consider how systems in healthcare can be transformed to resolve the paradoxes that we noted above. The chapters in this volume address systems to improve clinical quality and safety, development systems (e.g., for moving scientific ideas from the lab to the market, for developing medical technologies), operational systems (e.g., disaster response, information technology, and end-of-life care), and financial systems (such as the new "Massachusetts Plan" to cover all members of society). The volume also includes the voice of the patient in improving systems of care.

We are grateful to all of our chapter authors who volunteered scarce time to write about aspects of healthcare about which they are passionate. Our goal has been to provide works by experts that will engage stakeholders in discussions of issues important to our nation's health and economy. We hope that we have succeeded.

VOLUME 1: PRACTICE MANAGEMENT

It used to be that physicians could graduate from medical school, complete a residency, and be confident that they could start a practice that was financially and professionally successful almost from the first day. Those halcyon days are long gone, with the advent of constrained reimbursements, increased regulation, and real competition for patients. Today, physicians must run their practice as if it was a business—because it is. Although many physicians may be accidental business people, they must pay attention to the most critical operational aspects of their practice if they are to achieve their professional goals.

To that end, we asked our authors to bring forward the issues that they see from their experience as those most critical to the operational success of the medical practice. They responded with eight focused and insightful chapters on how to:

- Manage the continuing opportunities and challenges of solo practice
- Join and leave a practice
- Measure performance in a medical practice
- Build a culture of accountability in a practice
- Manage difficult physicians
- Promote a practice
- Create a practice marketing plan
- Manage the revenue cycle

In addition, two authors took a broader look at the environment of medicine, one exploring the potential and realities of the new pay-for-performance and the other considering the future of the medical practice.

In all, these chapters should provide physicians and practice administrators with the most up-to-date practical thinking on the effective management of physician practices.

VOLUME 2: LEADING HEALTHCARE ORGANIZATIONS

Leadership is the art of instilling in people the desire to strive together to create a better future. Leaders listen, observe, provide direction and meaning, generate and sustain trust, convey hope, and obtain results through their influence on other employees. The challenge is to energize people to push themselves beyond what they thought they could do (Cohn, Cannon, and Boswell 2006).

Nowhere are these principles more evident than in the chapters in Volume 2, where nationally known authors discuss the need for and evidence of leadership in healthcare. Diane Dixon begins this volume with an analysis of six healthcare leaders who embraced a positive, can-do mindset that enabled them to transform their institutions. Drs. Waldman and Cohn describe ways to transcend the adversarial relations that traditionally accompany physician-hospital relations and the dividends to patient care of engaging physicians in clinical priority setting, which Jayne Oliva and Mary Totten build on by describing the dual opportunity and responsibility of physicians serving on hospital boards.

The final six chapters highlight the need for and benefits of leadership in specific sectors of healthcare, including biotechnology, informatics, complementary and alternative medicine, supply costs, risk management, and pastoral care.

In healthcare, as in other fields that serve the public welfare, dedicated professionals prefer being inspired to being supervised. Through their influence on business strategy and especially on organizational culture, effective leaders:

- Create a safe environment for reflection and learning
- Improve the practice environment and hence practice outcomes
- Help people reconnect with the values that attracted them to healthcare in the first place

The purpose of this series and of Volume 2 in particular is to create a nurturing environment that stimulates further reflection, discussion, and action, resulting in improved healthcare for our communities. Only then can we consider our efforts successful.

VOLUME 3: IMPROVING SYSTEMS OF CARE

The imperative for improvement is clear for everyone who works in healthcare. Through breakthrough studies championed by the Institute of Medicine, we have learned that inadequate systems of care jeopardize the health and recovery of hundreds of thousands of patients annually, adding billions of dollars of expense to an unsustainable healthcare budget.

For people inside and outside the nonsystem of fragmented U.S. healthcare, the complexity can be overwhelming. A framework that treats a patient or healthcare processes as a number of mechanical parts, without paying attention to interactions of human beings with other human beings, is likely to fail.

We are fortunate in Volume 3 to have chapters written by experts who have created a platform for learning and discussion that can inform the healthcare debate, point out the choices we need to make, and help us maintain optimism about our future. Carl Taylor provides practical and organizational insights that can guide us in meeting the needs of patients, families, and healthcare workers during the next man-made or natural disaster. Michael Doonan and Stuart Altman use the recently enacted Massachusetts health plan to discuss a way forward for dealing with the needs of the uninsured and underinsured. Philip Buttell, Robert Hendler, and Jennifer Daley define quality and safety in operational metrics that permit tracking, improvement, and cultural change. Jack Barker and Greg Madonna analyze the similarities and differences between aviation and healthcare and offer promise that simple practical steps like briefing, debriefing, coaching, and team training can enhance skill sets in communication and improve safety outcomes, as they did in aviation nearly three decades ago.

Hospitals' success increasingly relies on sharing information to prevent adverse outcomes in medication administration and proactive disease management, as seen in the next three chapters on informational technology solutions, medical technology, and improving outcomes and reimbursement. In the final four chapters, Donald McDaniel, Anirban Basu, David Kovel, and Ian Batstone argue that despite the expense of our poorly coordinated (non)system of care, healthcare creates high-wage, high-tech, and high-touch jobs that form the backbone of the American economy. Rudy Wilson Galdonik, who has been a caretaker and a patient, offers practical suggestions for improvement of systems of care from a humanistic perspective. Lynn Johnson Langer notes the rapid uptake that accrues when scientists translate the results of their research to the business community to serve the interests and needs of society. Finally, Kenneth Fisher and Lindsay Rockwell point out the tremendous cost of care in the last year of life and the billions of dollars that could be freed to support systems improvement if we instituted practical changes in the way that we provided terminal care.

Although change may feel like failure when we are in the middle of it, we have reached a critical time when we can move from individual "blame-storming" to ways to ameliorate systems of care. This volume and indeed the entire three-volume series will only be successful if the insights contributed by our authors inspire us to create an environment conducive to questioning our past assumptions and learning new ways to study and improve patient care.

Kenneth H. Cohn, MD, MBA
Douglas E. Hough, PhD

REFERENCE

Cohn, Kenneth H., S. Cannon, and C. Boswell. 2006. "Let's Do Something: A Cutting-Edge Collaboration Strategy." In *Collaborate for Success! Breakthrough Strategies for Engaging Physicians, Nurses, and Hospital Executives*, ed. Kenneth H. Cohn, 76–77. Chicago: Health Administration Press.

CHAPTER 1

Leading Impact-Driven Disaster Response in a Healthcare Setting

Carl W. Taylor

Since the bombing of the Twin Towers of the World Trade Center in New York City on September 11, 2001, the United States has become increasingly focused on the response to sudden and impactful catastrophic events. Yet on August 29, 2005, Mother Nature played her own role in causing chaos and misery as thousands of people were impacted by the destruction of Hurricane Katrina along the Gulf Coast of the United States.

The seminal message of any chapter about planning for or participating in disaster response is the need to provide both emergent and nonemergent care to persons impacted by the event. Regardless of the cause—a malicious act, an accident, or Mother Nature—it is a given that healthcare will be delivered by providers under circumstances seldom seen during normal times.

Impact-driven disaster response means leading in a manner most likely to accomplish one's goals. General Colin Powell's definition of leadership recognizes "plans don't accomplish work. Goal charts on walls don't accomplish work.... [I]t is people who get things done."[1]

To accomplish the goal of finding and directing people to serve and to survive is to understand the issues around disaster response and be prepared to provide clarity of purpose, credibility of leadership, and integrity in organization.

In predisaster discussion with physicians and healthcare executives, the frequently heard comment is, "When 'it' happens, I will just do my day job of caring for patients, but perhaps just more of them." Unfortunately, disasters do not always allow the luxury of simply performing one's daily job. Rather, a complex series of factors also pressure the provider and/or executive to take on leadership roles and responsibilities that extend beyond clinical care.

Hippocrates advised any physician arriving in an unfamiliar town to "first examine its position with respect to the winds."[2] Isaac Cline, a physician and pioneer in medical climatology, was head of the weather service in Galveston, Texas, in September 1900, when Galveston was destroyed by an unpredicted hurricane. Of a storm that cost him his wife and home, he later wrote, "If we had known then what we know now of these swells and tides they create, we would have known earlier the terrors of the storms which the swells told us in unerring language were coming."[3]

Almost 105 years to the day, one could drive the Gulf Road in Mississippi from Ocean Springs to Bay Saint Louis and Waveland and suggest there are still lessons to be learned. Even now, there are reasons for the healthcare provider to examine the surroundings, evaluate the hazards, participate in the planning, and lead in any response. Leadership in disaster response is a dynamic, ever-changing process, a series of shared experiences of the best and worst practices in an effort to learn how to effectively act.

Consider the following issues, which form lessons learned from recent disasters. These are continuous threads in the sections that follow:

a. Social interactions are more valuable than processes and tools.

b. Interpersonal trust is preferred over policies and procedures.

c. Cooperation over competition is best.

d. Agility in response is even more effective than planning, but good planning produces dialogue. Dialogue produces thought and thought produces knowledge. Knowledge produces confidence, which produces agility.

e. Simplicity over complexity always works.

f. Reliability over capability prevails.[4]

This chapter will deal with disaster preparation and response from two perspectives. In the first section are lessons learned primarily from the local and state response viewpoint. To slightly misquote Yogi Berra, a New York Yankee baseball catcher and Hall of Fame inductee, "In theory there is no difference from practice and playing but in playing there is." What I think Yogi would mean, particularly along the Gulf Coast region in the post-Katrina days, is that experience is the best teacher, though not the kindest or most forgiving, but certainly the best. Hence these sections and the subsequent case studies draw heavily from a series of personal experiences and presentations by other leaders. There is also a federal—formal if you will—response structure.[5]

In the appendix that follows is an overview of that response structure. A wise reader of this chapter will spend time with the topics covered in the appendix, which highlights the basis for organized response.

In the event you choose not to read further, let me leave you with one guiding motto of disaster response: *Semper Gumby*—"always flexible." It is a motto to keep in mind when the power is out, communications are down, the water is not working, and three things remain: a stethoscope, assessment skills, and good leadership.

PRINCIPLES OF DISASTER LEADERSHIP: BUILDING COMMUNICATION AND EARNING TRUST

You are not alone in responding to a disaster. Your effectiveness to your community and your own recovery depend on the ability to communicate with others who need your assistance or can offer it to you. But why is it important to build preevent relationships with reliable partners? What barriers hinder access to this goal? What steps should be taken to ensure the development of a network of support? What must leaders do to create accountable communication bridges?

The cornerstone of disaster response is that most success in overcoming a disaster will ultimately depend on *communication* and *trust*. Communication is at the core of being able to ask for or offer help. Trust is about using communication ability to convey decisions, which promote effective response and individual and institutional survival. Communication strategies are built, whereas trust is earned. Achieving effective communication and earning trust will overcome many of the disaster response certainties that will be exposed during the catastrophe.

Among the certainties are these:

a. The disaster will always be more complex than your planning.

   Witness for a moment the chaos and confusion in New Orleans surrounding events at the Superdome and Convention Center. Loss of power, lack of food, questionable maintenance of general order, and safety failures all seemed to occur when preevent plans were overwhelmed by the gravity of the event. The lack of communication between agencies delayed their emergency responses and caused a lack of trust in the evacuees.

b. Many conflicting opinions will be voiced about the best courses of action that should be implemented, including some in opposition to yours.

   Ed Minyard of Unisys, a company based in New York, relates a story of his effort to create an emergency operations center in the week following Katrina's landfall. One of the unsung and underrecognized heroes of New Orleans, Ed and his team went to the city of their own volition and established the communication infrastructure that restored connectivity between the city and disaster responders. As Ed noted in a speech to city officials later, however, the real challenge in developing the correct response efforts in New Orleans was sifting through the varying opinions from competing agencies and individuals for the city's optimum evacuation plan.[6] Once the appropriate information was gathered, the actual deployment was monumental. In short, poor communication between perceived competing agencies exposed a lack of trust in the decision-making ability of some of the professionals sent in to assist in the disaster.

c. Much of the information received regarding the disaster will be incorrect or incomplete.

Following Hurricane Ivan in 2004, which greatly impacted Florida and Alabama, a review was undertaken to highlight both right and faulty actions. In interviews with hospital personnel in Alabama, there was a sense that the relief and assistance provided by the federal government disproportionately favored Florida. In subsequent interviews with federal officials, however, it was clear the aid provided was based upon how the hospitals gauged their needs. A phrase frequently uttered was, "Your hospitals could not see tomorrow," meaning the leaders' inability to anticipate problems from a lack of food, water, and power. Consequently, the available communication was frequently wrong, which impacted the response.[7]

d. Many of the individuals or organizations offering to help will be unknown to you.

Volunteers may appear at your facility or in your community willing to help but with uncertain skills, inadequate supplies, and, oftentimes, an ill-defined mission. Communication can assist in requesting well-trained, well-supplied volunteers whose capabilities and credentials are verifiable.

The challenges to good communication and earning trust are due to:

a. The very nature of healthcare, which is often fragmented.

Voluntary daily collaboration between facilities or providers is quite uncommon. Every hospital, no matter the size of the community, competes with other hospitals, freestanding facilities, and, occasionally, their own community doctors. Physicians are embedded within silos around their practices and specialties and thus rarely participate in disaster planning meetings because of time constraints. These factors often make communication and connectivity difficult topics to discuss—much less implement. At best, when communication and trust are taken on as an achievable challenge, the approach can best be described as *coop-etition*, the collaboration of competitors who work together during times of disaster.

b. A lack of prior experience with local, state, or federal response partners.

To many providers and/or facilities of care, their relationship with federal or state entities is normally viewed as a regulator or, perhaps, payer but rarely as a disaster response partner. Yet within many states it is the Department of Health or the Emergency Management Agency that is charged with facilitating predisaster communication and trust through its planning efforts.

c. The lack of good national examples in which an integrated, well-organized disaster response system has performed well against a backdrop of a real event.

Witness almost any congressional committee examining the response to a disaster and you will hear "a failure to communicate" frequently cited as the cause of poor response.[8]

d. Delaying until the event occurs to build communication channels.

The challenge of communication is further heightened by the nature of how or, perhaps better, when relationships are built. It is vital to develop communication and trust *before* the catastrophe hits. If the event has occurred, there are likely to be additional challenges to building effective communication. Not only are people not physically where they normally are, but their responses may well be impacted emotionally by events as they unfold.

Mass media, for instance, will filter the event information in different ways through diverse groups. There is a great deal of debate over just how much civil disorder occurred in New Orleans in the early days following Katrina. Regardless of where the truth lies, the media images displayed will be permanently etched in our minds. After seeing those images, you or your staff may feel differently about assisting during future disasters.

Leaders build communication and earn trust by seeking three steps:

a. Set clear goals for you and your staff/organization.

Setting goals requires a preevent commitment to define your role in disaster response and to communicate those goals before, during, and after an event has occurred.

For the provider or healthcare professional, for instance, it may be to serve on a Medical Reserve Corp as a volunteer medical response leader in the community or to agree to be part of a deployable Disaster Medical Assistance Team. It may also be to assume a role within the Incident Command System of your local hospital.

For state public health departments, that clear goal is defined by the Emergency Support Function 8 of managing and coordinating healthcare response during an event.[9] It is the role of the public health department in a disaster to actively assist in managing surge capacity[10] and surge capability.

Surge capacity is the term for managing large numbers of patients from a sudden impactful event. The goal, of course, is to manage them in a way that no hospital or provider site is overwhelmed by the sheer numbers of patients presenting for care.

Surge capability refers to the types of patients a provider can safely handle. An example would be an explosion at a school that causes a large number of pediatric burn cases. A local hospital may have plenty of empty beds but no pediatric burn capability.

Regardless of the goal chosen, leadership is best expressed against a clear mission. Whether your role is as a practitioner or other healthcare professional or public health leader, the common goal is to maximize the numbers of lives saved during the disaster while continuing to provide proper care for current patients. By communicating this goal, you are positioned to be a disaster leader and to earn trust by leaning forward into the event.

b. Lean forward and be proactive in implementing your goals.

This means to actively and proactively participate as a responder—not just an information gatherer. A good example from the public health arena comes from the Alabama Department of Public Health's (ADPH) use of a Medical Transfer Center during Hurricane Katrina. As large numbers of patients were being displaced by the storm, the ADPH deployed public health employees into the state of Mississippi to identify the source of the patients and direct them to hospitals or shelters that could optimally provide care. This lean-forward approach to "getting in the way of an event" gave rise to a clear understanding of the goal of "managing the many effectively, so providers could manage the one safely."

The Medical Transfer Center's other goal is to be a resource to all providers during and after the disaster, not only to manage the flow of patients but also to assist with supplies, resources, volunteers, and other issues to support medical care. Leaning forward capably earns trust and has centered the ADPH as an accountable partner in disaster response. Accountable partners are, of course, only as good as their accountable relationships.

c. Develop accountable relationships.

To become part of a disaster response from a leadership position means recognizing that successful disaster response requires assistance from many differing parties.[11] Look at the Incident Command structure in the appendix to obtain a sense of the operational, financial, logistics, planning, and communication requirements of effective response.

Although we will outline some of the specifics in the next section of this chapter, here are a few key points. First, before the catastrophe hits, leadership requires advising others in your community of your intended role when "it" happens. A few days after Katrina, Dr. Robert Galli, an emergency physician at the University of Mississippi Medical Center, took pictures of the disaster in the Gulf Coast. One particularly compelling photo was of Hancock Medical Center in Bay Saint Louis, Mississippi. Clearly evident from the photo was a water line indicating where four feet of water had stood only a few days before. Yet in the muck and mess, the most revealing part of the photo was not of the damage but of the line of patients—including one clearly pregnant woman—standing outside waiting to be treated.

Hal Leftwich, the excellent chief executive officer (CEO) of that hospital, remarked that events left him with little choice of his facility's response. As the water was retreating, patients began to arrive, some swimming in. He commented later, "We saw a Coast Guard helicopter landing and thought they were bringing help. Instead, they were dropping off patients for us to treat."[12]

Through a strong medical staff, outstanding professionals in the facility, good assistance from other response agencies, and outstanding leadership, Hancock Medical Center remained a hub of care for Bay Saint Louis and Waveland without interruption even while the facility was being rebuilt. Hancock Medical Center proved to be an accountable partner to its community when disaster hit.

Leaders who set a goal to remain or return quickly to their community accept that there are two key requirements to accomplish this task. First, develop a trusted information/communication network to gain knowledge about the event before, during, and after its impact. This knowledge creates a condition the military might call *situational awareness,* an accurate as possible understanding of events. Second, situational awareness then allows you to make correct decisions leading to positive outcomes. These actions create trust in the leader and his or her leadership decision making.

As an overall approach to gaining situational awareness, leaders need to create channels of trusted information. Again drawing from the Alabama experience, our unified incident reporting system collects real-time information of critical importance to healthcare providers. The status of beds, staff, utilities, supplies, structural challenges, ingress and egress blockages, and other community issues leads to correct decision making based on a statewide view of event issues and response capability. Pushing local disaster planners to create a system to obtain this vital information is an important first step.

Supporting the drive toward information clarity is the need to recognize four key issues:

a. Develop multiple ways to obtain information.

Two of the three Emergency Operations Centers along the Gulf Coast in Mississippi and the Emergency Operations Center of New Orleans were impacted by Katrina. Therefore, receiving good information immediately after the storm proved problematic and uncertain. Moreover, given the challenges of loss of power, movement of responders, and uncertainty of communication tools, more avenues to reach people who possess accurate information about the event become critical and essential to the decision-making process.

   b. Develop redundancy and interoperability.

Those you trust for information may themselves be unable to respond because of the disaster's impact on them personally. Clearly, Mother Nature does not exempt healthcare providers from her wrath, nor will a widespread pandemic. This means that leaders must develop redundancy and interoperability both in the communication devices at their fingertips and in the persons they rely on for support. This is true in the first few days after a disaster and in the days, weeks, and months afterward. Disaster response and recovery is quite often a marathon, not a sprint, and managing people through the information-gathering process in a catastrophe can prove to be difficult.

   c. Build information channels before the crisis occurs.

In natural disasters, the loss of power or transmission lines can reduce access to oral or written documents dramatically unless procedures for communication channels have been developed in advance.

   d. Develop relationships with people who can provide basic services, including food, water, laundry, and power during times of disaster.

During Katrina, for instance, West Jefferson Medical Center's central laundry facility was destroyed, leaving the hospital without clean linens at a time when its daily emergency room visits had tripled. Therefore, maximizing lives saved and maintaining care for existing patients can be as basic as finding food and clean laundry for them.

Being able to communicate with people you trust competently to assist during a disaster will be invaluable in a crisis; however, do not assume that the networks are already in place. Begin now to establish a relationship with public health officials and your provider community partners to build a plan to support one another in time of need. Set clear goals, lean forward by being proactive, agree to participate in one another's planning and exercises, and be an accountable partner when called upon.

LEADERSHIP IN ACTION: DEALING WITH SPECIFICS OF PROVIDING CARE

When disaster strikes, the surrounding infrastructure will change, from both human dynamics and internal operations standpoints. This section will highlight topics that may often be missed in planning, but they will prove critical in maintaining an adequate response to an event. Against the backdrop of maximizing lives saved in less than normal clinical conditions, the demands on leadership are to answer these 11 central questions:

What Is the Philosophy of our Clinical Organization?

Principle number one is to determine where you will be and what you will do personally and organizationally when "it" occurs. Does it matter what the nature of the event is, such as a man-made or natural catastrophe? Options include: Stay in the facility at all costs, return as early as possible, or do not return. That decision depends greatly on your leadership philosophy with the realization that experience and the actual event will influence that decision making over time.

For many of the Gulf Coast hospitals, including the three in New Orleans, West Jefferson Medical Center, East Jefferson Medical Center, and Ochsner Clinic, the decision to stay open regardless after Hurricane Katrina mirrored a philosophy of its leaders to stay in the community.

Many of the heroes who stayed the course during Katrina, however, may not have done so had a subsequent disaster occurred. I heard comments frequently from a number of healthcare professionals throughout the Gulf Coast who said they simply would not go through "this" again. The philosophy of your facility may vary, is experientially based, and must be reviewed at least once a year.

Principle number two is that circumstances will alter your philosophy. At the initial warning of Katrina's approach, none of the hospitals in New Orleans evacuated. Their philosophy was to stay and ride out the hurricane. Many of them, however, elected not to ride out the following flood.

Will our Staff Show Up?

From a leadership perspective, there are four challenges to staffing, which will determine if your office or healthcare facility is to remain open or recover from an event.

1. The first challenge is addressing the need for workers to come in and work during an event. Recent studies, for instance, suggest that approximately 42 percent of all healthcare workers would not show up for their shift in the midst of a pandemic.[13] A number of nurses during the severe acute respiratory syndrome (SARS) event in Canada did not report for their shifts, which caused staff and operational challenges.[14]

    As you attempt to get your staff to report for duty, you must recognize there are issues your employees are dealing with and by inference you must deal with them also.

    a. The primary issue is fear. Will I be safe? What steps are the leaders of my facility taking to ensure my safety? The fear can come from concern over infection to structural damage from a storm to concern over social disruption, which was experienced in New Orleans. Regardless of the cause, good leaders recognize the challenge of protecting the personal safety of the healthcare workers by communicating solutions and plans before and during the event.

    b. The second issue is concern for family members and loved ones. While working at a hospital during Hurricane Ivan, the major concern I heard from nurses was not of personnel issues but *personal* issues. Because the hospital did not allow family members to weather the storm in the facility as staff members worked, this decision created concern and anxiety. As one nurse told me, "I can be a nurse anywhere. Remember, there is a national nursing shortage."

You can find proponents and opponents of allowing staff to bring their families into a facility during a storm. Though proponents cite the overall morale benefits, opponents allude to issues of employee distraction, workplace disruption, and stress on food, water, and facilities. Regardless of your personal position, encouraging your staff to have a family plan in place can help ensure their availability to work immediately or to come in shortly thereafter.

   c. A significant issue in getting employees into work involves mission. A common complaint I hear is, "We have met the enemy and it is caller ID." This device allows the worker away from the facility to easily identify the caller as his or her employer. The worker knows full well the intent of the call and can choose whether to answer.

From a leader's perspective, you need to gauge the relationships with your staff. Will they put themselves in harm's way if asked? How deeply do they believe in the mission of your facility? Getting strong emotional commitment for the mission of healthcare in a disaster is vital to getting workers to respond favorably when called upon to work.

2. The second challenge is to determine the correct type of workers needed. Disaster responders often think initially in clinical terms for employees—physicians and nurses. However, food service workers, environmental service workers, and especially clerical staff are all critical personnel to keep the facility open and operational. Vital also are materials management, security, information technology support, and finance personnel.

3. The third, and often overlooked, issue is dealing with the psychosocial needs of your staff during the disaster. During the early days of Katrina with its enormous devastation, healthcare workers suffered the same loss of homes, family, businesses, and community as others. Long hours and altered environments, including lack of water, air conditioning, and basic creature comforts, all contribute to the stress on your workforce. Leaders plan early for dealing with the various types of additional demands on their employees, including creating flexible work rules to allow staff members to grieve or deal with personal losses.

After the hurricane season of 2004 in Florida, I discovered a number of hospitals had terminated workers who did not report to work during the storm. I personally do not support this action. In fact, at the height of the storm when no one is on the road, you will need fewer workers than in the hours afterward. A more enlightened approach would recognize that disaster response is both emotionally and physically draining, especially when the storm is at its peak. Perhaps those discharged workers could have provided welcome relief to the first phase of employees who reported for duty. These tired workers will eventually need a break to deal with their own physical and emotional challenges.

4. The fourth issue in leadership deals with worker retention. Healthcare costs along the Gulf Coast are up 25 percent following Katrina. Any trained healthcare worker, with a home and skills, is highly desired because of the exodus of many talented, though exhausted, caregivers. Employee retention strategies are required to deal with ongoing staffing challenges.

Where Will Supplies Come From?

Your healthcare team will depend on a reliable supply chain for both clinical and nonclinical supplies. Yet roads can be impacted during a natural disaster or the widespread nature of the event can cause suppliers to create delivery priorities. In a yet-to-be experienced pandemic, it is reasonable to assume supply-chain disruptions due to shortages in all areas of business operations: from truck drivers to janitorial personnel, from manufacturing of goods to actual inventory on hand, to concerns of ingress and egress into a healthcare facility, to name a few. In addition, most hospitals and providers have gone to a just-in-time inventory management approach, which means they no longer warehouse supplies.

From a leadership planning perspective, there are some commonsense and valuable recommendations that emerged from Katrina. These can be implemented in your facility, regardless of the disaster type.

1. Assume at least a normal or increased patient load.
2. Factor in additional people and pets, if your plan allows your staff to bring them into your facility.
3. Recognize that much of your patient load will be unmanaged chronically ill patients whose lives have been disrupted by events.
4. Engage in discussions with your suppliers about their disaster plans and potential events, which might cause delays in serving your facility. Supplies required for a minimum of 10 days include pharmaceuticals, food, water, and other mission-critical supplies. This dialogue needs to include a discussion about events outside of your area, which could still impact your supply chain.

   We learned long ago that a storm in Puerto Rico would disrupt our supply chain for certain items manufactured on the island. From a pandemic perspective, the need to understand and manage current suppliers and create alternative supply chains is essential.

5. A final recommendation is to discuss supply-chain assistance with your county or state public health departments. As part of the overall disaster preparedness, these entities have worked toward building supply caches and delivery capability. Their contacts will prove valuable during this time of unusual need.

How Do You Get Transportation and Fuel?

You and your staff will need to find a way to work, and your discharged patients will need transportation to home or alternative care facilities. Mother Nature often impacts roadways and interferes with the operation of gasoline stations. Viable transportation solutions include public service announcements for individuals with four-wheel drive vehicles or vans to pick up staff in a carpool type of arrangement. In addition, there may be social support organizations and county or municipal government entities that have transportation available. Your local emergency management agency and public health department can communicate this information and assist.

Fuel, on the other hand, often proves a difficult commodity. During Katrina, hospitals relied on an informal sharing of information based upon advanced knowledge of specific gasoline stations next in line for fuel shipments.

A more sophisticated approach implemented by Ocean Springs Medical Center in Ocean Springs, Mississippi, is to purchase fuel that would be delivered within 48 hours after landfall of any storm. Billing and invoicing options need to be addressed as well.

Will Our Facilities Be Appropriate?

There are a number of leadership considerations when facilities are reviewed. First, the structural integrity of the facility will be a fundamental determinant during a natural disaster of whether to remain or evacuate. Among the commonsense issues are those in or surrounded by low-lying flood-prone areas. One of the planning challenges to Ocean Springs Medical Center was the potential flooding of roadways in and out of the facility. Therefore, evacuation decisions must be timely made.

Another structural challenge is the ability of large glass atriums and other similar structures to withstand wind loads. Although a hospital or office building may choose not to evacuate because of an atrium, consideration must be given to altered traffic flow and other challenges.

Although there are a number of considerations regarding evacuation, it may not mean the entire facility should be evacuated. Possibly, only certain units should be moved from outside walls into interior spaces for safety. Regardless, all components of your facility must be evaluated to determine how to best use or preserve the space.

Facilities also play a role in a number of other issues. For instance, the need for a family plan for your staff is critical. If family members of your staff will not be allowed into your facility, then you must help them identify alternative sites to accommodate their family members or themselves if their own homes are impacted or unreachable.

Or your workers may not wish to bring their families into your facility because of infection risk and other dangers. If either occurs, alternate sites become critically important as a planning tool. These sites might include wellness centers on the hospital's property, the local YMCA and other gyms, and schools.

Finally, the need is paramount to recognize that alternate sites can play a strong role in surge capacity. Before Katrina struck and even before it landed on August 28, 2005, West Jefferson Medical Center's caseload averaged 150 patients daily. Since then, that number has climbed to more than 450. West Jefferson managed this increase in surge capacity through a number of novel approaches. One was identifying an available, abandoned nursing home across the street from the hospital and negotiating with a community health center to establish a presence there.[15]

Is Our Security Adequate?

Safety of your facility, patients, and staff is of paramount importance during and after an event. Amid reports of robbery, assault, and rape, there is much debate about what actually occurred at the Superdome and Convention Center in New Orleans. One definite outcome was the great fear of social disruption and personal safety that arose in the hearts of healthcare workers as hurricane reports were shown on television. Against this backdrop of social disorder, three hospitals—Ochsner Clinic, East Jefferson Medical Center, and West Jefferson Medical Center—were able to stay open because of their being able to locate dependable security.

There are four avenues to obtain personnel to secure your facility.

1. First, your own workforce could be employed during times of crisis. Hospitals, office buildings, and other locations often have existing guards or security personnel. Adequacy of numbers, training, and their own employee attendance should be evaluated ahead of time.
2. The second choice is to rely on local, county, or state police for assistance if there is a specific advance agreement for them to do so.
3. The third choice is to hire private companies for specific event protection. During natural disasters, large hotel chains often rely on these companies with great success.
4. The fourth choice is to negotiate a mutual aid agreement or use other creative means to provide security.

In New Orleans, West Jefferson Medical Center had a prior existing agreement with a military police unit of the Louisiana National Guard, which provided security throughout the duration of the early days of Katrina. Reciprocally, West Jefferson volunteered space and sleeping quarters to law enforcement personnel assigned to New Orleans to restore civil order.[16]

What Communication Tools Should We Use?

Can we talk? Or rather, why can we not talk? There are three principles to effective communication and each is equally important. The first principle is what is in your hand when you are trying to communicate. Do you have to rely on electric power as your energy source of communication? We know in a natural disaster that electric power is the enemy of communication. At the Strong Angel III exercise referenced earlier in this chapter, which was led by Commander Eric Rasmussen, MD U.S. Navy, he illustrated how the absence of electric power crashed virtually every communication system.

Oftentimes, cell phones are subject to power outages and will not operate, particularly if the cell tower (or the phone) loses battery power and digital phones lose data lines to the Web. Satellite phones will work at times, especially if you are outdoors. Analog phones and ham radios can also be operational, which proves that older technology can be a lifeline in desperate occasions.

Today, every hospital with a well-honed disaster plan has established a relationship with ham radio operators to use their expertise during times of disaster. In addition, most states are having dialogue with talk providers who will be delivering disaster-hardened networks. For instance, the Alabama Department of Public Health is using federal disaster funding to procure talk radios for every hospital and community health center in the state.

The second principle of communication is the language used. Basic English should be the standard protocol, but local, state, or federal responders often communicate with acronyms, no matter to whom they are speaking. A number of good Web sites offer a glossary of current terms, but another equally valued approach is to insist on an acronym free environment (AFE). Clarity and accuracy of communication in times of crises are far more important than following normal communication policies.

Finally, the most important principle of communication is knowing who to call when you are looking for help or offering to help. During these calls, you will discuss situational awareness, supplies, staffing, and patients.

The Alabama Department of Public Health has created a Patient Transfer Unit (formerly the Medical Transfer Center mentioned previously), a central entity designed to deal with disaster-related health events. Before a disaster strikes, leaders will identify a wide range of entities that can provide help when disaster occurs.

Who Sues?

Healthcare is a heavily regulated industry. At work against a system of integrated care during a disaster are three statutory/regulatory barriers or risk challenges.

The first is the Emergency Medical Treatment and Leave Act (EMTALA), which is found in the Social Security Act (42 U.S. Code 1395 dd) and requires an emergency patient to be treated and stabilized upon delivery and before being transferred to another facility. Although most emergency physicians view EMTALA primarily in the light of financial issues, it has other ramifications from a disaster perspective. If implemented as written, it can serve as a barrier to safe, effective patient routing from hospitals that have exceeded their surge capacity.

In an informal guidance by the Center for Medicare and Medicaid Services (CMS) on November 8, 2001, it was recognized that EMTALA had not contemplated public health emergencies. Through a series of subsequent pronouncements, the CMS intimated that initial screening requirements could be limited in presidentially declared disasters. During Hurricane Katrina, Section 1857 sanctions were waived for redirection of patients not stabilized.

Another perceived challenge to effective communication during disaster response is found within the Health Insurance Portability and Accountability Act (HIPAA), 45 C.F.R. Parts 160 and 164.

Recently, the U.S. Department of Health and Human Services (HHS) released a new Web-based interactive decision tool designed to assist emergency preparedness and recovery planners in determining how to access and use health information about some persons. This tool can be found at http://www.hhs.gov/ocr/hipaa/decisiontool/. As a general rule, HIPAA provides that covered entities (public health agencies and providers) may use or disclose protected health information for treatment, including the provision, coordination, and management of healthcare and related services.

Finally, there is the possibility of malpractice events arising out of the provision of care during a disaster. There is no safe, all-encompassing guideline that can cover every potential event and no guarantee prospectively or retrospectively that there will be broad agreement on any rule set. Good preevent communication and planning, however, can at least mitigate any postevent litigation risk. This planning should center on the following:

1. Triage efforts will need to focus on maximizing the number of lives saved.
2. Triage decisions will affect allocation of resources across the spectrum of care.
3. Current patients have needs also that must be met.
4. The usual scope of practice standards may not apply.
5. Equipment and supplies may have to be rationed.
6. There may not be enough staff or enough trained staff.
7. Surge capacity may create backlogs and delays.
8. Providers may have to make treatment decisions based on best clinical judgment without the help of lab or imaging studies.
9. Standards for documentation may be difficult to maintain.[17]

Who Pays?

The ability of any healthcare provider to provide needed services in a disaster will last only as long at its ability to make payroll and purchase supplies and services. Katrina demonstrated the fragility of the financial state of healthcare facilities, as will future pandemics. Well-directed leaders will take several steps before a disaster hits to meet the sudden interruption of cash flow and the associated increases in operational expenses.

The first step is to review the business interruption policies in force and in effect for the enterprise. Of particular note is the challenge embedded in some insurance policies that tie business interruption to physical damage. In a pandemic or for some facilities after Katrina, their businesses were interrupted and financial losses occurred. Because of lack of physical damage, however, their insurer was slow to respond.

Second, it is vital to review the facility's borrowing authority. For facilities, there are two keys: a good banking relationship and the borrowing authority approval in place before the disaster hits.[18]

A strong relationship with banks can also create an ability to literally have cash delivered when required. When the power goes out, we become a cash-driven society. Availability of cash will keep employees at work and mitigate the stress associated with the need to meet short-term obligations. Another short-term remedy is to establish a foundation that can raise cash and donations of both money and goods that can be distributed directly to the staff. It is rare that a donation plan is found in a hospital or healthcare-planning document, but it can truly have a significant impact in meeting the cash and clothing/supply needs in cases of emergency.

Third, consider the opportunity to create a disaster-ready foundation to solicit donations from others. Both West Jefferson Medical Center and Hancock Medical Center established foundations to ask for cash to assist in rebuilding. In West Jefferson's case, the money went to the employees.[19] Hancock Medical Center gave donors options of contributing to rebuilding the facility, to donating to the employees of the facility, or to assisting the community physicians with total losses of practices and homes.[20] Generous contributions from many Americans had a significant, positive impact on the individuals at these medical centers who had lost so much and yet even in their loss stayed in their communities to assist others.

Fourth, where there has been a sudden change to your county or region demographics a consideration changing the hospital's licensure or status might also prove valuable. After Hurricane Katrina, Hancock Medical Center realized its county had suffered a significant loss of population. The hospital leaders considered a number of options available to keep the facility open. For them, the correct decision was to convert to a critical access hospital and reduce its bed size from 100 to 24 beds to meet the needs of its much smaller community. Flexibility in sizing and creative measures in staff retention will pay dividends during the postevent recovery period.

How Do We Overcome Psychological and Psychosomatic Issues?

Leadership in a disaster recognizes that psychosocial issues will be present in patients, providers, and staff. In addition to post-traumatic stress disorders suffered by patients, there will be the need to deal with a sense of fear or dread about the event, particularly in events such as a pandemic or terrorist attack.

Finally, challenges around blame, stigmatization, isolation, and personal and even facility resilience must be addressed as patients continue to be fearful. As your own staff members experience a variety of emotions, personal counseling might be necessary to deal with loss, grief, and mourning. Fortunately, there are materials available through the Centers for Disease Control and Prevention entitled "Crisis and Emergency Risk Communications." These and other resources should be gathered before a catastrophe strikes.[21]

How Is a Level Playing Field Created?

Leadership in a disaster is about recognizing the source of possible assistance and asking for assistance when needed. Witness common comments from Katrina: "No one helped us" and "Why did they get evacuated first?" Frustration, discontent, and a sense of discrimination can erode confidence in leadership. In outbreaks, this will also include stigmatization, blame, and a collapse of social cohesion.

These challenges should lead to at least three steps to create a level playing field, in which individuals take as much responsibility for their own actions as possible.

First, we use a term in planning called *YOYO*, or "you are on your own," to create a sense of resilience. Though difficult to attribute the phrase to any one person, seasoned disaster professionals use it frequently to lower the expectation that the cavalry is going to ride over the hill to rescue those in distress. As the phrase resonates from their leader as a battle cry, staff members realize that they have much of the power in their hands to control much of their destiny.

The second recommendation is for leaders to adopt the so-called natural leader or soccer mom strategy.[22] Within your organization, identify formal and informal individuals who are trustworthy, calm, and controlled. They are emotional leaders who can be counted on during disasters to convey information, calm the fears of workers, and mitigate the personnel criticisms.

Finally, the need of the leader is to produce. It is vital for you to provide clear direction and articulate the needs of your organization to others who can help. During times of crisis, it is essential for the leader of the organization to draw upon his or her personal strengths to effectively lead.

Good leadership recognizes it will take more than a plan on paper to solve each of these 11 issues when a disaster hits. Deal with personnel issues in advance, anticipate challenges in your daily operations, prepare for the long term, and create a thoughtful approach to problem solving.

TOOLS THAT ENHANCE RESPONSE

Leaders lead best when planning and thought precede decision making. The tools of choice begin with a hazard, threat, and vulnerability analysis (HVA). An HVA is that moment when your leadership team gathers to discuss a wide range of prospective challenges, ranging from man-made to natural disasters.

The team begins to ask fundamental questions, including the likelihood of human, property, or business loss. Also to be addressed is your facility's ability to respond internally to the disaster and your community's ability to assist in your response. Most HVA forms offer a scoring methodology to highlight specific threats to review further. When completed, an HVA forms the chapters of your disaster plan. Although there are multiple schools of thought on the desired length, you should be more concerned with the initiation of the process. Once the initial document is developed, it will be reviewed and revised as necessary.

There are other tools useful to disaster response. In some states, there is a unified Disaster Response Incident Management System. These systems promote focused exchanges of staff, supplies, patients, and event data between providers and responders.

Another lesson learned from Katrina was the impact of a healthcare system existing more on paper than on servers. In all states, Katrina displaced more than 1 million persons on August 29, many of whom who were poor, underfunded, and beset with a litany of chronic diseases. Overall, 250,000 of those displaced persons ultimately required some type of care.

Among the challenges presented was the inability of the patients to articulate all of their known conditions and medications. In response, a truly Herculean effort by the Health and Human Services Office of the National Coordinator for Health Information Technology (ONCHIT), the Markle Foundation, and many others created a special Web site, http://www.katrinahealth.org. This Web site aggregated pharmacy data for many of those displaced and allowed providers an access point to search the medication history of these displaced persons.

Clearly, almost any disaster will put patients in motion. Patients with multiple comorbid conditions will present to your office, emergency room, or medical needs shelter. Many of these patients will be unable to fully articulate their conditions and perhaps even less likely to articulate their full complement of current medications. Because these are patients that will be new to you, gaining at least some information about their medication history or known conditions will be valuable in providing care. In the future, we will have a better electronic record system available to providers that will at a minimum contain medication histories of patients.

THE ROLE AND CHALLENGES OF THE COMMUNITY PHYSICIAN

Many of the previous suggestions and recommendations are well suited for hospitals and emergency department physicians who are often real heroes in managing through difficult events. But how should community-based physicians and their experiences move forward after a catastrophe?

Issues Relevant to Practicing Physicians

Hospitals and physicians must realize the sense of loss of the private practicing physician. Gone in an instant may well be his or her home, office, records, and patients. Not gone in an instant or at any other time are their debts and liabilities or the desire to determine as quickly as possible whether recovery is possible. Unlike hospitals, community-based private practice physicians often find that the disaster response and federal resources are not available to them. In many cases, well-intended volunteer help may negatively impact private practitioners trying to rebuild their practices. Attempting to compete with so-called free healthcare just down the street becomes a challenge and a source of contention.

To the private practitioner, the issue begins with "Where have my patients gone, and are they coming back?" Many physicians in New Orleans who witnessed the widespread movement of their patients to Baton Rouge now believe that a large segment of their practices will not be returning at all or at least in the short term. To those physicians, that realization means either relocating their practices to reunite with their patients or considering out-of-area recruiting offers.

To the physicians who choose to remain, there are three steps that should be considered concurrently to assist in their journey toward economic recovery:

1. Become involved early in the disaster response dialogue. Most emergency medical operations centers or community hospitals hold at least daily meetings on what is happening with patients, supplies, resources, assistance, and needs.

   Decisions about the need for out-of-town or out-of-state medical volunteers are often made at these meetings, many times without realizing that there are community-based private practitioners willing to become involved. Moreover, these meetings are a time for you to express your needs for supplies and assistance.

2. If you play a role in your hospital's emergency call roster and you see a diminution in your payer mix, as we have witnessed in New Orleans, then negotiate a paid call relationship with the hospital. Be sure to articulate your needs as often as possible so as not to be ignored during the long-term planning of the medical community.

   I make this recommendation knowing that the local hospitals will also be struggling with financial challenges, but it is far easier to create an ongoing permanent bond with private physicians who are committed to your community. For rebuilding to occur, healthcare will need to be present and there will be a time (perhaps too long in coming for many local physicians) when the volunteer medical care will return home.

3. If you are a physician who has lost nearly everything, there will be a time of personal and professional reconstruction.

   One solution that seemed to work at Hancock Medical Center in Bay Saint Louis, Mississippi, was to offer employment to physicians under terms that would allow an exit from the employment if the physician felt his or her practice had recovered. These agreements, although not perfect, seem to be a fair balance of the needs of the parties.

I summarize this particular section with an admonition that private practitioners are often the least prepared for disaster response and yet they often suffer the greatest impact from the event. Although many private physicians are other directed in volunteering for Medical Reserve Corps or other charities, time needs to be spent considering the rebuilding or relocating of your own practices.

Does your hospital have a plan to help you? Have you found where and how to make your voice heard? Are there untapped sources of assistance that can be channeled toward your practice in the event of a calamity? If you have to relocate out of the area, are there resources available to help with that decision? Today might be a good day to ask.

Case Studies in Preparedness and Leadership

West Jefferson Medical Center

The motto of West Jefferson Medical Center (WJMC) is "To CURE Sometimes, To RELIEVE Often, and To COMFORT Always."

During the early days of September 2005, that motto should have been amended to read: "and To SURVIVE Somehow." Located in Marrero, Louisiana, on the west bank of the Mississippi River in Jefferson Parish, this 425-bed hospital found itself as one of only three hospitals in the greater New Orleans area that remained continuously open throughout all of the difficult days of the Katrina recovery.

One common denominator with success stories in disaster is a strong leadership team. Gary Muller, the hospital's CEO; Erie Hebert, the chief operating officer; and Mitch Leckelt, head of risk and recovery, all provided strong leadership and steady hands during the difficult days in September.

Without power and water and with shortages of food and staff, WJMC remained open for business as usual; however, the staff saw its emergency room visits climb from an average of 150 daily patients to more than 450 daily patients for nearly every day in September and early October. In many ways, WJMC exemplifies many of the best practices in disaster response discussed within this chapter.

With an interesting sense of clairvoyance, WJMC had signed an agreement with the Louisiana National Guard to deploy a security unit at the hospital just prior to the storm. The presence of this unit gave the employees a sense of safety and security when televised reports and observed events showed an increasing element of social disruption in the city. These feelings made it easier for employees to remain on the job and care for patients during the time of extreme chaos.

As the patient numbers swelled, WJMC established relationships with both federal response entities, such as Disaster Medical Assistance Teams, and a community health center group that was able to establish a primary care center just slightly away from the WJMC campus.

WJMC was also able to create a drive-through form of triage to reduce the number of patients presenting for care at its emergency room. Nurses literally met cars in the parking lot or driveway to assess if the individuals needed care or were merely looking for a shelter.

Because of the chaos in and around New Orleans in those early days, WJMC looked more to its relationships with friends or contractors for assistance. For instance, a CEO of another hospital outside the area was able to reach WJMC with a truckload of supplies. Sodhexho, a hospital supply company, was able to provide emergency support, and the U.S. Navy provided generator fuel.

Creativity became the rule of operation for the hospital as red bags were used for personal body waste, flashlights helped illuminate operating rooms, and the concept of clean linens was but a memory as the hospital's laundry had floated away during the storm to downtown New Orleans.

To attempt to reduce staff exhaustion, the concept of A and B 12-hour shifts was introduced to employees. This allowed overworked personnel an opportunity to get some rest during this horrific time.

Many on the staff had suffered total loss or damage to their homes. WJMC, in turn, established a foundation to raise money, which was subsequently disbursed to staff members in need. To assist its community physicians who had seen a significant decrease in patients with means to pay for healthcare services, WJMC began to pay doctors to take call. This helped WJMC keep physicians in the community at a time when they were being recruited by other states or facilities.

Of critical import is also the recognition that Katrina recovery is ongoing even these many months later. New Orleans will be decades in its recovery, and decisions made in a healthcare setting must recognize the changed universe. As such, WJMC continues to seek collaborative relationships with other hospitals and universities.

Lessons Learned

- Good planning recognizes the need for physical and financial security during the disaster and the recovery.
- Good leadership recognizes the need to think both in the sense of immediate concerns and survival in the long term.
- Good leadership in a disaster recognizes that social networks among friends and suppliers are often more effective in responding than organized response structures.
- Cooperation with other facilities or providers (instead of competition) can often be invaluable in recovery.
- Creativity and resourcefulness are valued tools for survival.

Hancock Medical Center

On August 28, 2005, Hancock Medical Center (HMC), located in Bay Saint Louis, Mississippi, was a 104-bed full-service hospital employing more than 500 persons and enjoying an average daily census of approximately 60 patients. County owned, self-sustaining, and supported by a medical staff of 25 members, HMC was emblematic of the string of Gulf Coast hospitals stretching along the entirety of the coastline, which served retirees, vacationers, casino employees, and other workers

in the tourist industry. In addition, it serviced residents of a rising upscale development community nearby that was thriving before Katrina hit.

Hal Leftwich, the CEO, had come to manage HMC from Florida. As Katrina approached, neither he nor anyone on his staff could imagine that, within a few short
hours, life would drastically change—perhaps for decades—in Bay Saint Louis.

Katrina's landfall placed HMC in a head-on collision of her fury. Because the
hospital lies at the intersection of Bay Saint Louis and Waveland, it was ground
zero for the landfall of the storm. HMC has been recognized as the single most-
damaged healthcare facility among many along the Gulf Coast.

During the height of the storm surge, nine feet of water filled the outside of
the hospital grounds, washing away or covering all of the cars in the parking lot.
The water swallowed up and destroyed the emergency power generator and cut
HMC off from the outside world. Six feet of water made it into the hospital,
destroying all of its imaging equipment, walls, beds, commons areas, kitchen,
and emergency room.

As the storm passed and as the water receded, patients began to arrive, some
literally swimming in to seek care.

Against the backdrop of nearly total devastation, the leadership of the hospital
had to think of both immediate and long-term implications for disaster response.

Immediate Needs to Deliver Care

Without power, water, supplies, communication, or diagnostic equipment, the
hospital staff of about 80 who had weathered the storm undertook two tasks simultaneously. First, they had to consider the care and limited treatment of those
patients arriving. A hospital worker explained, "We were left with our stethoscopes
and assessment skills." Fortunately, that was enough for the first few hours, and
CEO Leftwich is quick to credit the emergency room doctors and emergency room
staff with calm, effective professionalism during this early time of catastrophe.

The task was made more difficult, however, as a result of poor communication with other agencies. Rather than receiving patients into their facilities, many
hospitals were actually dropping off rescued patients to HMC in the early hours
after the storm hit.

The second and more difficult task was seeking to transfer the 34 patients who
had remained at HMC when Katrina made landfall. This effort, though ultimately
successful, was made more difficult because of lack of communications, the temporary displacement of the Hancock County Emergency Management Agency as a
result of its own damage, poor support from outside agencies, and a lack of transportation vehicles.

Lessons Learned

- Priorities are critical in the early stages of disaster and, hopefully, will be covered in the facility's disaster plan.

- Communication must be redundant and should include ham radio operators or other options when normal telecommunications networks are not operational.
- Transfer agreements and hardened support functions around a designed incident management system are a requirement. These agreements should expand beyond the normal, territorial borders and should be supported by a state or regionwide patient transfer system capable of quick response in a widespread disaster.

Long-Term Needs and Recovery

Perhaps the most important decision made by Leftwich within hours of the storm's passing was to focus the efforts of his staff on the rebuilding of the facility. Hope and a promise of a future proved to be the most important commodity in holding his team together as they were surrounded by horror and fear.

Around the hospital was the total devastation of the Mississippi Gulf Coast. Pictures cannot do justice to the horrific images of miles of coastline suddenly swept clean of its buildings and people. The leadership of HMC had to make some difficult decisions to maintain its financial viability.

The community that HMC had served prior to Katrina no longer existed. Overnight, Hancock County had lost a large percentage of its population and had become a rural county in the eyes of Medicare. Therefore, the first decision was to apply for status as a critical access hospital, which would enhance the chances of financial survivability.

The second decision was to reduce the hospital's bed size from 104 to 20 and the staff to less than 50 percent of the prestorm employment. This task was made a bit easier because many of the staff had left the area; however, pink slips were distributed to about 25 percent of the remaining employees.

With fewer patients to treat, Leftwich and his board decided to use staff members to do much of the rebuilding of the hospital. Though this would later cause the Federal Emergency Management Agency (FEMA) angst and result in significantly less federal reimbursement grant dollars for the hospital, the decision nevertheless proved outstanding in that it gave the employees compensated work, a sense of rebuilding, a vision of the future, and a strong voice in the direction of recovery efforts. Given that more than 70 percent of the staff, including Leftwich, had lost their homes, hope for the future was greatly needed.

With this direction, HMC was able to reopen for surgical cases in only three months. No one would have dared believe this was possible in the wee hours after the storm hit!

During the rebuilding, the continuity of caring for the remaining community was provided through the presence of Disaster Medical Assistance Teams and faith-based or other not-for-profit community health centers that were spread around the county.

HMC was able to establish regular daily meetings with the response agencies at a set-up outdoor café, which was serving fresh baked cookies from a gas oven that was still working. This informal meeting setting proved invaluable to creating a supportive bond between the hospital and the responders. Though others along the Gulf Coast have less than positive stories to share about interactions with outside response agencies, HMC proved a model of collaboration in most cases.

The practices of private physicians were also greatly impacted. Admirably, more than 85 percent of the HMC community doctors returned to Hancock County, though other communities suffered a loss of their physicians to neighboring states or facilities. However, there was virtually no federal support to help Hancock County doctors rebuild their practices. The hospital itself was struggling with what would ultimately be a $30 million rebuilding cost—much of it unreimbursed.

Moreover, many of the same free clinics that had been deployed to Hancock County were now actually seeing patients who had previously been treated by the community doctors. Frustration built, and concerns were aired.

Clearly, physicians were critical to the future of the facility if the community was to be rebuilt. Once again, HMC came up with an appealing response to the challenge. It offered employment to the doctors at 60 percent of the Medical Group Management Association (MGMA) market basket index, plus a productivity bonus. The hospital also took on all of the risk of loss from unfunded patients. In addition, it offered easy opt outs if the physician desired to return to private practice.

Finally, in addition to using its foundation to raise funds for its hospital rebuilding and staff support, HMC also assisted in soliciting for contributions to assist these community doctors in rebuilding their practices.

Lessons Learned

- Have a postevent plan and vision and act upon it quickly.
- Be flexible and recognize that your employees will have needs—both financial and psychosocial—that must be met.
- Have a strong financial recovery plan that realizes that insurance, aid, or other traditional sources of dollars may not be enough.
- In the hospital business, doctors are the lifeblood of the facility and caregivers to the community. Have a plan that expands your efforts beyond the brick and mortar of your walls and reaches into the community.[23]

CONCLUSION

This chapter has provided a brief summary of major issues around disaster response. It is meant to be a guide to encourage practice and organization leaders on a path toward readiness. Every disaster is different, every community unique, and hence no chapter or book can, or even should, attempt to deliver canned solutions as if they were handed down from Mount Sinai. Rather, any writer on this subject should share lessons learned with others in need in hopes of providing a basis for asking questions, testing assumptions, and taking on the mantle of leadership when called upon.

One of the true strengths of healthcare providers is that they are problem solvers. Physicians are trained to examine patients and make recommendations for care. These same skills in examining events and making recommendations are the essence of disaster response. Good physicians, however, become great caregivers when their ability to examine a situation is supported by good training, valid experience, competent support, correct information, and appropriate tools.

Leadership in disaster response is organized from the basis that each of those components—training, experience, support, information, and tools—must be planned in advance and/or obtained during a disaster and managed in a way that achieves the overarching goal of healthcare leaders in disaster response. That goal, simply put, is: *to maximize the lives saved*. The following closing key concepts form a good beginning checklist for disaster leadership.

Key Concepts

- Communication before the event needs to be mission number one. This builds social interaction with your community around disaster response and exposes opportunities to work together during times of crisis.
- Trust is the most valued commodity. Can you count on others to assist when needed?
- Although healthcare is fragmented and competitive, it is the wise practitioner who finds ways to cooperate around disaster response.
- Remain flexible. Though the previous examples and case studies are merely guides, circumstances and the nature of the event will dictate your response and how you lead your facility.
- When in doubt, keep the response simple. Stay focused on the need to protect yourself and your employees and to maximize the numbers of lives saved.
- Look for redundancy in relationships and communication. Take time out of your busy schedule to meet individuals within the community who will be needed by your facility in times of disaster.
- Above all else, lead or follow well. Both are equally important—at different times.

ACRONYMS

ADPH: Alabama Department of Public Health.

CMMS: Center for Medicare and Medicaid Services.

DMAT: Disaster Medical Assistance Team.

DMORT: Disaster Mortuary Operational Response Teams.

EMA: Emergency Management Agency.

EMAEOC: Emergency Management Agency Emergency Operations
Center.

EMTALA: Emergency Medical Treatment and Leave Act.

EOP: Emergency operations plan.

ESF: Emergency support function.

FEMA: Federal Emergency Management Agency.

FRP: Federal response plan.

HEICS: Hospital Emergency Incident Command System.

HICS: Hospital Incident Command System.

HIPAA: Health Insurance Portability and Accountability Act.

HRSA: Health Resources and Services Administration.

HSPD-5: Homeland Security Presidential Directive 5.

HVA: Hazard, Threat, and Vulnerability Analysis.

ICS: Incident Command System.

JCAHO: Joint Commission on Accreditation of Healthcare Organization.

MMRS: Metropolitan Medical Response System Program.

MTC: Medical Transfer Center.

NIMS: National Incident Management System.

NPS: National Pharmaceutical Stockpile.

ONCHIT: Office of the National Coordinator for Health Information
Technology.

PTU: Patient Transfer Unit.

SNS: Strategic National Stockpile.

NOTES

1. Harari, 2005. *The Powell Principles—24 Lessons from Colin Powell.* New York:
McGraw-Hill, 79.

2 Larson, 2006. *Isaac's Storm.* New York: Vintage Books, 6.

3. Ibid., 14.

4. Mikawa, S., ed. 2006. "Integrated Disaster Response Demonstration." Paper
presented at Strong Angel III, San Diego, CA.

5. United States Department of Homeland Security. 2004 [2006]. "National Response Plan." Washington, D.C.

6. Minyard, E. 2006. "Mobile Emergency Communication Services: The New Orleans Experience." Presentation to Distributed Medical Intelligence Conference 9, New Orleans, LA.

7. Wallace, D. and C. Taylor. 2005. "After Action Report of Hurricane Ivan." Unpublished report prepared for the Alabama Department of Public Health.

8. Select Bipartisan Committee to Investigate the Preparation for and Response to Hurricane Katrina. 2006. *A Failure of Initiative: Final Report of the Select Bipartisan Committee to Investigate the Preparation for and Response to Hurricane Katrina.* Washington, D.C.: U.S. Government Printing Office.

9. U.S. Department of Homeland Security (DHS). 2004 [2006]. *National Response Plan.* Washington, D.C.: U.S. Government Printing Office.

10. The Joint Commission. 2005. *Standing Together: An Emergency Planning Guide for America's Communities.* Chicago: Joint Commission Resources.

11. McGlown, K. J., ed. 2004. *Terrorism and Disaster Management—Preparing Healthcare Leaders for the New Reality.* Chicago: Health Administration Press, 64–65.

12. Taylor, C., and H. Leftwich. 2006. Personal interview with the author, November 2.

13. Nordqvist, C. 2006. "Many Health Workers Would Not Respond to Flu Pandemic." Available at: http://www.medicalnewstoday.com/articles/41796.php. Accessed April 18, 2006.

14. Commission Established by the Government of Ontario Canada to Investigate the Introduction and Spread of Acute Respiratory Syndrome. 2003. Presentation of Barbara Wahl President of the Ontario Nurses Association, Toronto, ON, September 20, p. 13.

15. Hebert, E. 2006. "Lessons Learned from Katrina." Speech to Mobile Health Care Providers, Mobile, AL.

16. Ibid.

17. Agency for Healthcare Research and Quality. 2005. *Healthcare Research and Quality: Altered Standards of Care in Mass Casualty Events.* Gaithersburg, MD: AHRQ Publications, 9–10.

18. Loper, S. 2006. "Lessons Learned from Katrina." Speech to Advanced Regional Response Training Center Focus on Financial Resiliency in Disasters Meeting, Mobile, AL.

19. Herbert.

20. Taylor, C., and H. Leftwich. 2006. Personal interview with the author, November 2.

21. Center for Disease Control and Prevention. "Crisis and Emergency Risk Communication." Available at: http://www.bt.cdc.gov/erc.

22. Prior, S. D. 2006 "Managing In a Pandemic," Presentation to the Advanced Regional Response Training Center Focus Meeting on Pandemic Preparedness, Mobile, AL.

23. As I end these case studies, I would like to extend my sincere gratitude to the leaders of these two hospitals impacted by Hurricane Katrina: Gary Muller, Erie Hebert, Mitch Leckelt, and Jennifer Steele of West Jefferson Medical Center and Hal Leftwich of Hancock Medical Center. Both of these hospitals and their leaders graciously took time out of their busy schedules to provide information and insight into their disaster responses for this chapter. I wish you continued success with the operation and

recovery of your healthcare facility. Also Commander Eric Rasmussen MD U.S. Navy whose thoughts and leadership and suggestions are found throughout this chapter. Finally, thanks to Dr. David Wallace, the Director of Training at the Advanced Regional Response Training Center at the University of South Alabama, whose work gave rise to the appendix and whose classes formed the basis for many of the lessons learned and now shared.

APPENDIX: EMERGENCY OPERATIONS—FEDERAL, STATE, AND LOCAL STRUCTURES

You are not alone when disasters come, whether in planning, preparing, questioning, or responding. Although it is incomplete to suggest that all disaster planning falls into federal, state, and local efforts, understanding the continuum and the structure response is important. At the center of the national effort lies the National Response Plan; this dictates the lead agency accountable for certain emergency support functions.

At the base of this effort is Emergency Support Function 8, which requires the 50 state departments of health to be accountable for managing and coordinating medical care during emergencies. To facilitate this effort, all state departments of public health have received funding from the Health Resources and Services Administration (HRSA) to prepare both themselves and surrounding hospitals. Prudent states have used these dollars to improve public health, increase provider communication, and create a common organizational response chart for disaster response. This chart, called an Incident Command System, outlines the primary leadership positions required to manage catastrophes. These positions are discussed more fully later in this appendix. Visit the California Emergency Medical Services Authority (http://www.emsa.ca.gov/hics/hics.asp) to review the most recent version of a Hospital Incident Command System (HICS or HEICS).

THE THEORETICAL TIERED RESPONSE TO A HEALTHCARE DISASTER

Hospitals in the United States are self-reliant and self-sustaining, but many leaders of such organizations have been unaware of the vital need to fit into a comprehensive and coordinated community or regional disaster response system. The lack of recognition has resulted in an extremely inefficient way to manage surge capacity and capability during a mass casualty event. Soon after the first Gulf War ended in 1991, the federal government declared that the continental United States was at significant risk of a terrorist attack. At the same time, officials acknowledged that the public health and healthcare systems were woefully unprepared to respond and care for large numbers of casualties resulting from a catastrophic event, either natural or man-made.

As a result of these conclusions, the federal government began what is now a 10-year effort to improve the overall response capability of the United States healthcare system. In the mid-1990s, chemical and biological terrorist attack response training programs began to sweep the country. Millions of dollars were spent at the local level on personal protective equipment for hospitals and other healthcare facilities. For the first time, hospital personnel were expected to be proficient in taking care of patients while wearing fully protective chemical suits, a real change in the mindset of healthcare providers and administrators.

By 1996, the Metropolitan Medical Response System (MMRS) program had been established. The MMRS program set goals of creating uniform response networks using common plans laid out by the federal government with written assistance by local planners. The ultimate goal was to have the 120 largest metropolitan areas in the United States prepared to respond in a consistent manner. If federal assets were deployed to assist the local response, it was hoped those responders would better understand and fit into a system they had helped develop.

Out of the MMRS program evolved the National Pharmaceutical Stockpile (NPS) program, now known as the Strategic National Stockpile (SNS) program. Federal response teams were also created, most notably Disaster Medical Assistance Teams (DMATs) and Disaster Mortuary Operational Response Teams (DMORTs).

The healthcare disaster preparedness theme that continued into the latter half of the 1990s and the first five years of the twenty-first century were twofold: (1) to enhance a healthcare system that became advanced in its capability and capacity and (2) to improve coordination of all required agencies from the community level to the national level.

The terrorist attacks of September 11, 2001, were the first test for the so-called new healthcare disaster response system. The ultimate test of preparedness began in 2004, however, with multiple hurricanes devastating areas of Florida and culminating with the Hurricane Katrina catastrophe of New Orleans in 2005. There is still great debate on whether the National Response Plan helped or caused more harm and confusion during and after this disaster.

The relationship between federal responders and state and local governments has vacillated over the past 10 years. In the early 1990s, the governmental response was "We know best and we're here to take over" when called to become involved in local disasters. There were times when response coordination went well, but it is also fair to speculate those relationships were frequently strained. As time passed and the government promoted its emergency response programs, however, the relationship between the local and federal agencies began to develop positively. Naturally, the monetary awards associated with such governmental programs contributed to their relational reciprocation.

Until August 2005, it appeared a decade of disaster response planning had actually been successful. Some believe, however, the pendulum is moving back toward negative feelings as the aftereffects, disasters, and response failures of various agencies during the Katrina legacy continue to be evident. Hopefully, time will continue to heal all wounds and agencies at all levels will resume dialogue and work at preparing their city for the next disaster in a positive, planned, and organized way.

The National Response Plan (formerly the Federal Response Plan) lays out a global view for federal agencies by mandating: (1) their responsibilities to respond,

(2) their unique role, (3) their initiations and responses, (4) the organization and method of their responses, and (5) how the federal responders fit into regional, state, and local response plans.

Theoretically, the federal response is initiated by a request from a state governor upon the advice of health and emergency planners. This is the appropriate activation process, but it can create confusion, in particular to the levelness of the playing field.

The request for federal assistance during a catastrophic event may become politicized because of inadequate plans developed by local and state agencies and ineffectual leadership on their part. Though this is not the best option, requests may even be initiated by the federal government. Ideally, it will be crystal clear what is needed when a state has an effective and efficient plan, the planners and responders are well organized, and the federal government understands its role is to assist during times of disaster rather than take over and operate the disaster plan.

All emergency management response plans, specifically local, area, and state plans, commonly referred to as emergency operations plans (EOPs), follow the same format as the National Response Plan. The plans define 15 emergency support functions (ESFs). Each ESF is a predefined set of tasks and assigns those responsibilities to the appropriate department or agency to manage. The following is the most current list of ESFs, which are incorporated into emergency management response plans:

1. Transportation: Department of Transportation.
2. Communications: Department of Homeland Security/National Communications System.
3. Public works and engineering: Department of Defense/Army Corps of Engineers.
4. Firefighting: Department of Agriculture.
5. Emergency management: Department of Homeland Security/Federal Emergency Management Agency (FEMA).
6. Mass care, housing, human services: Department of Homeland Security/FEMA.
7. Resource support: General Services Administration.
8. Public health and medical services: Department of Health and Human Services.
9. Urban search and rescue: Department of Homeland Security/FEMA.
10. Oil and hazardous materials response: Environmental Protection Agency.
11. Agriculture and natural resources: Department of Agriculture.
12. Energy: Department of Energy.
13. Public safety and security: Department of Justice.
14. Long-term community recovery: Department of Homeland Security/FEMA.
15. External affairs: Department of Homeland Security.

These responsible agencies are national-level departments. State and local planners must apply these concepts and assign the authority to carry out these tasks to the appropriate state or local agencies or departments.

At the state and local level, the public health department is generally responsible for coordinating ESF 8, public health and medical services. Every tier of response under ESF 8 is organized, managed, or coordinated by public health. It is essential that each healthcare facility mesh its plans into ESF 8, set aside old habits of independent responses, cooperate rather than compete, share information and resources, and insist on an efficient community-wide healthcare system response.

There are six tiers or levels of healthcare response. Planning and coordination has to occur at each of the levels. Each level must know how to support the next lower level and how to access help from the next higher level.

The six tiers from lowest to highest are the following:

Tier 1: Individual Facility Level

Tier 1 is the individual healthcare facility, such as a hospital, public health department, community health center, or nursing home. These facilities will activate and manage their disaster plan in response to a local event. This is an everyday event in healthcare, because of surge capacity/surge capability minidisasters. At some point during the crisis, the local facility will return to regular activities or activate its hospital incident command system when the event surges beyond its capacity. When the event exceeds the capability of the facility, the next tier of response occurs by notifying other healthcare facilities, the public health department, and emergency management agencies.

Tier 2: Local Coalition or System of Individual Facilities Level

Tier 2 is a healthcare system, such as a collection of hospitals, community health centers, nursing homes, and the public health department(s) in a localized area. This organization of community healthcare assets gathers to respond in a systemwide manner. ESF 8 preevent planning and coordination must have already occurred at this tier. Common communications and incident command systems are critical for this level of response. If the event exceeds the capabilities of this local system, the next tier of response occurs by notifying the public health department and emergency management.

Tier 3: Area Coalition or System of Individual Facilities Level

Tier 3 is an area healthcare system, such as a collection of local systems in a larger area than Tier 2 (i.e., substate region). This area system will provide support and resources from a larger geographic area of the state without having to draw on all statewide resources. ESF 8 preevent planning and coordination must have also occurred at this tier and usually involves the state public health department, the state Emergency Management Agency (EMA), and other needed state-level agencies. Common communications and incident command systems are critical for this level of response. If the event exceeds the capabilities of this area system, the next tier of response occurs by area or substate regional public health departments and emergency management notifying the appropriate state agencies.

Tier 4: Statewide Coalition or System of Individual Facilities Level

Tier 4 is a state healthcare system made up of a statewide collection of healthcare facilities, resources, and personnel. The state system will provide support and resources from the entire state and will be a combination of governmental and private responders and volunteers. ESF 8 preevent planning and coordination must have also occurred at this tier and involves the state public health department, the state EMA, the state governor's office, and other state-level agencies. Common communications and incident command systems are absolutely essential for this level of response. If the event exceeds the capabilities of this state system, the next tier of response occurs by the state public health department, emergency management, or governor's office notifying the appropriate multistate and federal response agencies.

Tier 5: Multistate Coalition or System of Individual Facilities Level

Tier 5 is a multistate healthcare system made up of regional states' healthcare facilities, resources, and personnel. The multistate system will provide support and resources for a state or states impacted by a mass casualty disaster. ESF 8 preevent planning and coordination must have occurred at this tier and involves the state public health department, the state EMA, the state governor's office, other state-level agencies from numerous states, and regional national response agencies. Common communications and incident command systems are absolutely essential for this level of response. If the event exceeds the capabilities of this area system, the next tier of response occurs by regional national response agencies notifying the appropriate national response agencies.

Tier 6: Federal Regional or National System of Individual Facilities Level

Tier 6 is the federal regional and national healthcare systems. The regional or national response will provide federal healthcare resources and personnel to support the healthcare needs of a state or states. ESF 8 preevent planning and coordination must have also occurred at this tier and involves the state public health department, the state EMA, the state governor's office, other state-level agencies from multiple states, and federal response organizations, including FEMA, the

Department of Homeland Security, and the Department of Health and Human Services. Common communications and incident command systems are essential for this level of response.

Once a healthcare facility commits to implementing its role in a tiered response system, it is essential that incident management tools be developed and implemented that are consistent throughout the United States. The National Incident Management System (NIMS) and the Hospital Emergency Incident Command System (HEICS) are those two tools. NIMS was established in Homeland Security Presidential Directive 5 (HSPD-5) by President George W. Bush in 2004 and is a comprehensive national approach to incident management. It is basically creating and mandating simultaneously a National Incident Command System. It is the system to more effectively coordinate and integrate federal, state, area, and local plans and resources and responses. In the past, the federal government has encouraged healthcare disaster response planning in two ways: (1) awarding grants and contracts and (2) encouraging those involved to do the right thing when disaster hits.

NIMS has now tied participation of hospitals and other healthcare facilities to financial incentives, primarily a continuation of federal funding of healthcare disaster preparedness, including equipment, supplies, training, and exercises.

For hospitals and other healthcare facilities to be in compliance, they must do the following:

1. Adopt the concept of NIMS and become familiar with the National Response Plan.
2. Develop and adopt a Hospital Emergency Incident Command System (HEICS).
3. Make HEICS a part of their disaster plan.
4. Ensure the completion of training for key staff.
5. Participate in local and regional planning and exercises.

The first phase of compliance should have been completed by September 30, 2007. The Joint Commission on Accreditation of Healthcare Organizations (JCAHO) will continue to require emergency preparedness planning, training, and exercises. It will be critical for NIMS and JCAHO requirements to be synchronized.

It is central that all responding agencies at the local level, including healthcare, be represented at the county or city Emergency Management Agency Emergency Operations Center (EMAEOC). The Incident Command System (ICS) is the core of a coordinated local response. When an individual agency uses its incident management system, it is referred to as an *incident command*. When a group of agencies gather at the EOC and work together, it is referred to as a *unified command*. ICS and HEICS are the same system, but HEICS is the specific name given to the hospital version of ICS.

Hospitals are being asked to develop and incorporate HEICS into their disaster response plans. The purpose is to create a common incident management system for all hospitals, but it is also to have a tool in place to plan, prepare, respond, and communicate using the same language as other response agencies, particularly all public safety, EMA, and volunteer agencies.

HEICS is divided into five sections with corresponding personnel for each:

1. Command and Control Section: The facility incident commander is in charge; the public information officer disseminates the message to all facets of the public; the liaison officer of your facility communicates with other liaison officers of other agencies; and the safety and security officer secures both the facility and the personnel.
2. Logistics Section: The Logistics Team chief is responsible for the building, resources, supplies, food, transportation, and communications equipment.
3. Planning Section: The Planning Team chief is responsible for collecting and managing information, keeping all necessary personnel informed of the facility's status, managing the response plan, predicting the next steps, and providing personnel.
4. Finance (Administration) Section: The Finance Team chief is responsible for the budgeting for personnel time, procurement, claims, costs, and the business management of the facility.
5. Operations Section: The Operations Team chief provides healthcare during the disaster event. All other sections either provide overall command, control, and/or support to the Operations Section.

Disaster preparedness for healthcare facilities of all types, specifically hospitals, is not an option. Success or failure will depend on the facility's commitment of time, money, personnel, and philosophy of the need to be prepared. Recent events have made an impact on the medical community, and agencies of all levels are encouraging all healthcare facilities to implement necessary procedures for disaster preparedness. When, not *if*, the next disaster comes, we will see if hospitals are able to function and remain open independently or if they have planned to survive together. Hopefully, the healthcare system in the United States will be adequately prepared.

CHAPTER 2

Healthcare Insurance: The Massachusetts Plan

Michael T. Doonan and Stuart H. Altman

Health insurance protects against catastrophic loss and high medical costs associated with illness, accidents, or diseases. Health insurance is also paying for a larger share of preventive care and prescription drugs. Studies show that, all things being equal, people without health insurance are sicker and more likely to die earlier because of medical problems.[1]

In April 2006, Massachusetts passed a healthcare reform proposal with the goal of moving toward universal coverage. The plan is based on the principle of shared responsibility and asks more of government, business, and individuals. The most unique feature of the plan is a mandate that everyone who can afford it purchase health insurance. This plan builds off the base of the existing health financing system and earlier state reforms. It was a bipartisan proposal supported by a broad-based coalition. In the first year, more than 100,000 previously uninsured people obtained coverage as a result of these reforms.

This reform makes Massachusetts the first state since Hawaii in 1974 to enact a plan targeted at or near universal coverage. Massachusetts helped trigger a round of state healthcare reform initiatives across the United States and also holds potential lessons for future national reforms. Elements of the Massachusetts plan are being considered by a host of other states.

This chapter examines the goals and context behind this reform, including an examination of the history of healthcare reform in the state and the policy environment in Massachusetts. We then provide details of the plan and an initial assessment of the first year of implementation.

HISTORY

Massachusetts has a long history of innovation in the area of healthcare. The Boston Public Health Commission was the first in the newly founded nation and headed by Paul Revere in 1799. The first permanent marine hospital was authorized to be built in Massachusetts in 1803. The first state board of health was created in Massachusetts in 1869. Massachusetts is home to some of the most advanced medical research in the world and boasts world-famous teaching hospitals. The state also has some of the highest-ranked health plans in the country. Three of the largest health plans in Massachusetts were ranked in the top 10 nationally for quality and enrollee satisfaction. Massachusetts also has some of the highest healthcare costs in the country. Healthcare is also a huge part of the state's economy, responsible for the employment of more than 12 percent of the employment in the state.

Massachusetts has a history of innovation in the area of cost control and coverage expansion. Greater effort and success have been achieved in efforts to cover the uninsured than in controlling healthcare costs. In the 1970s, Massachusetts attempted to control healthcare costs by instituting government-regulated regional hospital rate setting. Toward this end, it also embraced managed care along with deregulation and competition between hospitals as rate regulation was repealed in the 1990s. Efforts to expand access to care can be seen in the development of the Uncompensated Care Pool, also know as the Free Care Pool, in 1985 and major healthcare coverage expansions and reforms in 1988, 1996, and 2006. These programs and policies demonstrate a commitment to innovation and experimentation and set in place program and political constituencies that could be built on over time. They are important to understanding the current reform.

In 1975, Massachusetts joined Maryland, New York, and New Jersey in establishing a hospital rate-setting program. This program set annual revenue caps for every acute care hospital in the state.[2] Rate setting was precipitated by the rapid rise of healthcare costs in the 1970s driven by public coverage expansions (Medicare and Medicaid), increases in medical technology, and inflation. This initiative was supported by business and their concern about spiraling healthcare costs. It was successful in curbing medical costs, but only in the short term.[3]

UNCOMPENSATED CARE POOL

In part to mitigate the impact of rate-setting regulations, the Uncompensated Care Pool was established in 1985. This pool pays hospitals for the care of low-income uninsured people and in effect made access to hospital and community health center services available to everyone in the state who meets residency and income criteria (less than 200 percent federal poverty level, or FPL, or $27,380 for a family of two in 2007). This program also made the cost of the uninsured explicit, and this helped shape and drive later reforms.

The Uncompensated Care Pool, funded at more than $800 million in fiscal year 2006, collects revenue through hospital assessments, surcharges on payers (insurers, health plans, and individuals), general state revenue, and federal Medicaid matching funds. Federal funds are secured through intergovernmental transfers that are part of an 1115 state waiver demonstration program with the federal government. The 1115 waivers allow states to disregard many of the rules of the traditional Medicaid program in order to expand coverage and/or reduce costs in an innovative way. The structure of the Uncompensated Care Pool changed in the 1990s from one that paid only for hospital services to a program with registration providing a broad range of inpatient and outpatient services to the low-income uninsured not eligible for other state programs. It still does not pay for physician services, nonacute hospitals, or prescription drugs. The majority of pool funds are for hospital outpatient services (61 percent in fiscal year 2001), followed by inpatient services (34 percent) and community health centers (4 percent).[4]

Although the program has had tremendous success in expanding access to care, there have been ongoing concerns about equity and accountability of pool funding at the state and national level.[5] First, although the uninsured are more evenly distributed throughout the state, most of the people covered by this program are in the Boston area and distributed to two large safety net providers, Boston Medical Center and the Cambridge Health Alliance. Second, since 1990 the cost of uncompensated care in most years exceeded available funds, so hospitals still needed to cover some uncompensated care.[6] Third, it has been difficult to track funding provided to these facilities and understand how the money is directly linked to services provided. Fourth, the federal government as part of the waiver renewal in July 2005 threatened to end this type of institutional funding. Federal officials wanted more of the money to go toward the direct purchase of insurance coverage for low-income individuals and families. As detailed in the following sections, this federal pressure helped ignite the latest round of reform.

EMPLOYER MANDATE AND DUKAKIS REFORMS IN 1988

The current round of reform builds on past efforts. In 1988, Massachusetts passed significant health reform including a so-called pay-or-play employer mandate requiring all employers with six or more employees to provide health insurance or pay into a fund. Employers with more than six employees would have to pay up to $1,680 per uninsured worker per year into a state fund. The legislation also included Medicaid expansions and new programs to cover children and pregnant women, children and adults with disabilities, and the long-term unemployed. It required that all full-time college and university students purchase health insurance. In addition, small businesses were offered tax incentives to help them offer coverage to employees. The law aimed to achieve universal coverage by April 1992.[7]

Those still without employer-sponsored coverage would be able to buy insurance through a newly created Department of Medical Security. Premiums were to be on a sliding scale based on income, but the subsidies were not specifically defined in statute. The new department was required to use managed care products to reduce healthcare costs. The program relaxed hospital rate-setting standards and hoped that competition between hospitals would help reduce excess hospital bed capacity and ultimately lower costs.[8]

This legislation passed with the strong support of the governor and presidential candidate Michael Dukakis. In contrast to the next two rounds of reform, however, there was significant opposition to this legislation in the state legislature, the small-business community, and the Republican Party. One person close to the process characterized this as "the most controversial and heavily fought battle in the past 25 years in the Massachusetts State House."[9]

Dukakis lost the presidential election in 1988, and the economy in Massachusetts went into recession. A Republican, William Weld, was elected governor in 1990. The employer mandate was to take effect in 1992 but was delayed three times by the legislature and finally repealed as part of a reform package in 1996. The threat of retaining the mandate was used as leverage by the legislature with Governor Weld to help propel the 1996 reforms.[10]

Some of the elements of the Dukakis reform that were retained include: Medicaid enrollment expansions, new programs for people with disabilities, assistance for the long-term unemployed, and coverage mandate for college students.[11] Without these earlier coverage expansions, passage of the current reform, including the viability of an individual coverage mandate, would have been more difficult.

MANAGED CARE GROWTH

Hospital rate regulation ended altogether under the Weld administration in 1991 in a general trend toward competition and managed care. Managed care growth exploded in Massachusetts during this period and for a time was successful in keeping medical inflation under control. Health insurance premiums were held flat in the late 1990s but would experience double-digit growth from 2000 to 2007. Throughout the 1990s, consumer and provider backlash against managed care and the assertion of hospital systems substantially weakened the ability of managed care organizations to manage care and costs. Signs that managed care was weakening could be seen even as it was continuing to grow. The decline in managed care actually started in 1994 when the state passed an "any willing provider" law requiring all HMOs to contract with all pharmacies willing to take their price.[12] Also in 1997, New England Medical Center won a battle with Harvard Pilgrim Health Care Plan to limit the health plan's ability to exclude hospitals from coverage.[13]

The development and success of integrated healthcare delivery systems helped push back against managed care. The largest integrated healthcare delivery system in Massachusetts is Partners HealthCare System. It was formed by the Brigham and Women's Hospital and Massachusetts General Hospital in 1994. It has been joined by a number of hospitals in eastern Massachusetts and has 4,000 affiliated physicians. An example of their growing strength in the market can be seen in the showdown between Partners HealthCare System and Tufts Health Plan in 2001.[14] In October 2001, Tufts and Partners terminated their contract. Partners wanted a 29.7 percent increase in payments over three years. Blue Cross Blue Shield of Massachusetts had previously agreed to double-digit increases in payments. Tufts, facing pressure from employers and enrollees about being excluded from the prestigious Partners HealthCare System, capitulated to the health system's demands. Later, Partners received significant payment increases from Harvard Pilgrim. This example reflected a shift in the balance of power from the health plans back to the providers, and this was reflected in sharp increases in private healthcare premiums.

MASSACHUSETTS MASSHEALTH WAIVER AND COVERAGE EXPANSIONS IN 1996

Another major round of reform was enacted in 1996. Massachusetts extended coverage to nearly all uninsured children through the creation of a waiver demonstration program and the adoption of the Children's Medical Security Plan. In an innovative approach, legislators combined an increase in coverage for kids with a cigarette tax. It was pitched as a "good versus evil" story that proved politically powerful. This reform was seen as a blueprint for other states and national reform.[15] It was a precursor to the 1997 federal State Children's Health Insurance Program (SCHIP), which is a nationwide program designed to provide health insurance coverage to millions of children.

As part of the waiver demonstration program, the state created the MassHealth program and began implementation in 1997. The waiver and state legislation extended Medicaid coverage to children younger than 19 with family income below 133 percent of the federal poverty level. It made coverage available to all children younger than 12 with family income below 200 percent of the federal poverty level. It also created the Children's Medical Security Plan, which would make primary and preventive care available to all children on a sliding fee scale based on family income. In addition, the law created a pharmacy assistance program for low-income seniors and maintained and extended coverage to disabled adults and the long-term unemployed. These coverage extensions, like the ones before, would build the foundation for the next round of reform in 2006. The program was funded through increased federal money, a 25 cent increase in the tobacco tax, and some general revenue.

The Weld administration had been working on a waiver since 1994.[16] One crucial success in negotiating with federal officials was setting the baseline level for budget neutrality. States seeking Medicaid waivers must meet the condition of budget neutrality, which requires Medicaid programs not to exceed what they would be without the waiver. How fast the program would have grown absent a waiver and many other variables for calculating a baseline are critical, and the process is often as political as it is mathematical. Federal officials agreed with the Weld administration that expansions for children and pregnant women would not be counted against the state's budget neutrality cap because states are allowed to increase coverage for these groups under federal law Section 1902a(r) (2). The bottom line is that the state could expand eligibility and capture significantly more federal funds.

These reforms were made possible in part by the governor's efforts to obtain a waiver and by strong and persistent leadership in the legislature for expanded health insurance. Representative John McDonough and Senator Mark Montigny, chairs of the legislature's Joint Committee on Health, brought together a broad coalition that was essential for passage. They developed the strategy of linking coverage for children with a tobacco tax. Seniors were brought into the coalition with the new prescription drug program. Business supported the legislation's repeal of the employer mandate. Providers and particularly pediatricians and children's hospitals were strong proponents. Massachusetts also has a strong consumer organization, Health Care for All, that coordinated a powerful lobbying campaign. Legislation passed by wide margins in both chambers. In the end, Governor Weld vetoed the legislation because it increased the cigarette tax. The veto was easily overridden in the House of Representatives by a vote of 117 to 40 and in the Senate by a vote of 32 to 7.[17]

This success was achieved through a sophisticated political strategy, bipartisan support, and a broad-based coalition. Passage was achieved through a broad-based bipartisan coalition that included support from advocates, seniors, healthcare providers, hospitals, and business. Finally, the coverage expansions were financed through the tobacco tax and with federal money secured through an 1115 waiver demonstration program. With the exception of the tobacco tax, each of these strategies would be used to achieve the 2006 reforms.

1115 State Healthcare Reform Waiver Demonstration Projects

The number of uninsured in Massachusetts and in the nation rose in the early 1990s. President Bill Clinton's healthcare reform plan in 1993 was designed to extend coverage and to protect people from the fear that they might lose the health insurance coverage they have when they most need it. With the defeat of the Clinton plan, attention turned toward the states. The Clinton administration was very supportive of 1115 state waiver demonstrations that could extend Medicaid coverage while keeping costs similar to what they would have been absent reform. Many states, including Massachusetts, took advantage of waivers to shift a substantial portion of their Medicaid populations from fee-for-service to managed care and used the savings to extend coverage to a greater portion of the uninsured.

The Massachusetts waiver resulted in major coverage expansions. The number of uninsured in the state rose to 683,000 in 1995. At this time, Medicaid enrollment was 655,000. By 2004, the number of uninsured was down to 460,000. The 1115 waiver was responsible for the additional coverage of some 300,000 people in the state's MassHealth Program. The number of total MassHealth enrollees grew to 972,000 by the late 1990s and today covers more than 1 million people of a total population of 6.4 million.[18]

MASSACHUSETTS HEALTHCARE ENVIRONMENT

This section provides background on the healthcare environment in Massachusetts. It examines the hospitals, health plans, healthcare costs, and the importance of healthcare to the local economy. It examines the problems and challenges that help prompt reform. This is followed by a discussion of the details of this plan and how it has influenced other state efforts to expand healthcare coverage.

Massachusetts has some of the most advanced and expensive healthcare in the world. Healthcare and education drive much of the Massachusetts economy, and they are related. The educational facilities and teaching hospitals help develop the personnel and technology that drives healthcare advancements and costs. Massachusetts has four medical schools at Boston University, Harvard, Tufts, and the University of Massachusetts. Massachusetts General Hospital (MGH), Brigham and Women's, and Beth Israel Deaconess Medical Center, all associated with Harvard Medical School, have international reputations and date back to the 1800s.[19]

In the greater Boston metropolitan region, 14 teaching hospitals generated an estimated $24.3 billion in economic activity in 2006. Teaching hospitals in the state are responsible for the direct and indirect employment of more that 200,000 people.[20] The Milken Institute ranked the Boston metropolitan area as the leading healthcare center in the United States.

Healthcare premiums in Massachusetts, as in the rest of the nation, rose by double digits each year in the 2000s. In Massachusetts, health insurance premiums for families rose 69.2 percent between 2000 and 2006.[21] Over the same period, median income rose just 10.7 percent. For the nation as a whole, the premium growth rate was 89 percent, with average wages growing at slightly less than 20 percent. In dollars, the average annual family premium in Massachusetts, including employer and employee share, rose during this period from $7,341 to $12,419. According to Mercer Health and Benefits, the average healthcare costs of an employee, including dental and dependent coverage, was $9,428 in 2006. Massachusetts is ranked fourth nationally behind Alaska, New Hampshire, and Wisconsin in healthcare costs.[22]

HEALTH PLANS

The Massachusetts healthcare system is dominated by not-for-profit hospitals and health plans. Compared to other states, the healthcare delivery system has traditionally had higher costs and lower provider margins. The state has higher than average income, traditionally higher rates of insurance coverage, disproportionately more specialists and physicians per capita than the nation, more and higher-cost teaching hospitals, and higher frequency of outpatient office visits and greater use of nursing homes.

Although the health plans in Massachusetts are routinely ranked among the best in the nation, they also suffered from the consumer backlash against managed care that developed in the mid-1990s. Thus the regional managed care organizations (MCOs) of today are less aggressive in their attempts to limit the growth in healthcare spending. It became difficult for managed care organizations to compel physicians to control costs by limiting access to specialists or being strong gatekeepers. In addition, MCOs no longer have the market clout to obtain deep discounts from physician groups, hospitals, and healthcare systems.

Currently, Massachusetts's health plans have open access to a broad range of physicians and hospitals. Toward the end the 1990s and into 2000, employers were limiting options to one plan, so, in order to accommodate employees, plan networks were widened. Plans no longer controlled networks, and premiums grew at double-digit rates throughout the 2000s. The top four health insurers by membership in the state are Blue Cross Blue Shield of Massachusetts (3 million), Harvard Pilgrim Health Plan (1 million), Tufts Health Plan (600,000), and Fallon Community Health Plan (less than 200,000). All four plans have announced double-digit increases for 2007, for the seventh year in a row.[23] Massachusetts health plans have consistently ranked among the best in the country by the National Committee on Quality Assurance annual assessment reported in *U.S. News and World Report*. For 2006, Harvard Pilgrim ranked number 1 nationally, Tufts number 2, Blue Cross Blue Shield number 4, and Fallon number 11.[24] Plans were ranked based on access to care, member satisfaction, delivery of preventive services, and treatment (outcomes or protocols).

IMPORTANCE OF HEALTHCARE TO THE ECONOMY

Healthcare is a vital and growing portion of the Massachusetts economy and employed 12.2 percent of the population in 2003, which represented an increase of 26.6 percent since 1990.[25] In 2004, Massachusetts received more funding for research ($2.3 billion) from the National Institutes of Health (NIH) than any other state but California ($3.6 billion). NIH funding accounted for 40 percent of total federal healthcare research funding in the state in 2004. Massachusetts is losing population as a percentage of total U.S. population. In 2004, per capita income in Massachusetts was $42,000, compared to the national average of $33,000.[26] The state has less poverty and is more highly educated than the nation as a whole. The state has one of the highest HMO penetrations in the United States (37 percent compared to 23 percent nationally).[27]

Massachusetts has 27.1 specialists per 10,000 people, compared to just 14.4 for the country.[28] Drugs and nondurable medical expenditures soared through the 1990s. In 1994, they accounted for 7.8 percent of medical expenditures; in 2004, they accounted for 12.0 percent of healthcare expenditures in Massachusetts.[29]

IMPETUS FOR REFORM

There was a confluence of political and economic factors that made 2006 an opportune time for healthcare reform in Massachusetts. The underlying problem was the number of uninsured and the likelihood that as healthcare costs continued to grow, this problem would worsen. Estimates of the number of uninsured in the state in 2004 were approximately 500,000, or close to 10 percent of the population.

The urgency behind reform in 2006 was the threat of losing significant federal money. The federal government 1115 waiver with the state was up for review and would not be renewed under the existing conditions. Specifically, the state was in danger of losing $358 million annually in federal funds if they did not make significant changes to the intergovernmental transfer mechanism used to capture federal funds to help fund the Free Care Pool. The state spends more than $1 billion a year to provide services to the uninsured through the Uncompensated Care Pool, Medicaid disproportionate share hospital payments, and other safety net supports.[30] Much of this money was federal, and it was in jeopardy. This existing safety net system was inefficient and unsustainable. The state was given a deadline of July 1, 2006, to modify its waiver and direct less of its money to large institutions providing uncompensated care and more money to provide or subsidize individual insurance.

A number of factors made healthcare reform easier in Massachusetts. First, the state has a strong safety net and an Uncompensated Care Pool. This pot of money could be drawn on to fund expansion. Second, it has a relatively low number of uninsured compared to other states (8 percent to 10 percent compared to 16 percent nationally). Third, it has one of the highest rates of employer-provided coverage. All firms with more than 50 employees in Massachusetts offer health insurance coverage, compared to 96 percent for the rest of the country. Furthermore, 52.4 percent of employers with fewer than 50 employees offer insurance, compared with only 41.9 percent for the rest of nation.[31] Fourth, insurance in the individual and small-group market is regulated and more broadly available than in other states. The state requires insurance companies in the small-group market to use a modified community rating system, making it easier for older people with preexisting conditions to purchase care. Fifth, Massachusetts has a strong Medicaid program that provides coverage to more than 1 million residents. Strong pubic and private coverage keeps the rate of uninsured down, reducing the number that would have to be covered through reform. Sixth, the state has a history of healthcare reform, and coverage expansions enjoy strong public support. Finally, the state is more affluent than average and at the time of reform had a strong economy and a budget surplus. In 2007, however, the budget surplus turned into a $1 billion shortfall, and an economic downturn could jeopardize coverage expansion progress.

LEADERSHIP AND THE ROADMAP TO COVERAGE

Political leadership helped move insurance reform onto the political agenda. Strong leadership was essential from the governor, legislature, advocacy groups, business, and health plan and healthcare system communities. Political leadership was prodded and given a stage by the Blue Cross Blue Shield of Massachusetts Foundation in a series of three events called the Roadmap to Coverage. Events were held at the John F. Kennedy Library, and healthcare leaders from all sectors were invited. These events garnered considerable media attention on local television, radio, and newspapers. Each event had three important elements: new research and data, a top-ranking official keynote, and an audience that included the range of healthcare leaders in the state.

The first event on November 16, 2004, featured Senate President Robert Travaglini. He previously did not have a significant health insurance reform plan.

He used this opportunity to promise to cover half the uninsured in the state in two years. Governor Mitt Romney was working on a plan and Speaker of the House Sal DiMasi was interested in significant reform, so the engagement of the Senate president dramatically increased the chances of reform. This pronouncement convinced many that a real opportunity existed to pass reform in the current legislative session. The Senate president's speech received considerable press attention, and Governor Romney, who had been working for some time behind the scenes, was quick to release his own plan in an Op-Ed in the *Boston Globe* shortly after this event.[32]

The first Roadmap event included a research piece from the Urban Institute, "Caring for the Uninsured in Massachusetts: What Does it Cost, Who Pays, and What Would Full Coverage Add to Medical Spending?"[33] This report outlined the current state and federal resources that could be reconfigured to help pay for coverage expansions. The report concluded that more than $2 billion was spent on care for the uninsured in 2004, including $1.1 billion in uncompensated care. This breaks down to $800 million spent by hospitals, $155 million by community health centers, and $123 million by physicians. The report further estimated that between $374 million and $539 million in new funding would be required to cover the uninsured if existing funding could be reallocated. Total economic and social benefits of covering the uninsured were estimated at between $1.2 billion and $1.7 billion annually. The greatest value of the report was that it made the cost of the uninsured explicit. Uncompensated care is never free, and this report documented how these funds might be redirected toward more rational and appropriate care.

The second Roadmap event on June 21, 2005, featured the governor, who used the opportunity to fill in some additional details of his plan, but much remained undefined. The governor's plan included an individual mandate with penalties of withholding tax refunds and garnering wages. He characterized this as a conservative proposal rooted in individual responsibility. It would provide low-cost limited benefit plans in a comprehensive, market-based approach to make insurance more available and affordable. He noted that 160,000 of the uninsured were currently eligible for Medicaid, many of the uninsured with incomes more than 300 percent of the federal poverty level could afford insurance, and a new program would be designed to help people with incomes less than 300 percent of the poverty level who cannot afford care. He believed this could be done with existing funds and without new revenue.

The Blue Cross Blue Shield of Massachusetts Foundation and the Urban Institute released its second report, which detailed a wide range of policy options for covering the uninsured. The report evaluated expanding access to MassHealth (the state Medicaid program), tax credits, individual mandates, employer mandates, voluntary purchasing pools, and government-funded reinsurance. The most significant finding was that voluntary programs even with significant subsidies would cover less than half the uninsured. They concluded that an individual mandate was necessary for substantial progress toward covering all the uninsured.

This report helped raise support for the individual mandate proposed by the governor.[34]

The keynote at the third event on October 7, 2005, was Speaker of the House Sal DiMasi. The speaker did not release details of the House plan. Details were released later in the month and then quickly passed by the House on November 8, 2005. Foreshadowing difficult negotiations between the branches of the legislature and the governor, the speaker warned against "fuzzy math" and to be realistic about the revenue that would be required to truly expand coverage. He emphasized the notion of shared responsibility of individuals, business, and government. The governor and the Senate president were reticent about new revenue and employer responsibility. These issues would stall progress until the legislation ultimately passed the legislature on April 4, 2006. At this meeting a report was also released on implementation issues.[35]

Equally important to the process was pressure for change from a coalition of consumer groups. Massachusetts has a strong healthcare advocacy organization, Health Care for All. The executive director, John McDonough, is an expert on state healthcare issues and also has firsthand experience in the legislature. As the House chair of the Joint Committee on Health, McDonough took the lead in orchestrating the political strategy and coalition building necessary for the 1996 reforms. In 2005, Health Care for All organized a larger association of advocates known as MassACT (Affordable Health Care Today). This association includes the Greater Boston Interfaith Coalition, labor unions, community health centers, pubic health advocates, and a wide range of organizations focused on consumers and healthcare coverage expansion. This was the first time the faith-based community was directly and actively involved in healthcare reform, and they added significantly to the political dialogue pushing for passage and actively monitoring implementation.

Advocates had a three-pronged strategy. First, Health Care for All introduced its own comprehensive plan. The plan expanded Medicaid to all people in families with income less than 200 percent of the poverty level, provided sliding-scale subsidies for people between 200 percent and 400 percent of the poverty level to purchase care, and strengthened the affordability of coverage for small business. It was financed through a 60 cent increase in the cigarette tax and a payroll tax assessment that would fall on employers that do not provide health insurance. Further, in an effort to reduce premiums, the bill would provide state-sponsored reinsurance for all high-cost patients. Under the reinsurance plan, the state would cover high-cost cases. This would make healthcare costs lower and more predictable for insurers and reduce health insurance premiums for the public.

Second, the coalition pressured the legislature and helped organize a grassroots campaign through a ballot initiative. The ballot initiative would have mandated much of what was in their legislative proposal. The coalition organized more than 2,000 volunteers and collected more than 112,000 signatures. They had enough signatures to put the initiative on the ballot but withdrew it when they saw significant legislative progress. The threat of going forward with the initiative helped spur legislative action. Third, the volunteers and network they created through the process of collecting signatures was used to lobby for coalition positions.

Massachusetts health reform was stalled for four months in a conference committee between the House and Senate as differences were ironed out. One major sticking point was employer responsibility. The House bill included a payroll tax of 5 percent for employers with 11 to 100 employees and 7 percent for employers with more than 100 employees. The tax would be refunded if the company provided health insurance. The Senate bill had limited employer responsibility. Employers with more than 50 employees would be required to contribute if their employees used the state's Free Care Pool. Business leaders, including health plans and healthcare systems, helped broker a compromise that broke the stalemate. The compromise was a $295 annual fair-share surcharge for employers not providing insurance for each full-time employee. The details are described in the following section. Surprising little debate and opposition developed around the individual mandate.

PLAN DETAILS

The plan[36] requires everyone who can afford insurance to purchase it. Government provides new programs, regulations, and a healthcare connector in order to make insurance more available and affordable. Businesses with 11 or more employees that do not provide insurance are subject to a fair-share assessment. Most businesses will also be required to establish cafeteria plans to enable pretax deductions of employee health insurance premiums. Many businesses will also be indirectly impacted by several provisions in this law. Employers that offer insurance that does not meet state standards may feel pressure to upgrade coverage. More employees will opt to sign up for employer-sponsored insurance, which could increase employer cost significantly.

INDIVIDUAL RESPONSIBILITY

The individual mandate for health insurance applies only to those who can afford it and began July 1, 2007. This begs a number of questions. What type of insurance can satisfy the requirements of the mandate? Would a catastrophic bare-bones plan suffice? What is considered affordable and for whom? What are the penalties for noncoverage?

The Connector Board determined the minimal coverage required to meet the mandate, and it is fairly comprehensive. No bare-bones plans were allowed. Minimum coverage must include:

- Prescription drug coverage.
- Annual out-of-pocket cap of $5,000 for an individual, $10,000 for a family.
- Deductibles cannot exceed $2,000 per individual and $4,000 per family unless combined with a medical savings account.

- Coverage of preventive physician visits prior to any deductible.
- No limits on per year or per sickness.

Plans may have a lifetime cap. Currently, an estimated 360,000 people in Massachusetts, including a Connector Board member, have lifetime benefit caps. Still with these stipulations, an estimated 240,000 currently insured people will have to increase their coverage to meet the requirements of the mandate. These reforms may also pressure employers to change coverage to meet these standards.

The penalty for noncompliance with the mandate in the first year is loss of the individual state tax exemption, worth about $200 per person. The second year, however, the penalty is half the cost of an available low-cost plan, which could run into thousands of dollars. Health plans and other insurers will be required to send individuals and the State Department of Revenue proof of coverage. Similar to a W-2 form, the proof of coverage must be attached to tax returns.

One of the most difficult decisions the Connector Board made was on affordability and who would be exempt from the mandate. In a unanimous vote, resulting from a series of compromises, the Connector Board recommended an affordability schedule that applies the mandate to 80 percent of the uninsured and close to 99 percent of the public. At the same time, the board provided full premium subsidies to qualified uninsured people with family income up to 150 percent of the federal poverty level (up from 100 percent of the federal poverty level, or FPL). They also increased premium subsidies for people between 150 percent and 200 percent of the FPL. For people less than 300 percent of the federal poverty level who qualify for subsidized coverage through the Connector, care is considered affordable and therefore mandatory. For people with family income greater than 300 percent, a sliding-scale affordability schedule was recommended. For example, an individual making three times the poverty level, $34,341, will be required to purchase coverage if it is available for $210 dollars a month or less. If an employer offers coverage and the employee's share is less than $210, the employee will be obligated to have insurance. If the employee's obligation is more than $210, he or she will be exempt from the mandate. The affordability standard increases to $500 for an individual at six times the poverty level, or $60,001 annual income.

The Connector will also develop a case-by-case waiver and appeal process for individuals and families at any income level who believe that insurance is unaffordable for them. The Connector staff's goal is for this process to be "lenient and efficient." With this safety value and the increased low-income subsidies, the individual mandate will be applied broadly to nearly 99 percent of the total Massachusetts population.

GOVERNMENT RESPONSIBILITY

The state took on responsibilities for substantially increasing its Medicaid program, MassHealth, and for developing two new programs to be run by the Commonwealth Health Insurance Connector Authority. The law also created the Health Safety Net Trust Fund to replace the Uncompensated Care Pool. The state expanded the Insurance Partnership Program, which provides subsidies and incentives for employers and employees to provide and enroll in employer-sponsored insurance. Further, it made significant reforms in the individual and small-group market. The law created a Cost and Quality Committee to implement sections of the law and make future recommendations.

MASSHEALTH REFORMS

A number of expansions to the MassHealth program were implemented shortly after reform passed on July 1, 2006. This resulted in new coverage for more than 40,000 uninsured and was an early success of the program. Further, the legislation restored MassHealth benefits that were cut in 2002 to help close a budget shortfall. This restored coverage for dental, vision, chiropractic, and prosthetics. Eligibility for children was raised from 200 percent to 300 percent FPL. The legislation also provided $3 million for MassHealth outreach funding targeted to community organizations. It increased the enrollment caps for several targeted programs that had been closed for enrollment. These changes will eliminate the waiting lists for these programs and will make all who applied and are currently eligible able to enroll.

- The MassHealth Essential cap, a program for the long-term unemployed, elderly, disabled, and special-status immigrants, was raised from 44,000 to 60,000.
- The CommonHealth cap, a program for children and adults with disabilities but with income too high to quality for MassHealth, was raised from 14,000 to 15,600. The program will be able to accommodate all people currently eligible.
- The HIV+ program enrollment caseload cap was raised from 1,050 to 1,300, and eligibility for this program was raised to 200 percent FPL.

Reform also included $3 million in new funding to reach out to uninsured people and enroll them in MassHealth or one of the new programs. Most of this money went to grassroots groups in the community, but some went to statewide advocacy groups to help organize and coordinate the message. These funds were rescinded by Governor Romney before leaving office and restored by incoming Governor Deval Patrick. This approach has shown early success. This is reflected in the better than expected enrollment of low-income uninsured people in the new Commonwealth Care program.

COMMONWEALTH HEALTH INSURANCE CONNECTOR

The Commonwealth Health Insurance Connector is an independent public authority with primary responsibility for implementing Chapter 25, Massachusetts Health Care Reform. The Connector is governed by a 10-member board that includes state administrative officials and representatives of various interests appointed by the governor and attorney general.

The Connector has a broad set of statutory requirements. Major responsibilities include:

- Develop and run the Commonwealth Care Insurance Program, which will provide subsidized insurance options for uninsured people with family income less than 300 percent of the federal poverty level.
- Develop and run the Commonwealth Choice Program, which will provide health insurance options for small businesses and uninsured individuals with family income greater than 300 percent of the federal poverty level.
- Provide a Seal of Approval for health plans offered through the Connector.
- Establish a young-adult plan for people between 19 and 26 years of age.
- Define minimum health insurance coverage required to meet the mandate "Minimum Creditable Coverage."
- Develop rules for implementing the individual mandate. The law requires everyone who can afford it to purchase health insurance.
- Support public outreach and awareness.
- Create a business strategy to be financially self-sustaining.
- Become a healthcare broker and purchasing agent.

The Connector has many faces. It acts much like a state agency when it is administering the subsidized Commonwealth Care program. Commonwealth Care makes subsidized insurance available to people with family income up to 300 percent of the poverty level. The Connector acts like a healthcare broker or purchasing agent when running Commonwealth Choice. This program will provide a range of plans through the Connector for the uninsured and small businesses with 50 or fewer employees, with enrollment to begin May 1, 2007, and coverage to start on July 1, 2007. This is also the date that the individual mandate takes effect. There are no subsidies, but the Connector has some leverage to negotiate lower premiums and has had some initial success.

The Connector has a staff of 45 with a mix of public- and private-sector experience reflecting the varied Connector responsibilities. It is overseen by Executive Director Jon Kingsdale and Chief Operating Officer (COO) Rosemarie Day. The organization is designed around staff and program functions. The COO, general counsel, planning and development officer, chief communications officer, and chief marketing officer report directly to the executive director. The director of human resources, chief financial officer, chief information officer, and directors of each of the major programs—Commonwealth Care and Commonwealth Choice—report to the COO. Contractors are used to determine eligibility, enroll people, and perform customer services for the Commonwealth Care program. The Connector also subcontracts with the Small Business Service Bureau in Worcester, Massachusetts, to assist with the implementation of Commonwealth Choice.

FINANCING THE CONNECTOR

The Connector is required to be self-funding and predicts that revenue will exceed costs by 2009. It received $25 million in initial funding from the legislature and will have spent $18 million over by the end of state fiscal year (SFY) 2007.[37]

Revenue will come primarily from administrative fees charged to health plans in both Commonwealth Care and Commonwealth Choice. Commonwealth Care administrative fees are equal to 5.0 percent, 4.5 percent, and 4.0 percent of premiums for SFYs 2007, 2008, and 2009, respectively. Commonwealth Choice administrative fees will be equal to 4.5 percent and 4.0 percent of premiums for SFYs 2008 and 2009, respectively. Projections are based on enrollment; staff run moderate and conservative estimates, but there is the possibility that estimates are inaccurate. In the event that the Connector experiences a temporary cash shortage, it has made arrangements with banks for short-term loans to fill any funding gaps. The Connector will be seeking an additional $1.5 million to $2 million from the legislature for providing new public information and responding to the appeals process.

COMMONWEALTH CARE

Commonwealth Care provides comprehensive coverage to people with incomes less than 300 percent of the FPL with no deductibles or coinsurance. In the first three years of the program, bidding to offer coverage to these people was restricted to the state's four Medicaid Managed Care Organizations. Two of these plans, Boston Medical Center and Cambridge Health Alliance, will be able to enroll people they previously treated through the Free Care Pool. Type one plans, comprehensive coverage with no premiums, are available to people with family income less than 100 percent of the FPL. This type of coverage was extended to people with incomes up to 150 percent of the FPL on April 12, 2007. The first phase of the program began enrolling qualified people with incomes less than 100 percent of the FPL on October 1, 2006, less than four months after the first Connector meeting. They were already enrolled in the Free Care Pool that made them easier to reach. These people are also more likely to have chronic illnesses and have the most to gain from greater access to primary care. Commonwealth Care plans two through four, available for eligible people with family income between 100 percent and 300 percent of the FPL, became available on January 1, 2007.

The Connector negotiated capitation rates with the four Medicaid managed care organizations (MMCOs) eligible to bid on Commonwealth Care. Bids came in two stages with a 10-day window between rounds. The difference between initial and second bids resulted in $50 million in savings for the state. The Connector had negotiating leverage by guaranteeing the lowest-cost plan the automatic assignment of people who fail to select a plan. This was modified by the so-called spitting-distance rule that allows plans close to the lowest bid to receive a portion of automatic enrollment assignments. MMCOs will be paid different capitation rates based on age, sex, and geography, but the enrollees in plans two through four will pay the same premium. If enrollees who have a choice of plans (types two through four) and chose a more expensive plan, however, they will pay the difference. This provides additional incentives to be the low-cost plan. Negotiations were so successful that there was concern that the plans bid too low. As a safeguard, the Connector instituted stop-loss and other protections to safeguard the health plans if they significantly underestimated costs in order to gain market share.

The issue of how much of the premium should be charged to people with family income between 100 percent and 300 percent of the FPL was the subject of considerable debate. A compromise was reached between stakeholders and is reflected in the premium schedule in the following list. The schedule was changed on April 12, 2007, when the board defined affordability for the mandate. People with incomes up to 150 percent of the FPL will pay no premiums, and premiums for people with incomes less than 200 percent of the FPL will have premiums reduced by $5. These new rates are considered affordable, and so the mandate for coverage and penalties will apply to people at these income levels.

Commonwealth Care Monthly Premium
Contribution Schedule, January 2007

Percentage of the FPL	Adult Contribution	Two-adult Family
100.1%–150%	$18 or 1.76% of the FPL	$36 or 2.6% of the FPL
150.1%–200%	$40 or 2.8% of the FPL	$80 or 4.2% of the FPL
200.1%–250%	$70 or 3.8% of the FPL	$140 or 5.6% of the FPL
250.1%–300%	$106 or 4.7% of the FPL	$212 or 7.0% of the FPL

COMMONWEALTH CHOICE

The Connector also faces the challenge of becoming a broker and purchasing agent while becoming financially self-sufficient. The vehicle for doing this is the Commonwealth Choice program, which will provide a range of health plan options to the uninsured and small businesses with 50 or fewer employees. The Connector may also serve larger companies by helping provide coverage for part-time or seasonal workers. The challenge is to find an advantage in a market already providing these services. Moreover, the statute requires that products available inside the Connector must be available outside the Connector at the same price, so they cannot compete on price. Legislators included this provision to protect the existing health insurance marketplace. The hope is that the Connector will provide value through administration and the range of plans it can offer to employers, employees, and the uninsured. People who have multiple employers or shift from one small business to another, may still be able to retain the same healthcare coverage through the Connector.

It is hoped that value will be created through choice of health plans and various options within particular health plans. In negotiations with the plans, the Connector staff encouraged health plans to develop options with selective provider and hospital networks in order to lower costs. Four plans came in with limited networks, and others are considering doing so as well. No real limited network plans are currently offered in the marketplace. In the current market, employers generally have reduced choices of health plans, and are often limited to one, and this requires health plans to have broad networks to meet the diverse needs of employees. This trend reduces the leverage of health plans and leads to higher costs and fewer choices of health plans for enrollees. The Connector can offer a choice of health plans, and employees can select limited network plans that include providers of their choice. The employer will contribute a set amount per employee (at least 50 percent of the cost of coverage), and employees will pay more for more expensive plans. This may push efficiency, broaden options, and possibly make lower-cost, limited network plans available outside the Connector. The value proposition remains untested.

There was a compressed schedule for receiving bids, evaluating submissions, and awarding the Connector Seal of Approval. This seal enables plans to offer products through the Connector. Interested bidders were required to submit five coverage options: one premier plan, two value plans, one basic plan, and one young-adult plan. All plans provide similar benefits (with the exception of the young-adult plan). Differences comprise monthly premiums, deductibles that need to be paid before coverage begins, coinsurance or a percentage of costs for which members are responsible, co-payments that are paid at the time of services, and how broad or narrow the provider and hospital networks are. The premier options have the highest monthly premiums but very limited cost sharing with no deductible. The value plans have midlevel premiums with deductibles between $500 and $1,000, possibly limited networks, and higher co-payments. These plans are similar to what most people with insurance have today. The basic plans will have the lowest premiums and the highest out-of-pocket costs. Unlike the other plans, the young-adult plan has limited benefits and will only be offered through the Connector.

Plans were evaluated based on costs and plan design, which included innovation, network, marketing, network coverage, and geographic coverage. The Connector Seal of Approval was provided to 7 of 10 plans that applied: Blue Cross and Blue Shield of Massachusetts, ConnectiCare, Fallon Community Health Plan, Harvard Pilgrim Health Care, New England Health, Neighborhood Health Plan, and Tufts Health Plan. The MEGA Life and Health Insurance Company, the Mid-West National Life Insurance Company, and United HealthCare received scores significantly below the top seven and did not receive approval at the time this chapter was published.[38]

The Connector conducted research on the market and held focus groups with target customers and found that people wanted choice but a limited set of high-quality plans. They also wanted individual attention and assistance with plan choice. At this point, seven plans each offer five options for a total of 35 possible options. Not all options will be available in all regions, however, and the young adult plans are targeted to 19- to 26-year-olds, and it is not expected that there will be a high demand for premier plans. This will reduce the number of choices. The availability of help in plan section, experience, and enrollment patterns will be necessary to determine if this is the right amount of choice for consumers.

The Connector will also use a subconnector as well as brokers to make these plans more widely available. After bidding the project, the Connector selected the Small Business Service Bureau of Worcester, Massachusetts, as the subconnector. It has experience in servicing this community and was by far the lowest bidder. Responsibilities will include:

1. Customer service.
2. Eligibility determination/enrollment.
3. Web portal online enrollment.
4. Premium billing.
5. Collection remittance.
6. Helping businesses establish cafeteria plans that will enable the pretax premium contributions.
7. Liaison between brokers and the Connector.

The Connector will also work with individual brokers who will receive a $10 per member per month fee for the people they help enroll in insurance through the Connector. This rate is near the bottom of what brokers generally receive.

The law also calls for the Connector to make a young-adult-only plan available through the Connector for people between the ages of 19 and 26 who have no other source of health insurance. This will be the only place where such plans can be purchased. These plans may have more limited coverage and include caps on of $50,000 per illness or per calendar year. They must provide all mandatory state benefits, and insurers offering in this market must have one plan that offers prescription drugs. Bids submitted to the Connector show a range of prices for these plans between $100 per month without prescription drugs to more than $200 per month. The goal is to make insurance affordable for this group and make having insurance a habit. The downside is that there will be some people in this group who have expenses over the limits who will be underinsured.

EMPLOYER IMPACT AND UNDERSTANDING

Business in Massachusetts will be affected by reform in a number of direct and indirect ways. Direct requirements include: fair-share assessment contributions, efforts to extend tax deductibility to more employees, reporting requirements, and new antidiscrimination provisions.

Indirectly, as the individual mandate kicks in, employers may experience a jump in the number of employees enrolling in company-sponsored coverage. This may significantly increase costs and may have a far greater economic impact than the $295 assessment described in the following section. Further, reform sets minimum coverage levels that all people will need to have to satisfy the mandate. Employers that currently do not provide insurance that meets this standard may want to adjust coverage to meet this standard.

Employer awareness and response will be critical to the future success of reform. To that end, the Connector partnered with Associated Industries of Massachusetts (AIM) to hold information sessions for small businesses throughout the state. These forums are expected to reach a minimum of 500 small employers. Other information is available through the Connector Web site, but the extent to which businesses are aware of and prepared for these changes is still uncertain.

Fair-Share Assessment

Companies with 11 or more employees that do not make a "fair and reasonable" contribution to their employees' health insurance will be assessed a maximum fee of $295 per uninsured employee. The $295 amount was established to equal the per capita costs to the Uncompensated Care Pool of employees currently uninsured. This provision broke a major logjam over what employer responsibility should be.

The state Division of Health Care Finance defined *fair and reasonable* as having a minimum of 25 percent of a company's full-time employees enrolled in their health plan or paying at least 33 percent of employees' premiums. *Full time* was defined as 35 or more hours a week. Consumer groups, labor, and key legislators objected that these regulations were too narrowly configured. Legislative leaders believed legislative intent was to take into consideration part-time employees or full-time equivalents and that employers' contribution should be more on the magnitude of 50 percent.

Section 125 plans

Reform legislation required businesses with more that 10 employees to establish Section 125 cafeteria plans. These plans would enable insurance premiums to be deducted from employee wages on a pretax basis. This money is not subject to federal, state, or Social Security taxes. It will result in significant savings for employees and also reduce the payroll taxes businesses have to pay. Failure to comply with this requirement may subject employers to a "free rider surcharge." This charge will be calculated, in part, based on the money uninsured employees draw from the Free Care Pool, now known as the Health Safety Net Trust Fund.

Health Insurance Responsibility Disclosure Forms

The Division of Health Care Finance and Policy held hearings on draft regulations regarding the information that would be required from employers with respect to employee coverage. Regulations were subsequently withdrawn, in part, because of concern about the magnitude of information required. In technical corrections legislation, the reporting requirement date was postponed from

January 1, 2007, to July 1, 2007. This legislation also required employers to provide an annual written statement to employees with employer-sponsored coverage by January 31 each year. Employers must also report similar information to the Commission on Revenue. Falsification of this information could result in fines between $1,000 and $5,000.

Nondiscrimination Rules

Nondiscrimination rules will effectively require employers to provide the same benefits and make the same contribution to all full-time employees. Employers will not be able to pay more of the health insurance costs for employees making higher wages. Specifically, the legislation prohibits health plans from contracting with employers that do not make their products available to all full-time employees and that do not make a similar contribution to all company enrollees. The technical corrections legislation extended the compliance date to July 1, 2007, and further details are expected from the Department of Insurance.

Insurance Partnership Program

The Insurance Partnership program helps small businesses (50 or fewer employees) provide insurance to their uninsured employees. It also assists low-income self-employed people who are uninsured. Reform expanded eligibility for employees with family income up to 300 percent of the FPL. This brings subsidies in line with those offered through the Commonwealth Care program.

INSURANCE REFORMS

The new law merges the individual and small-group insurance markets but has created a commission to conduct a feasibility and impact study prior to implementation. A small group is defined as coverage of 50 or fewer employees. The commission hired an actuarial firm and released its findings in December 2006.[39] The study found that rates in the individual or nongroup market would decrease by 15 percent as a result of moving individuals into a larger group, but rates in the small-group market would increase by 1 percent to 1.5 percent as more higher-risk individuals join this group. Nongroup reductions vary by carrier, and savings from certain health plans could be as high as 50 percent. On the other end, increase in some small-group insurance rates could increase as much as 4 percent. Because the findings did not predict major increases in the small-group market, the merger went ahead as scheduled on July 1, 2007. At this date, the nongroup or individual market was closed to all new enrollees.

The law also requires Massachusetts licensed carriers to allow young adults to remain covered on a parent's insurance plan for up to two years after the loss of dependent status or until their 26th birthday, whichever comes first. This went into effect on January 1, 2007. Health plans may restrict coverage to young adults who remain in the plan's service area.

QUALITY AND COST

The legislation created a number of councils and committees. The Quality and Cost Council is charged with setting cost and quality goals for the State of Massachusetts and developing strategies in these areas. It is chaired by the secretary of Health and Human Services and will report its recommendations by the end of 2007.

The law provides $1 million in new funding to the State Department of Public Health to create an infection prevention and control program. A task force was developed to recommend mechanisms for collecting and reporting data on infection rates and best-practice guidelines for prevention.

Healthcare reform also increases Medicaid payment to hospitals but makes these payments contingent on meeting quality standards. The Executive Office of Health and Human Services is charged with setting quality benchmarks and pay-for-performance measures. The statute requires that benchmarks include improvement in racial and ethnic disparities in healthcare services.

FUNDING AND SUSTAINABILITY ASSUMPTIONS

Financial sustainability will require a reduction in uncompensated care costs, enhanced federal and state funding, high enrollment in the new programs, and macroeconomic stability. It may also require stability in the rate of healthcare inflation. Reform is partially funded by transferring funds from the Uncompensated Care Pool, which was replaced by the Health Care Safety Net Trust fund. Successful funding will require uncompensated care spending to decrease to subsidize insurance coverage. Federal safety-net funds made possible through the 1115 waiver and additional federal matching for the increased Medicaid and State Children's Health Insurance Program (SCHIP) funding are also essential to fund this program. The state 1115 waiver program needs to be renewed again by July 2008, the SCHIP program is up for renewal in 2007, and current levels of funding will need to remain at approximately the same level. In addition, $129 million per year for three years in new state general revenue was pledged for this program. This funding will need to be maintained at or around the same level, unless an alternative revenue source can be identified. Surveys show that many of the uninsured are unaware of the coverage requirement and that there is the possibility that a portion of the population will balk at the individual mandate. Finally, an economic downturn could increase the number of uninsured and reduce the availability of state funding.

CONCLUSION

Massachusetts has a long history of healthcare innovation. The current round of reform builds on a solid foundation of public and private health insurance. It also builds on a strong safety net, the costs of which were made explicit through the state's Uncompensated Care Pool. The number of uninsured is low compared to the nation. Many are still without health insurance, however, which entails social and economic costs and consequences. The healthcare sector in Massachusetts is a driver of the state's economy. The state has a number of world-class medical schools and teaching hospitals. This educational system has advantages, but the state also has high healthcare costs. The dominant health plans in the state are not for profit and rank at the top in the United States in terms of quality and member satisfaction.

The latest round of reform was driven by political leadership, activist consumer organizations, and the threat of losing significant amounts of federal money. Legislative success was achieved through a broad-based coalition of consumers, providers, health plans, healthcare systems, and the business community. The strategy was shared responsibility, asking more of individuals, government, and business. The individual mandate is the most innovative piece and is essential to getting near-universal coverage. The coalition that made reform possible has held together through the first year of implementation. Compromise on key issues kept reform on track. These included setting subsidy levels, outlining benefits, and defining affordability and the required minimum level of insurance.

The current Massachusetts experiment is being closely followed by other states and may help spark the next round of national reforms. Although other states can learn from the particulars, more can be learned from the process. Because Massachusetts builds off the base of its existing system, it would be difficult to adopt wholesale. What can be replicated is the notion of shared responsibility, developing broad coalitions, and building on the success of existing programs. Mandates are difficult but essential to sustained progress. Massachusetts also separated coverage expansion from cost and quality reform. Many believed that they had to be addressed together, but it was not politically viable at the time. Dealing with access brings more people under the tent but does not hold the uninsured hostage to these more difficult issues. Ultimately, continued progress and sustainability at the state level are predicated on financing, which may drive necessary national reform.

NOTES

1. Collins, S. R., C. Schoen, D. Colasanto, et al. 2003. *On the Edge: Low-Wage Workers and Their Health Insurance Coverage*. New York: The Commonwealth Fund.

2. McDonough, J. E. 2004–2005. "The Road to Universal Health Coverage in Massachusetts." *New England Journal of Public Policy* 20: 57–62.

3. Ibid.

4. Seifert, R. 2002. "The Uncompensated Care Pool: Saving the Safety Net." *Massachusetts Health Policy Forum* 16: 5.

5. Office of the Inspector General Commonwealth of Massachusetts. 2005. "Ongoing Review of the Uncompensated Care Pool Pursuant to Chapter 240 of the Acts of 2004." Publication No. CR-1111-69-25-11/05-IGO. Boston: Office of the Inspector General.

6. Seifert, 16.

7. McDonough, J. E. 2006. "The Third Wave of Massachusetts Health Care Access Reform." *Health Affairs—Web Exclusive,* September 14: 421.

8. Sager, A. 1989. "Making Universal Health Insurance Work in Massachusetts." *Law, Medicine and Health Care* 17 (3): 270.

9. Ibid., 269.

10. McDonough, J. E. 2004–2005. 57–62.

11. Ibid., 60.

12. Massachusetts Division of Health Care Finance and Policy. 2006. *Massachusetts Health Trends: 1990–2005.* 3rd ed. 2. Boston: Massachusetts Division of Health Care Finance and Policy.

13. Ibid.

14. Strunk, B. C., K. J. Devers, and R. E. Hurley. 2001. "Health Plan-Provider Showdowns on the Rise." Center for Health Care System Change, Issue Brief No. 40: 3.

15. Greenberg, J., and B. Zuckerman. 1997. "State Health Care Reform In Massachusetts: How One State Expanded Health Insurance for Children." *Health Affairs* 16 (4): 188–93.

16. Massachusetts Medicaid Policy Institute. 2005. *The MassHealth Waiver.* Boston: Massachusetts Medicaid Policy Institute.

17. Greenberg and Zuckerman, 190.

18. McDonough, 2004–2005. 60–61.

19. DeVol, R., and R. Koepp. 2003. *The Economic Contributions of Health Care to New England.* Cambridge, MA: Milken Institute, New England Health Care Institute Cambridge.

20. Ibid.

21. Families USA. 2006. "Premiums versus Paychecks: A Growing Burden for Massachusetts Workers." Families USA Publication No. 06-106MA (October, 2006).

22. Krasner, J. 2006. "Study: Mass. Healthcare Costs Are 4th Highest." *Boston Globe* (November 20). Available at: http://www.boston.com/business/globe/articles/2006/11/20/study_mass_healthcare_costs_are_4th_highest/.

23. Ibid.

24. "Best Health Plans 2006." 2006. *U.S. News and World Report.* Available at: http://www.usnews.com/usnews/health/best-health-insurance/hr_commercial_plan_2006.htm. Accessed May 20, 2007.

25. Massachusetts Division of Health Care Finance and Policy. 2006. *Massachusetts Health Trends: 1990–2005.* 3rd ed. 8. Boston: Massachusetts Division of Health Care Finance and Policy.

26. Ibid., 15.

27. Henry J. Kaiser Family Foundation. 2006. "Trends and Indicators in the Changing Health Care Marketplace Project." The Henry J. Kaiser Family Foundation Publication No. 7031, Washington D.C.

28. Massachusetts Division of Health Care Finance and Policy. 2006. *Massachusetts Health Trends: 1990–2005.* 3rd ed. 38. Boston: Massachusetts Division of Health Care Finance and Policy.

29. Ibid., 58.

30. Holahan, J. L. J. Blumberg, A. Weil, et al. 2005. "Road Map to Coverage: Synthesis of Findings." *Blue Cross Blue Shield of Massachusetts Foundation.* Available at: http://www.roadmaptocoverage.org/pdfs/Roadmap_Synthesis.pdf.

31. Agency for Healthcare Research and Quality, Center for Financing. 2004. "Access and Cost Trends: 2004." Washington, D.C.: Medical Expenditure Panel Survey-Insurance Component, Agency for Healthcare Research and Quality, Research in Action Issue 17.

32. Romney, M. 2004. "My Plan for Massachusetts Health Reform." Op-Ed, *Boston Globe* (November 21).

33. Holahan, J., R. Bovbjerg, J. Hadley, et al. 2004. "Caring for the Uninsured in Massachusetts: What Does It Cost, Who Pays and What Would Full Coverage Add to Medical Spending." *Blue Cross Blue Shield Foundation of Massachusetts*. Available at: http://www.roadmaptocoverage.org/pdfs/roadmapReport.pdf. Accessed June 1, 2007.

34. Blumberg, L., J. Holahan, A. Weil, et al. 2005. "Building the Roadmap to Coverage: Policy Choices and the Cost and Coverage Implications." *Blue Cross Blue Shield Foundation of Massachusetts*. Available at: http://www.roadmaptocoverage.org/pdfs/BCBSF_Roadmap2005.pdf. Accessed June 1, 2007.

35. Weil, Alan. 2005. "You Can Get There from Here: Implementing the Roadmap to Coverage." *Blue Cross Blue Shield Foundation of Massachusetts*. Available at: http://www.roadmaptocoverage.org/pdfs/Roadmap_Implement.pdf. Accessed June 1, 2007.

36. Massachusetts Legislature. 2006. "An Act Providing Access to Affordable, Quality, Accountable Health Care." Acts of 2006, Chapter 58.

37. Kingsdale, J. 2006. "SFY 2007 Budget and Preliminary Three-Year Financial Projections Commonwealth Health Insurance Connector Authority." Board of Directors Meeting; Holland, P. 2007. Personal interview with the author, March 13.

38. More detailed information can be found on the Commonwealth Connector Web site. Available at: http://www.mass.gov/?pageID=hichomepage&L=1&L0=Home&sid=Qhic. Accessed July 27, 2007.

39. Gorman Actuarial LLC, DeWeese Consulting Inc., Hinckley, Allen & Tringale LP. 2006. "Impact of Merging the Massachusetts Non-Group and Small Group Health Insurance Markets." Report prepared for the Massachusetts Division of Insurance and Market Merger Special Commission.

CHAPTER 3

Quality in Healthcare: Concepts and Practice

Phil Buttell, Robert Hendler, and Jennifer Daley

In the healthcare industry, quality of care is more than a concept. It has become essential to patient well-being and financial survival. This chapter will discuss the complex concept and multiple definitions of quality of care and evaluate how it has become an increasingly important factor in the delivery of healthcare. We will start by providing a historical perspective to help readers understand the evolution of quality in the healthcare industry. This perspective will include landmark reports and events that have helped shape the role quality of care currently plays in the industry. We will then explore the key principles and definitions that are essential to healthcare quality. After reviewing the key principles, we will explore a case study that illustrates the impact that quality improvement is having on a particular company within the industry. Last, we will speculate on the role quality will play as the healthcare industry continues to evolve.

The authors of this chapter are involved daily in the complexity of designing systems and motivating people to achieve the desired goal of high-quality, highly safe, and efficient healthcare. We believe that this goal is important for both human and business reasons. Imagine a hospital system in which proper processes are delivered in a timely fashion for the many different types of patients and disease processes. Imagine a hospital with no hospital-acquired infections, no staff-related oversights leading to complications during difficult deliveries, no wrong-site surgeries, and no medication errors. A system that demonstrates this type of success has lowered the cost of providing care while maximizing the quality of care. We all want to be treated at such an institution. Employers would demand that their patients use this system because they no longer wish to bear the cost of poor outcomes, complications such as congestive heart failure following inadequate or delayed reperfusion of a coronary vessel in an acute heart attack, or hospital-acquired infections. Clearly, hospitals and physicians that provide cost-effective quality care will have made the business case for quality of care and be rewarded with higher volumes of patients and better reimbursement.

QUALITY IN HEALTHCARE: WHAT IS IT?

To begin this discussion, we must have a shared definition of quality and understand the strengths, weaknesses, and misconceptions of commonly held concepts about quality in healthcare. When a group of healthcare professionals is asked what quality means, there may be as many definitions as people in the room. And differing definitions can and will lead to different priorities and different goals, depending on the perspective of the constituent: patients, their families, healthcare providers and professionals, regulators, insurers, and employers. W. Edward Deming, who led the quality revolution in Japan and the United States, said, "A product or service possesses quality if it helps somebody and enjoys a good and sustainable market."[1] Note that he does not define quality directly but references the value of a product or service in terms of its ability to both help the consumer as well as its marketability.

Donabedian, a leading figure in the theory and management of quality of healthcare, has previously suggested that "several formulations are both possible and legitimate, depending on where we are located in the system of care and on what the nature and extent of our responsibilities are."[2] Different perspectives on and definitions of quality will logically call for different approaches to its measurement and management.[3] Another author recognizes the inherent problem in defining quality by stating, "It would be difficult to find a realistic definition of quality that did not have, implicit within the definition, a fundamental expression or implied focus of building and sustaining relationships."[4] Understanding differing perspectives about quality does not prevent success in achieving quality of care as long as key principles and concepts of quality are identified, understood, and used.

The most durable and widely cited definition of healthcare quality was formulated by the Institute of Medicine (IOM) in 1990. According to the IOM, quality consists of the "degree to which health services for individuals and populations increase the likelihood of desired health outcomes and are consistent with current professional knowledge."[5] Other authors have recognized Deming's appreciation of the importance of the market. They refer to care that meets the expectations of patients and other customers of healthcare services.[6] Therefore, for the purposes of this discussion, we have expanded the IOM definition. Quality consists of the degree to which health services for individuals and populations increase the likelihood of desired health outcomes (quality principles), are consistent with current professional knowledge (professional practitioner skill), and meet the expectations of healthcare users (the marketplace).

THE EVOLUTION OF AWARENESS OF QUALITY IN HEALTHCARE AMONG THE PUBLIC

The public has become more aware of the role quality of care plays in healthcare. The definition has not changed, but the public and the industry's awareness certainly has. High-profile patient safety failures have had a profound impact on the evolution of the public's awareness of quality of care. Patient safety plays an important role in quality performance, but it is important to note that quality and safety are not the same thing. Patient safety is a subset of the larger, much more complex and multidimensional concept of quality. Highly publicized patient care failures, however, were the catalysts that prompted a national evaluation of the patient safety issues troubling healthcare.

On December 3, 1994, a 39-year-old cancer patient died of complications of an overdose of cyclophosphamide, a chemotherapeutic agent she received at the Dana-Farber Cancer Institute (DFCI) in Boston for treatment of widely metastatic breast cancer. Another patient at DFCI also suffered an overdose of cyclophosphamide and experienced serious heart damage. According to James B. Conway, DFCI's chief operating officer, and Dr. Saul Weingart, director of the Center for Patient Safety at DFCI, "Both errors involved breakdowns in standard processes, and both raised issues of trainee supervision, nursing competence, and order execution."[7] The media reported the event with 28 front-page headlines over the next three years, partially because the patient who died, Betsy Lehman, was a healthcare reporter for the *Boston Globe*.

Although medical professionals have always known about deadly errors in complex healthcare systems, the public at large reacted to the events at Dana-Farber with shock and disbelief. They want a safe environment for themselves and their families, and these incidents were clear examples that hospitals are often unsafe, even at highly respected institutions. Regardless of the magnitude of the errors or the ability of the media to relay the message to a local community or an entire nation, these incidents and medical errors put quality and patient safety on the front page of every newspaper in the United States. Numerous other high-profile and fatal medical errors continue to be reported on an almost weekly basis, contributing to a general loss of trust among patients and their families when they experience serious illnesses.

THE INSTITUTE OF MEDICINE RESPONDS: *TO ERR IS HUMAN*

In response to the incident at Dana-Farber and many other facilities, the IOM began a thorough examination of patient safety, which resulted in the report *To Err Is Human: Building a Safer Health System*.[8] *To Err Is Human* brought patient safety into the mainstream of healthcare in academic centers, community hospitals, physician and nursing professional meetings, as well as on the front page of every newspaper in the United States. This report had a tremendous impact on the safety of healthcare delivered in the United States. As we will later see, the impact has not been as deep or as significant as one might have hoped, but the report changed the way people think about healthcare and their fundamental perceptions of the safety of healthcare delivery.

This report was the first in a series of reports produced by the Quality of Health Care in America Project. "The Quality of Health Care in America project was initiated by the Institute of Medicine (IOM) in June 1998 with the charge of developing a strategy that will result in a *threshold improvement* in quality over the next ten years."[9] The authors of *To Err Is Human* suggested that anywhere from 44,000 to 98,000 Americans die each year as a result of medical errors in hospitals. This number was derived from two parallel studies, one of which was conducted in Colorado and Utah hospitals and the other was a study based on data from New York State hospitals. The numbers were staggering and equivalent to a 747 airliner full of patients crashing every day. The New York study analysis suggested that serious adverse events occur in 3.7 percent of all hospitalizations.[10] The New York study was replicated in Colorado and Utah and found that serious adverse events occurred in 2.9 percent of hospitalizations.[11] Although many healthcare professionals were aware of the potential for serious safety problems in U.S. hospitals, few lay people realized the full magnitude of the risk and the deadly outcomes of flawed hospital systems. Academics, lawyers, state and federal legislators, and healthcare professionals involved in the complex workings in healthcare organizations were faced with the realization that something was broken in a system in which the goal was to alleviate suffering and save lives.

The IOM report made the following (see table 3.1) recommendations based on their review of patient safety:

1. Improve leadership and knowledge.
2. Identify and learn from errors.
3. Set performance standards and expectations for safety.
4. Implement safety systems in healthcare organizations.

These recommended actions are critically important to the development of a safe healthcare environment. A continued focus on these objectives will help create a much more quality-driven industry and a much safer environment in which to receive care.

The recommendations made by the IOM serve as useful starting points to improve patient safety, and several changes have been made to address these recommendations. Not enough, however, has been accomplished to change the culture of patient safety in the industry overall. Leadership is vital to improving the focus as well as the performance in patient safety. Leaders help shape the agenda in our industry by a single-minded focus on patient safety that is shared among all participants and constituents in the healthcare system. An increased focus on patient safety in the industry will need to be supplemented with additional knowledge and understanding of the specific elements that promote patient safety. This single-minded goal drives the evolution of policy and creates a culture that values the role quality and patient safety play in the care of patients.

Identification of serious errors is also important when attempting to improve patient safety through root cause analysis. In addition, so-called near misses—patient safety system failures that do not result in injury to patients—also provide

Table 3.1
To Err Is Human **Recommendations**

Improve Leadership and Knowledge

Recommendation 4.1: Congress should create a Center for Patient Safety within the Agency for Healthcare Research and Quality. The Center for Patient Safety should:

- Set the national goals for patient safety, track progress in meeting these goals, and issue an annual report to the president and Congress on patient safety.
- Develop knowledge and understanding of errors in healthcare by developing a research agenda, funding Centers of Excellence, evaluating methods for identifying and preventing errors, and funding dissemination and communication activities to improve patient safety.

Identify and Learn from Errors

Recommendation 5.1: A nationwide mandatory reporting system should be established that provides for the collection of standardized information by state governments about adverse events that result in death or serious harm. Reporting initially should be required of hospitals and eventually should be required of other institutional and ambulatory care delivery settings.

Recommendation 5.2: The development of voluntary reporting efforts should be encouraged.

Recommendation 6.1: Congress should pass legislation to extend peer review protections to data related to patient safety and quality improvement that are collected and analyzed by healthcare organizations for internal use or shared with others solely for purposes of improving safety and quality.

Set Performance Standards and Expectations for safety

Recommendation 7.1: Performance standards and expectations for healthcare organizations should focus greater attention on patient safety.

- Regulators and accreditors should require healthcare organizations to implement meaningful patient safety programs with defined executive responsibility.
- Public and private purchasers should provide incentives to healthcare organizations to demonstrate continuous improvement in patient safety.

Recommendation 7.2: Performance standards and expectations for health professionals should focus greater attention on patient safety.

Recommendation 7.3: The Food and Drug Administration (FDA) should increase attention to the safe use of drugs in both pre- and postmarketing processes through the following actions:

- Develop and enforce standards for the design of drug packaging and labeling that will maximize safety in use.
- Require pharmaceutical companies to test (using FDA-approved methods) proposed drug names to identify and remedy potential sound-alike and look-alike confusion with existing drug names.
- Work with physicians, pharmacists, consumers, and others to establish appropriate responses to problems identified through postmarketing surveillance, especially for concerns that are perceived to require immediate response to protect the safety of patients.

Table 3.1
To Err Is Human Recommendations *(continued)*

Implementing Safety Systems in Healthcare Organizations

Recommendation 8.1: Healthcare organizations and the professionals affiliated with them should make continually improved patient safety a declared and serious aim by establishing patient safety programs with defined executive responsibility. Patient safety programs should:

- Provide strong, clear, and visible attention to safety.
- Implement nonpunitive systems for reporting and analyzing errors within their organizations.
- Incorporate well-understood safety principles, such as standardizing and simplifying equipment, supplies, and processes.
- Establish interdisciplinary team training programs for providers that incorporate proved methods of team training, such as simulation.

Recommendation 8.2: Healthcare organizations should implement proved medication safety practices.

---

an opportunity to prevent errors. The industry has the ability to learn much from errors and near misses, and those learning opportunities need to be identified and capitalized on at the time of the safety system failure. Unfortunately, in our society, it is difficult to create a blame-free environment without incurring legal liability for negligence. Safety theory in other high-reliability industries such as commercial aviation and nuclear power strongly suggests that human error is typically related to system problems and human behavioral and cognitive patterns rather than mistakes by individual providers because of lack of knowledge or carelessness. To compound the naturally occurring problem of human error, healthcare providers have a professional and humanitarian responsibility for human life in which doing no harm is a basic ethical principle. Take, for example, an individual in an assembly line responsible for making stuffed animals. If this individual makes an error, there are few complications that will result, except perhaps lower productivity and an unhappy customer. In healthcare, mistakes can cause loss of life. Creating an environment that embraces error as an opportunity for improvement rather than an opportunity for blame and punishment is essential to promoting patient safety and safer healthcare for both patients and healthcare workers. The authors of the *To Err Is Human* report recognized the capacity for forgiveness and healing by choosing the title of the IOM report from a common phrase, "To err is human; to forgive, divine."[12]

According to the IOM, setting performance standards and expectations is another essential element to improving patient safety. This is an area that has been somewhat disorganized, as institutions were often responsible for setting their own patient safety agenda resulting in great variation among facilities. Resources were not always uniform, nor were they utilized in appropriate ways to set a safety agenda. There is value to creating standards and expectations that are universal. Creating standards and universal areas of focus help provide legitimacy and a target area. The Joint Commission on the Accreditation of Healthcare Organizations (JCAHO) has taken a leadership position in setting the patient safety agenda by promulgating new patient safety goals every year around common patient safety problems in hospitals (e.g., wrong-site surgery, illegible and nonstandard abbreviations, and preventions of falls among hospitalized and nursing home patients).

The last area of focus the IOM recommended was the implementation of patient safety systems in healthcare organizations. Implementing reliable systems that prevent human error in emergency rooms and intensive care units will improve patient safety in the U.S. healthcare delivery system.

AFTER *TO ERR IS HUMAN:* WHAT HAVE WE LEARNED AND WHAT HAVE WE DONE?

It is clear that the healthcare industry is not where it needs to be when perceived from a patient safety perspective. Medical errors continue to happen every day, and people are still at risk whenever they enter the healthcare system for care. The public is more aware of issues that have been played out in the media, and the IOM report has improved the awareness of the problem, but still too little is being done to transform healthcare. The patient safety agenda has been promoted by accrediting bodies, professional and hospital associations, and the myriad of public and private institutions whose main goal is to improve patient safety and the quality of healthcare in the U.S. system.[13] Five years after *To Err Is Human*, "the impact on attitudes and organizations has been profound. . . . In sum, the groundwork for improving safety has been laid these past 5 years but progress is frustratingly slow. Building a culture of safety is proving to be an immense task and the barriers are formidable."[14] Still, problems exist. "Little evidence exists from any source that systematic improvements in safety are widely available."[15] Improvements are happening every day, but the changes are limited to small improvements at local and individual levels. Some hospitals are achieving groundbreaking improvements in patient safety, but these are the exception rather than the rule. The changes need to be industry-wide for the value to really be seen by the public.

CROSSING THE QUALITY CHASM: A ROAD MAP FOR IMPROVING QUALITY OF CARE

A second major report by the IOM's Committee on the Quality of Health Care in America—*Crossing the Quality Chasm*—followed *To Err Is Human*. This report focused on the quality of care currently present in the U.S. healthcare system. The first sentence of the report reads, "The American health care delivery system is in need of fundamental change."[16] The committee outlined an agenda to improve quality. Table 3.2 outlines this agenda.

This report expands the work outlined in *To Err Is Human* in regard to improving patient safety because it focuses on a redesign of the entire industry around

Table 3.2
Crossing the Quality Chasm Agenda

- That all healthcare constituencies, including policy makers, purchasers, regulators, health professionals, healthcare trustees and management, and consumers, commit to a national statement of purpose for the healthcare system as a whole and to a shared agenda of six aims for improvement that can raise the quality of care to unprecedented levels.

- That clinicians and patients and the healthcare organizations that support care delivery adopt a new set of principles to guide the redesign of care processes.

- That the Department of Health and Human Services identify a set of priority conditions upon which to focus initial efforts, provide resources to stimulate innovation, and initiate the change process.

- That healthcare organizations design and implement more effective organizational support processes to make change in the delivery of care possible.

- That purchasers, regulators, health professions, educational institutions, and the Department of Health and Human Services create an environment that fosters and rewards improvement by (1) creating an infrastructure to support evidence-based practice, (2) facilitating the use of information technology, (3) aligning payment incentives, and (4) preparing the workforce to better serve patients in a world of expanding knowledge and rapid change.

a culture of improving quality of care. The committee proposed six components that define quality in healthcare. High-quality healthcare should be:

- *Safe:* Avoiding injuries to patients from the care that is intended to help them.
- *Effective:* Providing services based on scientific knowledge to all who could benefit and refraining from providing services to those not likely to benefit (avoiding underuse and overuse, respectively).
- *Patient centered:* Providing care that is respectful of and responsive to individual patient preferences, needs, and values and ensuring that patient values guide all clinical decisions.
- *Timely:* Reducing waits and sometimes harmful delays for both those who receive and those who give care.
- *Efficient:* Avoiding waste, including waste of equipment, supplies, ideas, and energy.
- *Equitable:* Providing care that does not vary in quality because of personal characteristics such as gender, ethnicity, geographic location, and socioeconomic status.

Arguably, hospitals and other healthcare institutions have been addressing these areas of quality improvement for decades. Yet, in 2003, the RAND Corporation published a study of representative populations of patients in the United States and discovered that only 54 percent of the recommended treatments were provided.[17] Why have we seen little progress? The use of measurement for the continuous improvement of high-quality process—quality management—that revolutionized manufacturing and service industries in the 1980s appears to have had little or no effect on the healthcare sector.[18] Once an innovation has been adopted by the first 15 to 20 percent of a field or industry, it becomes an almost unstoppable process.[19]

Despite the enormous efforts to date, the strong resistance to change in healthcare suggests we have not reached the breakthrough point. Resistance can occur for many reasons. Among them are the technical challenges in distinguishing quality across physicians and other healthcare providers; the unwillingness of hospitals, patients, and physicians to use the information derived from quality management; and the fear among physicians that quality indicators may increase litigation risks if plaintiffs' attorneys use the information as evidence to bolster malpractice claims.[20] Probably the most compelling reason we have seen little progress is that medicine is still a so-called cottage industry with very little standardization across physicians, nurses, or hospitals in how to deliver high quality of care. In fact, autonomy among individual providers—the ability to practice individual discretion within professionally accepted boundaries in the care of an individual patient—is a treasured value. Reinertsen and Schellekens pointed out the paradox of physician autonomy, in that as patients suffer injury, physician autonomy is reduced through regulatory and health plan oversight of medical decision making.[21]

PRINCIPLES ESSENTIAL TO PROMOTING QUALITY OF CARE

Improving quality of care in the healthcare system is still a work in progress. Having a robust definition of the dimensions of quality care is insufficient to accomplish the goal of continuous improvement. As stated earlier, quality consists of the degree to which health services for individuals and populations increase the likelihood of desired health outcomes (quality principles), are consistent with current professional knowledge (practitioner skill), and meet the expectations of healthcare consumers (the marketplace). Successful healthcare organizations—be they hospitals, physicians' offices, pharmacies, nursing homes, or ambulatory centers—will have understood, identified, and put into practice all of the following essential principles:

1. Leadership.
2. Measurement.
3. Reliability.
4. Practitioner skills.
5. The marketplace.

KEY PRINCIPLE 1: LEADERSHIP

In its simplest definition, leadership is the ability to influence behavior. The reason for changing behavior is to reach specific goals within an organization. The published literature on leadership is based on anecdotal and theoretical discussions. Less than 5 percent of these articles are empirically based, and most are based on demographic characteristics or personality traits of leaders.[22] Despite this, publications describing methods of personal development of leadership skills fill the shelves of bookstores. This discussion attempts to summarize briefly the basic and practical elements consistently associated with strong leaders.

a. Theories of Leadership

In 1977, a long-standing debate among the faculty of U.S. business schools began when a Harvard Business School professor published an article entitled "Managers and Leaders: Are They Different?"[23] In 1990, Kotter, a highly regarded thought leader in change theory, differentiated leadership from management and cautioned businesses to avoid confusing the two.[24] Management copes with the existing and growing complexity of our organizations, and leadership copes with change and transforming organizations to a vision with specific goals.[25] Kotter asserted that most U.S. corporations were overmanaged and underled and that both strong leadership and management were essential to success.[26] Leadership is not managing a spreadsheet but, rather, dealing in a disciplined manner with the complex world of human drives, desires, inspiration, and vision.

Berwick—a pediatrician and international thought leader in quality improvement in healthcare—questioned the common practice of defining healthcare improvement as changing regulatory, payment, and organizational structures under which care is given.[27] In many cases, this results in an emphasis on cost management and organizational downsizing with an associated loss of quality and safety. Berwick, now president of the Institute of Healthcare Improvement, stated that the failure to move the quality agenda forward was due to the failure of leadership and the inability of medical administrators and the professional workforce to innovate.[28] In 2005, Freed, in his detailed review of hospital turnovers, summarized the issue of leadership and management succinctly. He stated that hospitals that are underled may not do the right things and can find themselves at an eventual competitive disadvantage.[29] Hospitals that are undermanaged may not do things right and can find themselves eventually unable to execute.[30]

b. The Individual Characteristics of Successful Leaders

Harsdorff and colleagues evaluated approximately 800 acknowledged leaders from different U.S. business sectors, including healthcare.[31] The universal finding or traits that correlate with successful leaders are:

- Absolute personal integrity, including the ability to keep confidences.
- The ability to innovate.
- The ability to build partnerships in times of limited resources.
- Superior intelligence.
- The ability to hire and develop the best talent available.

Personal integrity must include an uncompromising approach to matters of safety, service, and quality of care. Careful listening to what physicians, consumers and patients, and the hospital staff desire and expect is required. *Innovation and superior intelligence* include the ability to project a specific vision and its practical goals to every individual in the organization as well as generate a very high percentage of strong buy-in by the employees. "The process of developing a winning strategy is...messy, experimental, and iterative and it is driven from the bottom up."[32] So-called transformational leaders, as opposed to those who manage by command and control, have the ability to transform cultures to create a context more conducive to the integration of evidence into clinical and management practice.[33] *The ability to build partnerships* through personal relations and highly effective meetings can lead to the empowerment of staff and a sense of ownership that drives the passion for high-quality care as well as high sensitivity to possible areas of risk. This unleashes the innovative potential of the staff in a way that is not common in healthcare. *The ability to hire and develop the best talent available* provides amplification of all of the previous activities and moves the organization toward a continuous cycle of improvement in multiple areas of caregiving, quality service, safety, and cost-effectiveness. All of these steps help lead to a highly effective organizational memory.

Other characteristics of transformational leaders include discipline and humility. "Disciplined attention is the currency of leadership" summarizes one of the characteristics contributing to a turnaround agent's efficacy in getting the attention he or she needs.[34] "The most powerfully transformative executives possess a paradoxical mixture of personal humility and professional will. They are timid and ferocious. Shy and fearless. They are rare—and unstoppable."[35] The turnaround agent is Level 5; he subordinates his role to that of the hospital for which he is clearing a safe path.

c. Leadership and Change

Coping with change is an essential focus of the effective leader. Every healthcare leader rapidly discovers that making a significant change (to transform or transition) is usually difficult to achieve and even harder to sustain. Often the toughest task for a leader in effecting change is mobilizing people throughout the organization to do adaptive work. "Adaptive work is required when our deeply held beliefs are challenged, when the values that made us successful become less relevant, and when legitimate, yet competing, perspectives emerge."[36] "You don't have to be managing people for long before you find out that people don't like change."[37]

Hospital medical staff members' failure to follow national guidelines to provide beta blockers or aspirin after a heart attack, failing to immunize patients with pneumococcal vaccine under Centers for Disease Control and Prevention and Medicare guidelines, or continuing antibiotics longer than recommended by their own surgical societies with the associated risk of resistant organisms are examples of resistance to change. Some medical staff meetings can become war zones of resistance as checklists to remind physicians of evidence-based care are denounced as so-called cookbook medicine. Of interest, when education and negotiation have failed, regulation, such as incorporating quality goals into hospital policies or medical staff bylaws and increasing peer accountability, makes these issues vanish with no evidence of patient injury. If resistance is a consequence of the lack of clear goal setting and compelling objective information,[38] the essential role of the leader is to provide clear goals as well as the empirical information to help in clinical and administrative decision making.

Individuals in hospitals, as in many other organizations, find it hard to believe that "change is the only constant."[39] But other industries have gone further than healthcare in recognizing that "individuals and organizations that are good react quickly to change. Individuals and organizations that are great create change."[40] The rapid rate of change in healthcare makes the ability to accomplish appropriate change an essential skill for all healthcare administrators, medical staffs, and clinical staffs. An important role of leadership is to set organizational goals and through communication (dissemination) guide the organization to accomplish the needed change (adherence).[41]

Kotter's eight-stage process is an effective tool for coping with change.[42] In brief, his eight-stage process to create change can be summarized as:

1. Establish a sense of urgency.

2. Create the guiding coalition.

3. Develop a vision and strategy.

4. Communicate the change vision.

5. Empower broad-based action.

6. Generate short-term wins.

7. Consolidate gains and produce more change.

8. Anchor new approaches in the culture.

In many situations, however, an effort to improve a process may stall for unknown reasons. A practical and useful tool called the ADKAR model has been developed by Prosci, an independent research company. More than 300 organizations were surveyed, and Prosci found that there are five stages that a group must pass through to accomplish a sustainable change.[43] Different members of the group may be at different stages at different times, causing the process to stall. The ADKAR psychological model can be used to accelerate the change process.

- Awareness of the need to change.
- Desire to participate and support the change.
- Knowledge of how to change.
- Ability to implement the change.
- Reinforcement to keep the change in place.

In evaluating a hospital management team or any group of people essential to a change process, each element can be rated on a scale of 1 (no awareness) to 5 (complete awareness). The strength of this tool is that it turns opinion into observable fact and can be used by anyone involved in the change process for self-assessment or for organizations undertaking transformation. After the rating process (which can include averaging several observers' ratings), any element with a rating of 3 or less needs attention. The focus must be sequential, and awareness of each step is a prerequisite to the next. Complete implementation of change is highly unlikely until each element is accomplished. This simple tool allows the quantification of each stage, understanding what awareness or skills the group or individuals possess or lack. It also guides priority setting because teaching new skills to individuals who have neither the awareness nor the desire for change is a futile effort.

Examples of airline success in safety and innovation are being discussed more frequently in healthcare. It is worthwhile to read about the early days of Southwest Airlines and note that all the elements of leadership noted previously are now considered routine in their company culture.[44] The durability of the Southwest Airlines culture appears to be because of these elements. But after the early days of struggle, one element seems to stand out in the employees' interactions with customers, both as a reason for initial success and sustainability. The paramount key to Southwest Airlines' success is the employees taking pride of ownership in the service they provide. Compare the Southwest approach to the healthcare industry with its shortage of workers, intense bidding for personnel such as nursing, declining revenues leading to cutbacks in benefits, and a premium on productivity to the point of mandated nursing-patient ratios. If a healthcare organization does not state outright that ownership of the process and outcome of the services we deliver is impossible, we certainly act as if it is. In fact, the concept of providing and promoting job security to a permanent core of employees as a form of ownership for healthcare workers is simply not part of the culture in many healthcare institutions. Many healthcare institutions act as if they are entitled to their patients' loyalty because of their mere presence in the marketplace and do not act as an entrepreneurial organization trying to earn and retain the loyalty of their patients and their families.

Genuine leadership in healthcare drives success through all the elements mentioned previously, but it is sustained by the promotion of a sense of personal ownership of the processes and outcomes for the patients cared for in our institutions. Personal ownership is an extraordinary potential force in healthcare organizations. It drives process improvement, risk awareness, communication, and innovation to achieve the levels of service and clinical performance that patients desire and that we all want for ourselves and our loved ones. Kotter clarifies: "What's crucial about a vision is not its originality but how well it serves the interests of important constituencies—customers, stockholders, employees—and how easily it can be translated into a realistic competitive strategy."[45] No one is better qualified than those same constituencies to participate actively in vision formulation. Participation in vision formation generates personal and organizational ownership.

KEY PRINCIPLE 2: MEASUREMENT

Quality of care can theoretically be measured by outcomes (a healthcare outcome is the change in the health status of the patient that is a direct result of care provided) or process (what providers do to and for patients). Outcome measurements have been a powerful tool in cardiovascular surgery and hospital-acquired infections (see figure 3.1).

Figure 3.1 An Example of Coronary Artery Bypass Graft Mortality Variation among California Hospitals[1]

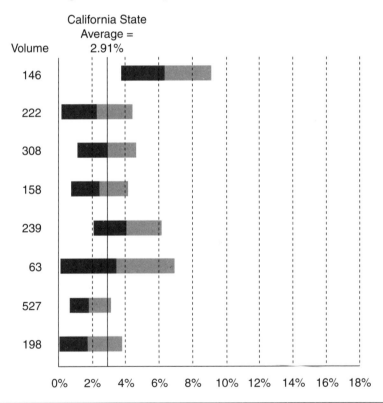

[1] Parker, J. P., Z. Li, B. Danielsen, J. Marcin, et al. 2006. *The California Report on Coronary Artery Bypass Graft Surgery 2003 Hospital Data.* Sacramento, CA: California Office of State-wide Health Planning and Development. Available at: http://www.oshpd.state.ca.us/HQAD/Outcomes/Studies/cabg/2003Report/2003Report.pdf. Accessed December 17, 2006.

The majority of our discussion, however, will be describing process measurements because they are the most common and are more easily measured than changes in patient health status. Measurement of process is often preferred because process is under relatively greater control of providers, needs a shorter time frame for results, can directly inform improvement, and may not require statistical adjustment for severity of illness.[46] Stated simply, certain evidence-based interactions with the patient are performed appropriately in a timely fashion or they are not. In a patient with pneumonia, either the antibiotic was given on time or it was not. In a patient with a heart attack, either an aspirin was given within a specific time period or it was not. These processes are examples of the nationally reported core measures reported by hospitals on a quarterly basis to JCAHO and the Centers for Medicare and Medicaid Services (CMS). The quality indicators have become a significant part of hospital and physician assessment. Clinical studies are appearing correlating quality of care with patient survival.[47] When paired with cost or efficiency of care, quality indicator graphs provide striking visual correlations (see figure 3.2).

Who is the doctor in the upper right quadrant offering risk-adjusted high-quality care at the greatest efficiency? These individuals are good for the healthcare system and provide evidence that high-quality care can be given without increases in marginal costs.

Figure 3.2 Physician Performance Disclosure Using Quality and Cost Metrics (adapted from Regence Blue Shield)[1]

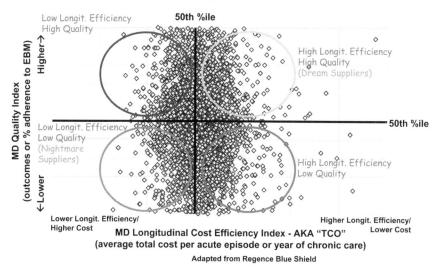

Adapted from Regence Blue Shield

---

[1] Milstein, Arnold. 2004. "Clinical Climate Change: How Purchasers Will Hinge Provider Revenue on Superior Cost Efficiency and Quality." Available at: http://council.brandeis.edu/pubs/Princeton%20XI/Arnold%20Milstein.pdf. Accessed December 12, 2006. Reproduced by permission of the author.

The government and commercial payers have identified the value of measurement, whereas healthcare providers are less certain. Quality measures are reportable to the public in the form of core measures. These indicators have had a tremendous impact on how our industry cares for patients and are directly related to the IOM's "effective" characteristic of quality care. There has always been resistance when anyone in the industry (hospitals, patients, or payers) suggests that medicine should be practiced in a more predictable and reliable way. So-called cookbook medicine has developed a negative connotation to some healthcare providers. Opponents of practicing evidence-based medicine claim that practicing medicine cannot be defined in such simple terms as these evidence-based processes. But the use of processes demonstrated in randomized controlled trials that lead to better patient outcomes promote better health and outcomes.

The CMS has helped bring about a change in the acceptance of the process-defined approach to quality. The publicly available core measures are a set of processes that improve the care we provide patients. To date, these measures have improved clinical outcomes in some of the highest-volume illnesses, namely pneumonia, congestive heart failure, and acute myocardial infarction, and surgical-site infection. New measures in surgical care improvement, childhood asthma, and behavioral health are also in development. The measures are based on extensive clinical research, are evidence based, and have a focus on improving patient outcomes. The core measures have created the foundation for evidence-based metrics that meet the IOM definition of effective care in some prevalent medical conditions.

CMS makes these metrics transparent to the public on the Department of Health and Human Services Hospital Compare Web site, http://www. hospitalcompare.hhs.gov. They require participation by the hospital in order to receive yearly payment increases for the care of Medicare patients. The Web site allows any individual with access to the Internet to compare how hospitals perform these certain processes. According to the Web site, "Hospital Compare is a consumer-oriented website that provides information on how well hospitals provide recommended care to their patients." CMS has partnered with the Hospital Quality Alliance (HQA) in this project. The HQA is a public-private collaboration established to promote reporting on hospital quality of care. The HQA consists of organizations that represent consumers, hospitals, doctors, employers, accrediting organizations, and federal agencies. Similar public reporting initiatives are being promoted by states and multiple managed-care payers.

KEY PRINCIPLE 3: RELIABILITY

Underlying nearly every identified problem in the hospital setting is the problem of reliable process. In evaluating highly reliable organizations, five principles have been found to be universal. They are command and control, risk appreciation, a specific quality component of the industry, metrics driving management, and reward.[48]

- *Command and control:* Performance goals shared and agreed upon throughout the organization.
- *Risk appreciation:* Whether there is knowledge that risk exists, and if there is knowledge that risk exists, the extent to which it is acknowledged and appropriately mitigated and/or minimized.
- *Quality:* Policies and procedures for promoting high-quality performance.
- *Metrics:* A system of ongoing checks to monitor hazardous conditions and used as the basis for accountability.
- *Reward:* The payoff an individual or organization receives for behaving one way or another; expected social compensation or disciplinary action to correct or reinforce a behavior, and the most powerful is recognition.

Of interest, the term *command and control* was used originally because preceding studies on reliability were on aircraft carriers.[49] This is not intended to suggest that each hospital leader should function in an inflexible military command and control demand mode. In fact, a highly reliable organization (HRO) must have mechanisms to support flexibility, organizational support for constrained improvisation on the part of lower level people, and cognition management methods.[50]

The principles of an HRO have been applied and monitored for a decade in one healthcare organization and may be used as its own control to compare outcomes once the principles were stopped. A large pediatric intensive care unit (PICU) providing care for a large geographic area applied the Libuser principles of an HRO to support the bedside caregiver from 1989 to 1999. Admissions, daily census, ventilator use, and pediatric transports to the unit went up, and mortality and consequential events (events that lead to an increased level or amount of care, neurological injury, or death) went down. Additionally, nursing turnover was very low (approximately 5 percent). After the two champions of HROs left the PICU, the new intensivists did away with the high-reliability strategy. Admissions, daily census, transports, and children on ventilators went down, whereas mortality, consequential events, and employee turnover went up.[51]

Although reliability has been successfully achieved by anesthesiologists[52] and discussed by the Agency for Healthcare Research and Quality[53] in its effort to promote patient safety, healthcare in general has not applied all of the Libuser principles consistently. This may be one of the reasons for the lack of progress pointed out previously by Leape and Berwick.[54] The organizational efforts of identifying the rules and principles essential to reliable care and institutionalizing them in job descriptions, measuring adherence to these job elements, allowing constrained or supervised innovation at the bedside, and rewarding good results are not standard in the healthcare industry. Healthcare has been moving in a better direction through the work of the Institute for Healthcare Improvement (IHI) and the IOM, however. Further study into successful high reliability organizations and innovative appropriate application of their ideas into healthcare may accelerate the process of beneficial change.

In figure 3.3, different areas of healthcare are compared with other industries and activities. The relative risk of death in an airplane crash is 1 in 1 million, whereas the risk of death from climbing in the Himalayas is 1 in 100. Note that anesthesiology and the transfusion process are ultrasafe as opposed to the other healthcare areas. These ultrasafe areas have evolved through a focus on reliable and standardized processes similar to the airline industry.

One of the challenges in creating reliable processes is variability. When measured, healthcare processes and outcomes have always demonstrated wide variability. The principles of risk adjustment in large samples have provided a degree of comparability previously unavailable. The use of easily understandable visual presentations have allowed physicians to compare their performance against what they may or may not agree is a best practice.

Figure 3.4 demonstrates wide variability in the total charges and length of stay in a single diagnosis related group (DRG) among a group of physicians. Five variables are presented in this simple picture: physician (each circle), number of cases for each physician (represented by the size of the circles), adjusted length of stay, and adjusted charges (as a surrogate for cost). Length of stay and total charges are adjusted for patient risk. The graph demonstrates wide variability in both adjusted length of stay and total charges. Potential causes of the wide variability are different practice patterns among the physicians, inappropriate utilization of services, inefficient consultative services, or prolongation of hospitalization for social reasons.

Figure 3.3 Average Rate per Exposure of Catastrophes and Associated Deaths in Various Industries and Human Activities[1]

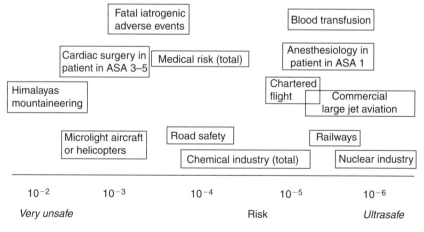

[1] Amalberti, R., Y. Auroy, D. Berwick, and P. Barach. 2005. "Five System Barriers to Achieving Ultrasafe Health Care." *Annals of Internal Medicine* 142 (9): 756–64. Copyright ©2005, American Medical Association, Chicago, IL.

Hospitals have approached these issues primarily through utilization management that appears to have been most successful following the institution of DRGs. Because physicians have often been reluctant to judge their colleagues' practice patterns, the effectiveness of utilization management and review in hospitals is far from consistent. Because of the complexity of utilization management and review, the primary approach of healthcare payers has been to deal with cost control rather than the complex underlying causes of cost expansion. Policies to reduce inappropriate variation in processes—be they HMOs with their own medical management programs, capitation, discounted contracting, or federally mandated reductions in physician payments—may have slowed the rise in medical costs and reduced inappropriate variation in utilization, but they have been far from successful.[55]

Value-based purchasing—achieving the highest possible quality at the lowest possible cost—is being adopted by Medicare and many managed care payers as the next wave in healthcare purchasing. The concept is intuitively powerful to patients and insurers; this will be the standard against which all hospitals and physicians will be measured for the foreseeable future. Purchasers and consumers will seek the providers with the highest possible quality at the lowest possible cost and reward them with both volume and incremental bonuses of money or

Figure 3.4 Variability in DRG 89 at a Single U.S. Hospital (information derived from public data)[1]

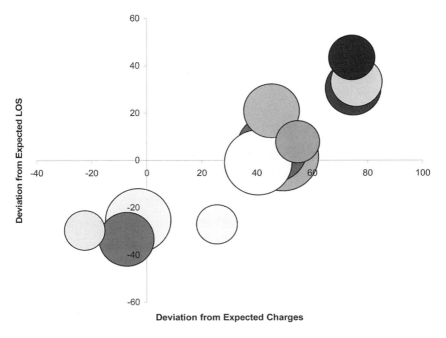

Deviation from Expected Charges

---

[1]Variability similar to this can be seen in almost any DRG measured at any facility.

access to service (e.g., clinical information technology). Those providers who have low-quality scores and high costs will be assumed to have less value to purchasers and consumers, and those providers, be they physicians or hospitals, will see their market share shrink. Transparency to the public on both cost and quality through public reporting on Web sites and in the media will presumably encourage consumers to make educated choices about seeking value in their choices about where to seek care. The advent of high-deductible insurance products and health spending accounts may encourage consumers to act more rationally—in the economic sense—in choosing providers.

KEY PRINCIPLE 4: PRACTITIONER SKILLS

The process of achieving consistently high quality of care in a reliable way consists of "doing the right thing right." To do the right thing requires that physicians, nurses, and all healthcare providers make the right decisions about appropriateness of services and care for each patient (high-quality decision making), and to do it right requires skill, judgment, and timeliness of execution (high-quality performance).[56]

The IOM characterized the threats to quality into three broad areas that affect practitioners: overuse (receiving treatment of no value), underuse (failing to receive needed treatment), and misuse (errors and defects in treatment).[57] The physicians and practitioners that are making treatment decisions must be doing so in a way that appropriately utilizes resources without overuse, underuse, or misuse. This is difficult to control because of variability in physician treatment practices. Evidence-based medicine has made its way into mainstream health decision making to reduce this variability. The concept relies on evidence to help practitioners decide on the appropriateness of services and care and how to execute the patient's care appropriately.

Both overuse and underuse represent limitations in the practitioners' decision making ability. Both areas focus on the competence of the practitioners and their ability to utilize resources appropriately. Questions to ask when evaluating whether overuse or underuse has occurred are:

1. Do they utilize resources appropriately?
2. Are they ordering too many tests?
3. Are they ordering too few tests?
4. Is therapy appropriate and consistent with individual patients' risk-benefit calculus?

Once a treatment decision is made, the duty of quality falls on the performance of the individuals providing the care to the patient (high-quality performance) and the systems in which they work. In the treatment phase of the care cycle, the providers must have processes and practices in place to ensure the treatment protocols are completed and there is no misuse. When errors and defects occur, quality is suboptimized (not an on-off switch but, rather, a spectrum) and patient safety is at risk.

KEY PRINCIPLE 5: THE MARKETPLACE

The marketplace has had a profound effect on moving hospital quality forward, and it is essential to understanding the role of quality of care in the current environment of healthcare. Despite the studies cited earlier,[58] quality metrics have been improving primarily by public transparency and the promise of improved payment and patient volumes. The value proposition of quality and efficiency and tying reimbursement to reporting or excelling in performance on specified quality metrics (pay for performance) has been accepted by nearly all third-party payers and has become a significant force in healthcare. This model has gained considerable attention by employers and payers for the following reasons. First, healthcare premium costs have continued to rise at rates as high as 14 percent per year. Although there have been some decreases in recent years in premium costs, workers are still only earning an additional 2.1 percent to 3.8 percent per year (see figure 3.5). The additional costs must be absorbed by one of two parties: the individual or the insurer. Additionally, the number of uninsured has continued to rise to a high of 45 million Americans, and that number is expected to increase to 51 million by 2010.[59]

The basic economics in healthcare are similar to most industries and involve the management of three main principles: cost, volume, and revenue. We must understand the role quality plays in the market because it is fundamental to the environment in which we operate. Quality is an important component in several areas: from the basic business model of healthcare and the financial impact on the industry (practitioners, facilities, and customers) to the public opinion driving decisions for treatment plans and treatment locations. For the industry to adopt changes, institutions must "realize a financial return on investment in a reasonable time frame, using a reasonable rate of discounting. This may be realized as 'bankable dollars' (profit), a reduction in losses for a given program or population, or avoided costs. In addition, a business case may exist if the investing entity believes that a positive indirect effect on organizational function and sustainability will accrue within a reasonable time frame."[60]

The industry faces many challenges when it comes to costs. One problem is the significant variation of cost in U.S. healthcare.[61] Some hospitals perform better quality care at a much lower cost than others. The industry also faces high fixed costs and a highly paid professional workforce, so it takes significant economies of scale to realize all the value. In addition, the cost of treating clinical complications is very high and contributes significantly to the rising cost of healthcare. One study indicated that between 10 percent and 20 percent of patients receiving greater than 48 hours of mechanical ventilation will develop ventilator-associated pneumonia (VAP). Treatment of VAP costs between $10,019 and $13,647 in additional hospital costs during the prolonged hospital stay.[62]

One key element to the economic model that quality should help improve at facilities is volume. Practitioners and treatment facilities are consistently judged by visitors based, in large part, on the quality of care they are providing. Although some practitioners are able to thrive because of their technical proficiency, patients

Figure 3.5 Yearly Percentage Increase of Wages Compared to Healthcare Premiums[1]

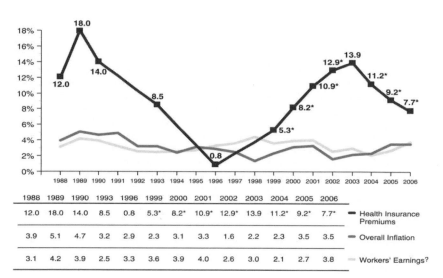

1988	1989	1990	1993	1996	1999	2000	2001	2002	2003	2004	2005	2006	
12.0	18.0	14.0	8.5	0.8	5.3*	8.2*	10.9*	12.9*	13.9	11.2*	9.2*	7.7*	▬ Health Insurance Premiums
3.9	5.1	4.7	3.2	2.9	2.3	3.1	3.3	1.6	2.2	2.3	3.5	3.5	▬ Overall Inflation
3.1	4.2	3.9	2.5	3.3	3.6	3.9	4.0	2.6	3.0	2.1	2.7	3.8	▬ Workers' Earnings?

[1] Henry J. Kaiser Family Foundation and the Health Research Educational Trust. 2006. "Employer Health Benefits: 2006 Annual Survey." This information was reprinted with permission from the Henry J. Kaiser Family Foundation. The Kaiser Family Foundation, based in Menlo Park, California, is a nonprofit, private operating foundation focusing on the major healthcare issues facing the nation and is not associated with Kaiser Permanente or Kaiser Industries.

* Estimate is statistically different from estimate for the previous year show at $p < .05$. No statistical tests are conducted for years prior to 1999.

' Data on percentage increase in workers' earnings are seasonally adjusted data from the Current Employment Statistics Survey (April to April.)

Note: Data on premium increases reflect the cost of health insurance premiums for a family of four.

Source: Kaiser/HRET Survey of Employer-Sponsored Health Benefits, 1999–2006; KPMG Survey of Employer-Sponsored Health Benefits, 1993, 1996; Health Insurance Association of America (HIAA), 1988, 1989, 1990; Bureau of Labor Statistics, Consumer Price Index, U.S. City Average of Annual Inflation (April to April), 1988–2006; Bureau of Labor Statistics, Seasonally Adjusted Data from the Current Employment Statistics Survey (April to April), 1988–2006.

return and also refer their friends based on the quality experiences they have had. If a patient has a bad experience and receives the wrong drug at a facility (a misuse) or finds out a physician did not order a test another physician thought was indicated (underuse), the patient may be less likely to seek care at that facility or from that physician in the future. Additionally, patients will tell their friends about the bad experience they had. Although opportunities for service recovery exist, many patients and managed care plans are not returning to physicians and hospitals that provide poor quality of care.

All healthcare providers, physicians included, will soon be impacted by the financial impact of improving quality of care. Many have already felt the impact of pay for performance. Managed care plans and Medicare are offering financial and volume referral incentives to physicians and hospitals that demonstrate superior adherence to evidence-based practices and better outcomes. In some pay-for-performance plans, the higher performing entities receive greater than average payments, whereas the poorer performers will receive less than the average payment. The federal government is committed to developing more quality metrics in more diagnostic and therapeutic categories and is poised to implement pay-for-performance bonuses to hospitals and physicians in 2008 or 2009.[63]

Tenet Healthcare and the Commitment to Quality: A Case Study

Formed in 1996 in the merger of two for-profit healthcare systems, American Medical International and National Medical Enterprises, Tenet Healthcare enjoyed rapid growth with the subsequent acquisition of more than forty hospitals until 2002. Hospital volumes were growing rapidly, and the profitability of its hospitals and the holding entity was at an all-time high. In fall 2002, however, Tenet faced serious and, to some observers, fatal charges against it and some of its hospitals. Based on analysis by independent observers, Tenet was reported to have escalated its charges so that, in a substantial minority of its hospitals, the hospitals were receiving an unacceptably high proportion of Medicare outlier payments. In the same week, the Federal Bureau of Investigation raided a Tenet hospital in Redding, California—Redding Medical Center—based on allegations of overuse and inappropriate utilization of invasive cardiac procedures such as cardiac catheterization and coronary artery bypass graft surgery. Subsequently, in 2006, Tenet settled with the federal government for $750 million to settle all charges lodged against it by the federal government related to these and other issues. In late 2005, Tenet also settled multimillion dollar liability claims by patients who had been treated for cardiac disease at Redding Medical Center.

In early 2003, the new senior leadership of Tenet recognized that perceptions of the quality of care in its hospitals constituted a serious threat to its long- and short-term viability. Supported by the board of directors, Tenet and its leadership committed to making substantial improvements in the quality of care provided in its hospitals and associated healthcare institutions. This new initiative—known as the Commitment to Quality (C2Q)—had as its sustaining mission the improvement of every aspect of care. Recognizing the rising demands for both improvement and transparency in quality and safety of care from regulators, payers, patients, and employers, Tenet and its leadership committed to supporting and sustaining improvement in six dimensions of quality of care: evidence-based medicine, patient safety, physician excellence, nursing excellence, patient flow and capacity management, and clinical resource management. Subsequently, in 2005, additional dimensions of improvement were added to the Commitment to Quality. Service excellence, which had been a focus of improvement in Tenet Healthcare since 2000 in its Target 100 program, merged with the Commitment to Quality.

Senior management requested an evaluation of the quality of care for each hospital in the identified dimensions as well as a plan to improve the quality of care—consistent with evidence-based goals for quality and safety—that Tenet hospital leaders would be held accountable for achieving. Senior leaders recognized that the change management process around the Commitment to Quality programs would be both significant and difficult but insisted on sustainable and measurable progress in return for providing the resources to improve the quality of care.

Establishing ongoing communication and dialogue about the strategic implementation plan for the Commitment to Quality among senior and midlevel leaders in the corporate and hospital leadership structure was a critical first step in the implementation of C2Q. Daylong meetings were held in national and regional venues to vet the initiative and solicit input and feedback from corporate and hospital leaders.

Initial reactions to the initiative were enthusiastic but tempered by concerns about draining resources from bedside care to improve quality. Financial officers were skeptical that the proposed investment in improving quality and safety did not have sufficient financial return to the hospitals. Historically, Tenet had a decentralized model of corporate oversight in clinical care and quality improvement. Some leaders expressed concern about a broad initiative developed by corporate management being undermined by staff and leadership in the hospitals. They requested the right to prioritize the quality initiatives based on both the hospitals' baseline performance and readiness for change.

One apparent barrier to launching the Commitment to Quality was the lack of standardized metrics in many of the dimensions of the program across the hospitals. Although many of the higher-level metrics that were reported through common reporting systems (e.g., length of stay) to regional and corporate leaders, in some dimensions—especially in detailed operational metrics such as emergency room dwell time or operating room start and stop times—little or no standardization across the hospitals existed. One of the first tasks was to establish a common set of metrics for each goal and objective and provide standard rationales, definitions, data collection protocols, as well as data reporting guidelines. Each hospital spent one month collecting and validating each metric in the complete list prior to beginning implementation.

The hospital leadership teams also raised significant issue about the resources available at each hospital to implement the changes necessary to achieve rapid but sustainable change in quality and safety. They expressed concern that diverting hospital resources toward improvement compromised the ability to deliver care by midlevel managers and frontline staff. They also acknowledged that detailed expertise in change management, improvement methods and techniques, and deep knowledge of hospital systems was not uniformly available or of the same quality across all Tenet facilities. They did agree that the transfer of such knowledge to the senior leadership, midlevel managers, and frontline staff would be required to create a sustainable improvement in performance as well as a change in the culture of improvement in the hospitals. To address these concerns, an implementation vehicle known as the C2Q Transformation Team was created. Each of the four geographic regions in the Tenet Healthcare system has an improvement team known as a Transformation Team. Each team is staffed by a regional team leader, typically an experienced hospital senior manager (e.g., hospital chief operating officer, chief nursing officer). The team is also staffed by subject matter experts—typically nurse leaders—in case management, emergency room management, and operating room management.

After the in-depth monthlong self-assessment, the C2Q Transformation Teams spend eight weeks full-time on-site at each hospital working side-by-side with their hospital counterparts to achieve improvement on a set of mutually agreed upon goals established during the first week on-site. The regional Transformation Team is then available to the hospitals through multiple communication vehicles and returns to conduct sustainability visits every 8 to 12 weeks. A second round of four-week on-site visits was begun in 2005 with the goals of integrating Tenet's service quality initiatives with C2Q and focusing on length of stay reduction and pharmacy safety as well as continuing to improve performance in the initial six C2Q dimensions. Examples of specific projects and goals in each dimension of quality are described in table 3.3.

Table 3.3
Quality: Goals and Targets

Commitment to Quality Dimension	Example of Goal	Associated Metric	Example of Target
Evidence-based medicine	Improve core measure performance in acute myocardial infarction (AMI)	Number of times the patient received appropriate treatment/Number of opportunities to provide evidence-based treatment appropriate for the patient	Greater than or equal to 95% adherence to evidence-based standards
Patient safety	Reduce hospital-acquired infections (e.g., central venous catheter–associated bloodstream infections (CVCBSI)	Number of patients with central venous catheter–associated bloodstream infections /1,000 patient days with device in place	Reduce CVCBSIs to top decile performance in national comparative databases

Table 3.3
Quality: Goals and Targets *(continued)*

Physician excellence	Implement and monitor timely physician privileging and credentialing	Percentage of all new and reappointment credentialing and privileging completed within time specified by hospital and medical staff bylaws	100% timely and accurate credentialing and privileging
Nursing excellence	Improve nursing satisfaction and increase nursing retention rates	Employee satisfaction scores for nurses Percentage turnover for new hires (within year one) Percentage turnover for all nurses	Improve nursing satisfaction scores by 20% Reduce new-hire and veteran turnover rates to 10%
Capacity management and patient flow	Improve capacity management in the emergency room (ER)	Left without being seen (LWBS) Patient dwell time in ER for patients who are discharged from the ER Patient dwell time in the ER for patients who are admitted to the hospital	LWBS ≤ 2% ER dwell time (discharged) ≤ 2 hours ER dwell time (admitted) ≤ 4 hours
Utilization management and review	Insure that all patients undergoing percutaneous angioplasty and/or coronary artery bypass graft and/or cardiac valve replacement receive the procedure consistent with American College of Cardiology/American Heart Association (ACC/AHA) appropriateness guidelines	Percentage of patients undergoing the procedures that are Class I or Class IIA (ACC/AHA guidelines)	95%
Clinical resource management	Reduce variable cost per case of high-volume, high-cost procedures while maintaining clinical effectiveness for patient process and outcome (e.g., total hip replacement)	Percentage of all first-time total hip replacements using clinician-approved cost-effective prostheses	90%

Among the positive forces at work in the Commitment to Quality in Tenet Healthcare is leadership. Involvement by the most senior leaders at Tenet in communicating and reinforcing key strategies and demanding accountability for results has been vital to the success of the C2Q initiative in promoting change. The board of directors has adopted an incentive compensation system based on a so-called balanced scorecard of results that emphasizes clinical quality, safety, and service excellence equally with financial results. Transparency among the hospital leaders about their quality performance has also promoted healthy competition to achieve higher and higher levels of performance. Both transparency and accountability have accelerated change and improvement in the hospitals. Commencing with the collection of core measure data for heart attack in mid-2003 with adherence rates of about 50 percent for the initial measure set, adherence to the CMS expanded core measures in heart attack was 95 percent among the 20,000 patients treated in 2006 in Tenet hospitals.

Leadership and commitment must be accompanied by resources to achieve results. Tenet commits more than $60 million a year in corporate and regional resources to supporting quality and quality-related initiatives on an annual revenue base of $9.5 billion. More than one-third of these resources are committed to developing informatics infrastructures that enable consistent and accurate data collection, information transfer, and rapid sharing of both results and improvement strategies over a corporate-wide intranet. Significant investments are made in supporting the regional quality improvement infrastructure, including regional chief medical officers and regional directors of clinical quality improvement, who work collaboratively with the regional Transformation Teams to sustain and improve quality, safety, and cost-effectiveness. Collaboration between the hospitals and the regional teams has promoted a 33 percent to 50 percent reduction in hospital-acquired infections such as catheter-associated bloodstream infections with almost half the hospitals recording no catheter-associated bloodstream infections for more than a year.

Initially, the Commitment to Quality was envisioned as a corporate initiative that would be implemented in similar ways in each hospital. Acceptance at the hospital level was markedly enhanced by standardized metrics and goals but with customization of the improvement initiatives at the local level. In order to prevent each hospital from reinventing the wheel, so to speak, when addressing similar issues, success stories and failures are shared among the hospitals, creating a virtual network of improvement teams that share strategies, tactics, and knowledge. For example, in order to achieve 95 percent adherence to the acute myocardial infarction (AMI) core measures, several hospitals redesigned their relationships with their local emergency medical services to permit transmission of electrocardiogram tracings from the field to the emergency department, allowing identification of ST-segment elevation heart attacks in the field. Hospitals alerted to a ST-segment elevation AMI are able to mobilize cardiac catheterization teams that are ready when the patient arrives at the hospital and have reduced the average so-called door-to-balloon time to an average of 45 minutes. The emergency department and cardiology staff in those hospitals conduct national

Web-enabled presentations to all the other hospitals and are available to mentor other Tenet hospitals that are working to reduce door-to-balloon times.

These strategies are shared among regional improvement teams and utilize the Tenet intranet to catalog the experiences and lessons learned across the system. Many common improvement ideas and strategies evolved, but unique and innovative solutions to common problems continue to be reported after several years of implementation. One hospital, which had implemented the Institute of Healthcare Improvement bundles to reduce catheter-associated bloodstream infections, was frustrated by its inability to reduce the rate of infection. In frustration, the chief medical officer insisted that every physician placing central venous access be retrained and recertified. A core team of four physicians was certified and observed by infection-control practitioners to monitor technique and the sterility of the placement process. Within eight weeks, the rate of bloodstream infections associated with placement of central catheters had dropped 90 percent and achieved performance equal to the lowest decile performers in the National Nosocomial Infections Surveillance (NNIS) database.

Providing an initial assessment for each hospital granted excellent opportunities for the hospital medical staff and clinical and administrative leadership to address issues they mutually determined to be important to the success of the hospital and the care of the patients. Although many hospitals faced similar challenges in improvement in evidence-based medicine and patient safety, different challenges were observed in capacity management and patient flow. Standardized goals and metrics help identify opportunities for improvement, but the solutions—although having some common features—are primarily the result of frontline employees and midlevel managers conducting multidisciplinary improvement efforts. One hospital experienced unacceptably high rates of diversion of ambulances from its emergency room—in some months approaching 200 hours. Careful mapping of the flow and timing of patient movement from entering the emergency room through admission to a patient care floor or intensive care unit identified several barriers to patient flow, including poor communication between the emergency room staff and the receiving units and long delays in the turnover of rooms by environmental services. Mapping and measuring the times associated with each part of the patient flow process resulted in new communication protocols between the emergency room and the receiving care units and service standards about response time. Hospital managers also reorganized the staffing and team structure of environmental services to meet peak demand in patient room cleaning and turnover. As a result, the hospital has less than ten hours of diversion a year and has consistently met the established goals of fewer than 2 percent of all patients entering the emergency department leaving without being seen and average dwell times of less than two hours for patients seen and discharged and less than four hours for patients seen and admitted.

Continuous communication at every level of the organization and through multiple mechanisms is also vital to the success of C2Q. Repetition of the key messages in multiple forums and through e-mails, conference calls, regional and national meetings, corporate and local hospital written and in-person presentations, and in face-to-face meetings is vital. Presentations and question-and-answer periods with the hospital governing boards and medical staff, as well as employee forums with frontline employees and midlevel managers, proved invaluable.

THE BUSINESS CASE FOR QUALITY

Healthcare has had a difficult time demonstrating the business case for quality because of the complexity of care and difficulty in capturing the real fixed and variable costs of caring for patients. Other industries have long accepted the theory first described by Deming that improvement in quality leads directly to a decrease in cost. Better quality results in less rework, fewer mistakes and delays, and a better use of time. Productivity improves as a result. By improving quality, the industry captures the market with better quality and lower price, is able to innovate in the business and clinical practice of medicine, and so can provide more jobs.[64]

The difficulty in demonstrating the business case in healthcare may be the result of healthcare not having yet reached the level of quality that triggers the results as defined by Deming. Healthcare lags significantly behind many industries in rates of errors and the ability to capture the measures that permit maximal management of the complex healthcare process. The ability to provide timely and detailed measurement in healthcare is time and personnel intensive because of insufficient real-time information technology. In fact, as overburdened as healthcare workers feel while manually gathering quality-related data, we are obtaining and using only a small fraction of the information necessary for maximizing the management of high-quality care.

What is the cost of quality? Does it raise the price of goods and services? Are huge savings possible by implementing continual improvement efforts? These questions are not easy ones, but quality is becoming increasingly measurable as are its costs. In healthcare, the failure to prevent serious complications, such as a hospital-acquired infection, may cost the patient his or her life, prolonged disability, and thousands of dollars in treatment. Avoidable surgical complication may prolong hospitalization, result in disability or death, and cause great expense and repeated procedures.

Healthcare organizations, however, have been reluctant to implement improvements because better quality has not been accompanied by better payment or improved profitability. The most recent business case for quality has been driven by employers and third-party payers seeking value-based purchasing. Serious doubts about the long-term sustainability of rising healthcare costs, the accelerating numbers of uninsured, and the double-digit increases in healthcare premiums are driving employers and health plans, as well as federal and state governments, to demand cost-effective, safe, and patient-centered care. Both physicians and hospitals are being assessed with a combination of quality and efficiency (cost) measures and these measurements are being used to include or exclude both hospitals and physicians from healthcare plans.

The current business case for quality is straightforward. Access to the patient (both by volume and payment level) is being determined by demonstrating high quality and cost efficiency. A clear understanding of the history and development of the concept of quality patient care and the ability to understand, identify, and utilize the key principles will help create successful healthcare organizations.

CONCLUSION

There has been a change in healthcare since the mid-1990s that will shape the future of the industry. As Leape stated, "Ten years ago, no one was talking about patient safety. Five years ago, before the IOM report, a small number in a few pioneering places had developed a strong commitment, but its impact was limited and most of health care was unaffected. Now, the majority of health care institutions are involved to some extent and public awareness has soared."[65] Many exciting changes have occurred in the industry because of the increased focus on safety and quality. Some of these changes may be short-lived, but some will truly revolutionize the way healthcare is provided. Quality and safety are important factors shaping the future of the industry for hospitals and medical care providers. Quality metrics will shape physician practices as well as the processes in place at the hospitals in which they practice. Quality will define both success and failure for physicians, hospitals, and the executives who lead in the healthcare industry.

Key Concepts

- Quality consists of the degree to which health services for individuals and populations increase the likelihood of desired health outcomes (quality principles), are consistent with current professional knowledge (professional practitioner skill), and meet the expectations of healthcare users (the marketplace).
- Successful healthcare organizations—be they hospitals, physicians' offices, pharmacies, nursing homes, or ambulatory centers—will have understood, identified, and put into practice all of the following essential principles: leadership, measurement, reliability, practitioner skills, and the marketplace.
- Access to the patient (both by volume and payment level) is being determined by demonstrating high quality and cost efficiency. A clear understanding of the history and development of the concept of quality patient care and the ability to understand, identify, and utilize the key principles will help create successful healthcare organizations.
- Quality metrics and practices will help define both success and failure for physicians, hospitals, and the executives who lead in the healthcare industry.

NOTES

1. Deming, W. E. 1994. *The New Economics*. 2nd ed. Cambridge, MA: SPC Press.

2. Donabedian, A. 1988. "The Quality of Care: How Can It Be Assessed?" *Journal of the American Medical Association* 260: 1743–48.

3. Ibid.

4. Winder, Richard E., and Daniel K. Judd. 1996. "Organizational Orienteering: Linking Deming, Covey, and Senge in an Integrated Five Dimension Quality Model." Available at: http://www.ldri.com/articles/96orgorient.html. Accessed August 3, 2007.

5. Lohr, K. N., M. S. Donaldson, and J. Harris-Wehling. 1992. "Medicare: A Strategy for Quality Assurance. V. Quality of Care in a Changing Health Care Environment." *Quality Review Bulletin* 18: 120–26.

6. Laffel, G., and D. Blumenthal. 1989. "The Case for Using Industrial Quality Management Science in Health Care Organizations." *Journal of the American Medical Association* 262: 2869–73.

7. Conway, J. B., and S. N. Weingart. 2005. "Organizational Change in the Face of Highly Public Errors. I. The Dana-Farber Cancer Institute Experience." *Agency for Healthcare Research and Quality, Morbidity and Mortality Rounds on the Web*. Available at: http://webmm.silverchair.com/perspective.aspx?perspectiveID=3. Accessed August 3, 2007.

8. Kohn, K. T., J. M. Corrigan, and M. S. Donaldson. 1999. *To Err Is Human: Building a Safer Health System*. Washington, D.C.: National Academy Press.

9. Ibid., p. 5.

10. Brennan, T. A., L. L. Leape, N. M. Laird, et al. 1991. "Incidence of Adverse Events and Negligence in Hospitalized Patients: Results of the Harvard Medical Malpractice Study I." *New England Journal of Medicine* 324: 370–76.

11. Thomas, E. J., D. M. Studdert, H. R. Burstin, et al. 2000. "Incidence and Types of Adverse Events and Negligent Care in Utah and Colorado." *Medical Care* 38(3): 261–71.

12. Pope, A. 1711. *An Essay on Criticism 1*. Line 525.

13. Leape, L., and D. Berwick. 2005. "Five Years after *To Err Is Human*: What Have We Learned?" *Journal of the American Medical Association* 293: 2384–90, 2384.

14. Ibid., 2384–85.

15. Ibid., 2384.

16. Institute of Medicine. 2001. *Crossing the Quality Chasm: A New Health System for the 21st Century*. Washington, D.C.: National Academy Press, 1.

17. McGlynn, E. A., S. M. Asch, J. Adams, et al. 2003. "The Quality of Health Care Delivered to Adults in the United States." *New England Journal of Medicine* 348: 2635–45.

18. Coye, M. J. 2001. "No Toyotas in Healthcare: Why Medical Care Has Not Evolved to Meet Patients' Needs." *Health Affairs* 20 (6): 44–56.

19. Rogers, E. M. 1995. "Lessons for Guidelines from the Diffusion of Innovations." *Journal on Quality Improvement* 21 (7): 324–28.

20. Kesselheim, A. S., T. G. Ferris, and D. M. Studdert. 2006. "Will Physician-Level Measures of Clinical Performance Be Used in Medical Malpractice Litigation?" *Journal of the American Medical Association* 295 (15): 1831–34.

21. Reinertsen, J., and W. Schellekens. 2005. *10 Powerful Ideas for Improving Patient Care*. Chicago: Health Administration Press, 36–37.

22. Vance, E., and E. Larson. 2002. "Leadership Research in Business and Health Care." *Journal of Nursing Scholarship* 34 (2): 165–71.

23. Zalesnik, A. 1977. "Managers and Leaders: Are They Different?" *Harvard Business Review* 15 (3): 68–78.

24. Kotter, J. P. 1990. "What Leaders Really Do." *Harvard Business Review* 68 (3): 103–11.

25. Ibid.

26. Ibid.

27. Berwick, D. M. 1994. "Eleven Worthy Aims for Clinical Leadership of Health System Reform." *Journal of the American Medical Association* 272 (10): 797–802.

28. Galvin, R. 2005. "Interview. A Deficiency of Will and Ambition: A Conversation with Donald Berwick." *Health Affairs Web Exclusive*. January 12. Available at: http://content.healthaffairs.org/cgi/content/full/hlthaff.w5.1/DC1. Accessed August 3, 2007.

29. Freed, D. H. 2005. "Hospital Turnarounds: Agents, Approaches, Alchemy." *Health Care Manager* 24: 96–118.

30. Ibid.

31. Harsdorff, C., and D. Hamel. 2005. Personal communication with the authors.

32. Campbell, A., and M. Alexander. 1997. "What's Wrong with Strategy?" *Harvard Business Review* 75 (6): 42–51.

33. Schein, E. H. 1985. *Organizational Culture and Leadership.* San Francisco: Jossey-Bass.

34. Heifetz, R. A., and D. L. Laurie. 1997. "The Work of Leadership." *Harvard Business Review* 75 (1): 124–34.

35. Collins, J. 2001. "Level 5 Leadership: The Triumph of Humility and Fierce Resolve." *Harvard Business Review* 79 (1): 66–76, 67.

36. Heifetz and Laurie, 124.

37. Miller, J. 1997. "Lead, Follow, or Get out of the Way." *Hospital Material Management Quarterly* 19 (1): 63–67.

38. Rhydderch, M., G. Elwyn, M. Marshall, and R. Grol. 2004. "Organizational Change Theory and the Use of Indicators in General Practice." *Quality and Safety in Health Care* 13: 213–17.

39. Cohen, W. D., and M. H. Murri. 1995. "Managing the Change Process." *Journal of American Health Information Management Association* 66 (6): 40, 42–44, 46–47.

40. South, S. F. 1999. "Managing Change Isn't Good Enough." *Clinical Laboratory Management Review* 13 (1): 22–26.

41. Redfern, S., and S. Christian. 2003. "Achieving Change in Health Care Practice." *Journal of Evaluation in Clinical Practice* 9: 225–38.

42. Kotter, J. P. 1996. *Leading Change.* Boston: Harvard Business School Press, 21.

43. Hiatt, J. M., and T. J. Creasey. 2003. *Change Management.* Loveland, CO: Prosci Research.

44. Freiberg, K., and J. Freiberg. 1997. *Nuts? Southwest Airlines' Crazy Recipe for Business and Personal Success.* New York: Bantam Doubleday Dell.

45. Kotter, J. P. 1990. "What Leaders Really Do." *Harvard Business Review* 68 (3): 103–11.

46. Higashi, T., P. G. Shekelle, et al. 2005. "Quality of Care Is Associated with Survival in Vulnerable Older Patients." *Annals of Internal Medicine* 143: 274–81.

47. Ibid. See also Bradley, E. H., J. Herrin, et al. 2006. "Hospital Quality for Acute Myocardial Infarction: Correlation among Process Measures and Relationship with Short-Term Mortality." *Journal of the American Medical Association* 296 (1): 72–78.

48. Libuser, C. B. 1994. "Organizational Structure and Risk Mitigation." PhD dissertation, University of California, Los Angeles.

49. Rochlin, G. I., T. R. La Porte, and K. H. Roberts. 1987. "The Self-Designing High-Reliability Organization: Aircraft Carrier Flight Operations at Sea." *Naval War College Review* 40 (4): 76–90.

50. Bigley, G. A., and K. H. Roberts. 2001. "Structuring Temporary Systems for High Reliability." *Academy of Management Journal* 44: 1281–1300.

51. Roberts, K. H., V. Desai, and P. Madsen. 2006. "Reliability Enhancement and Demise at Back Bay Medical Center's Children's Hospital." In *Handbook of Human Factors and Ergonomics in Health Care and Patient Safety,* ed. P. Carayon. Mahwah, NJ: Erlbaum.

52. Amalberti, R., Y. Auroy, D. Berwick, and P. Barach. 2005. "Five System Barriers to Achieving Ultrasafe Health Care." *Annals of Internal Medicine* 142 (9): 756–64.

53. Pizzi, L. T., Goldfarb, N. I., and Nash, D. B., eds. 2001. "Promoting a Culture of Safety." In *Evidence Report/Technology Assessment No. 43, Making Health Care Safer: A Critical Analysis of Patient Safety Practices.* AHRQ Publication No. 01-E058. Rockville, MD: Agency for Healthcare Research and Quality.

54. Leape, L., and D. Berwick. 2005. "Five Years after *To Err Is Human*: What Have We Learned?" *Journal of the American Medical Association* 293: 2384–90, 2384. See also Freed, D. H. 2005. "Hospital Turnarounds: Agents, Approaches, Alchemy." *Health Care Manager* 24: 96–118.

55. Catlin, A., C. Cowan, S. Heffler, B. Washington, and the National Health Accounts Team. 2007. "National Health Spending in 2005: The Slowdown Continues." *Health Affairs* 26 (1): 142–53.

56. Palmer, R. H. 1991. "Considerations in Defining Quality of Health Care." In *Striving for Quality in Health Care: An Inquiry into Policy and Practice,* ed. R. H. Palmer, A. Donabedian, and G. J. Povar, 1–53. Ann Arbor, MI: Health Administration Press. See also Blumenthal, D., and A. C. Scheck, eds. 1995. *Improving Clinical Practice: Total Quality Management and the Physician.* San Francisco: Jossey-Bass.

57. Chassin, M. R., R. W. Galvin, and the National Roundtable on Health Care Quality. 1998. "The Urgent Need to Improve Health Care Quality: Institute of Medicine National Roundtable on Health Care Quality." *Journal of the American Medical Association* 280: 1000–1005.

58. McGlynn, E. A., S. M. Asch, J. Adams, et al. 2003. "The Quality of Health Care Delivered to Adults in the United States." *New England Journal of Medicine* 348: 2635–45. See also Coye, M. J. 2001. "No Toyotas in Healthcare: Why Medical Care Has Not Evolved to Meet Patients' Needs." *Health Affairs* 20 (6): 44–56.

59. Commonwealth Fund Commission on a High Performance Health System. 2005. *A Need to Transform the U.S. Health Care System: Improving Access, Quality, and Efficiency.* New York: Commonwealth Fund.

60. Leatherman, S., D. Berwick, D. Iles, et al. 2003. "The Business Case for Quality: Case Studies and an Analysis." *Health Affairs* 22 (2): 17–30, 18.

61. Davis, K., C. Schoen, and S. C. Schoenbaum. 2004. *Mirror, Mirror on the Wall: Looking at the Quality of American Health Care through the Patient's Lens.* New York: Commonwealth Fund. See also Fisher, E. S., D. E. Wennberg, and T. A. Stukel. 2003. "The Implications of Regional Variation in Medicare Spending: Part I. The Context, Quality, and Accessibility of Care." *Annals of Internal Medicine* 138: 273–311.

62. Safdar, N. 2005. "Clinical and Economic Consequences of Ventilator-Associated Pneumonia: A Systematic Review." *Critical Care Medicine* 33 (10): 2184–93.

63. Centers for Medicare and Medicaid Services. 2005. "Medicare 'Pay for Performance (P4P)' Initiatives." Press release, January 31. Baltimore, MD. Available at: http://www.cms.hhs.gov/apps/media/press/release.asp?Counter=1343. Accessed December 18, 2006.

64. Deming.

65. Leape, L., and D. Berwick. 2005. "Five Years after *To Err Is Human*: What Have We Learned?" *Journal of the American Medical Association* 293: 2384–90, 2387.

CHAPTER 4

Adapting Proven Aviation Safety Tools to Healthcare: Improving Healthcare by Changing the Safety Culture

Jack Barker and Greg Madonna

At about 6:15 P.M. Pacific standard time on December 28, 1978, United Airlines flight 173 crashed into a wooded, populated area, killing 8 passengers and 2 crew members and seriously injuring 21 passengers and 2 other crew members. The National Transportation Safety Board (NTSB) determined that the probable cause of the accident was the failure of the captain to monitor properly the aircraft's fuel state and to properly respond to the low fuel state and the crew members' advisories regarding fuel state. This resulted in fuel exhaustion to all engines. Contributing to the accident was the failure of the other two flight crew members to fully comprehend the criticality of the fuel state or to successfully communicate their concern to the captain. The NTSB believes that this accident exemplifies a recurring problem: a breakdown in cockpit management and teamwork during a situation involving malfunctions of aircraft systems in flight.[1]

HISTORY OF AVIATION SAFETY CULTURE CHANGE

Flying has always been a high-risk endeavor. In the early days of aviation, airplanes would frequently crash because of a sheer lack of understanding of aeronautics as well as because of technological limitations. Engineering technology such as metallurgy of aircraft materials, as well as operational technology such as navigation and meteorology, was in its infancy. Airplanes would often fly into conditions that overwhelmed their performance capabilities and crash or literally fly off never to be heard from again.

As commercial aviation matured in the post–World War II years, there were an alarming number of aircraft accidents. Airplanes were becoming more reliable, yet the number of fatalities grew exponentially. Aviation safety developed into a science, and researchers found increasing evidence that human factors played a major role in causing accidents. After several costly and preventable high-profile crashes in the 1970s, the science of Crew Resource Management (CRM) was developed to provide solutions to the human aspect of aviation safety.[2] CRM is a system that teaches teams to make optimum use of all available resources—equipment, procedures, and people—to promote safety and enhance the efficiency of flight operations.

Large commercial aircraft have multiple crew members, and this fact presented a perplexing phenomenon:

> In aviation, analyses of aircraft accidents and incidents indicate that the majority of civilian accidents result from failures in crew coordination and that lack of technical proficiency, equipment problems, and environmental factors such as severe weather are of secondary importance.[3]

Why would more than one pilot in the same cockpit all agree to a decision, which would ultimately lead to their doom? The answer to this question was not clear. In many of the accidents, it was found that at least one member of the crew knew something of the situation was going awry but failed to effectively communicate it to the captain. Because of professional cultural pressures and a hierarchal societal structure, subordinate crew members were hesitant in probing a questionable decision made by the much more senior captain or, worse yet, failing to point out an error.

As the result of numerous aircraft accidents not related to mechanical failures, United Airlines developed and instituted the first CRM program in 1979 integrated with their ongoing simulator training.[4] They used a novel training concept called line-oriented flight training (LOFT) that involved a complete mission without interruption during simulator training. Previous training was focused more on the individual pilots' technical skills and their ability to effectively deal with many different contingencies that at times became unrealistic. The LOFT scenarios were realistic and required the crew to work as a team to complete the missions safely. It was recognized that checking for technical skills alone in the simulator was not a guarantee of safety in the real-world environment. LOFT scenarios created subtle problems that required pilots to work as a team in order to successfully reach a safe conclusion to the flight. These scenarios were modeled after actual incidents that, depending on the crew's teamwork and decision making, could result in either a safe landing or a catastrophe. The scenarios allowed for either result, which was entirely up to the crew. This enabled the crews to utilize their newly developed CRM skills and, moreover, see the consequences of successfully using CRM skills.

Initially, CRM was met with resistance from financially conscious managements and even more so from old-school captains who resented the concept, or rather misconception, of having to bring others into the decision-making process.[5, 6] CRM was born out of the necessity to establish clear channels of communication among the crew members. The human-factor mistakes they were making were costly. Ultimately, the correctness of teamwork, collaborative decision making, and CRM was recognized by the Federal Aviation Administration (FAA) and became mandated for the entire industry. Since the inception of CRM, aviation accidents have decreased.[7] Air travel, as we know it today, has become the safest mode of transportation as a result of changing the culture of safety.

DOES CRM WORK?

The aviation industry has dedicated training resources to safety programs and in particular CRM. The question remains, "Does CRM decrease errors and reduce accidents?" Airline accidents are an infrequent event, with only 2.6 accidents per 1 million flight hours occurring in 2001[7] and therefore make for criteria that are difficult to study via the scientific method. Controlled studies such as implementing CRM at airline X and not at airline Y and comparing their accident rates a few years later go against FAA regulations. We are left with anecdotal evidence that CRM initiatives improve safety.

Figure 4.1[8] summarizes the impact of CRM training on accidents by several flying organizations. A significant reduction in accidents occurred in these disparate organizations following CRM training. Additionally, since United Airlines began CRM training, it has not experienced any crew-caused accidents. The NTSB report on the United Airlines DC-10 that crashed-landed in Sioux City, Iowa, in 1989 stated that the flight crew interactions were "[i]ndicative of the value of Cockpit Resource Management Training."[8, 9]

CONTINUED CRM TRAINING

Figure 4.2 illustrates an important consideration for organizations that attempt to change their safety culture utilizing CRM concepts. The U.S. Army

Figure 4.1 Impact of Various CRM Training Programs on Accidents

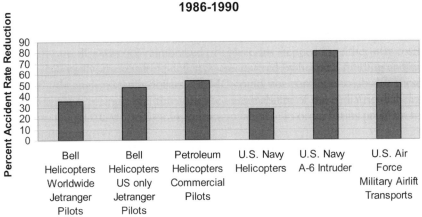

Figure 4.2 Army Aviation Accidents by Year, 1993–1999

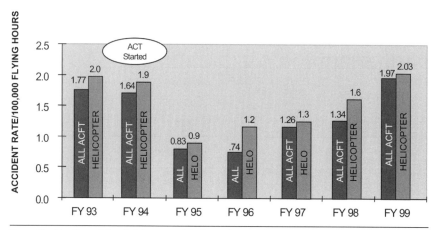

From Grubb, Gary, John C. Morey, and Robert Simon. 2001. "Sustaining and Advancing Performance Improvements Achieved by Crew Resource Management Training." In *Proceedings of the 11th International Symposium on Aviation Psychology*. Columbus: Ohio State University, 4. Used with permission.

initiated their CRM training called Aircrew Coordination Training (ACT) in 1994 for both their fixed-wing aircraft and helicopters. This program included only a one-time training event with no continuation or refresher training. The following year's results showed a significant decrease in overall accident rates. By 1999, however, the accident rates had increased back to baseline. Therefore, any attempt to use CRM training should contain a comprehensive plan to reinforce and build on the initial training.[10]

RELEVANCE TO HEALTHCARE

Since the mid-1990s, there have been several attempts to adapt aviation safety practices, including some aspects of CRM, to healthcare. One of the first programs involved team-based collaborative rounds at Concord Hospital in Concord, New Hampshire.[11] The results of this program included a 50 percent decrease in mortality rates for cardiac surgery patients, patient satisfaction rates above the 97th percentile nationally, and an increase in provider quality of work life. Another study found that teams practicing good leadership and team skills learned new procedures faster than other teams.[12] At Johns Hopkins, average length of patient stay in the intensive care unit was reduced by one day by improving communication through the use of daily patient goals.[13] Beth Israel Deaconess Medical Center in Boston, Massachusetts, had a 53 percent reduction in adverse events for their obstetrics department following team training.[14] The following case presentation illustrates how aviation safety tools can be implemented in a healthcare setting and some of the expected results.

Case Presentation and Analysis

The following case and analysis is used with permission from Health Administration Press: Kenneth H. Cohn and Jack Barker, "Improving Communication, Collaboration, and Safety Using Crew Resource Management," in *Collaborate for Success! Breakthrough Strategies for Engaging Physicians, Nurses, and Hospital Executives* by Kenneth H. Cohn (Chicago: Health Administration Press, 2006), 35–40.

Leaders of a northeastern otolaryngology department selected a CRM approach to improve communication and teamwork in their department of more than 150 surgeons, nurses, audiologists, psychologists, office staff, and physician assistants. The metrics that they sought to improve included throughput, patient and worker satisfaction, and safety culture perception, measured by the Agency for Healthcare and Research Quality (AHRQ) safety climate survey.[15] Everyone in the department completed the survey, which surveyed agreement with statements such as, "I would feel safe being treated here as a patient." Survey data provided a baseline measurement of the organization's safety culture. The survey was repeated at the end of program implementation to determine the efficacy of the interventions. Only 69 percent of the survey respondents initially viewed the safety climate in the department as positive.

Approximately 10 percent of the department was interviewed to identify core issues that surfaced in the survey data, such as teamwork challenges, disagreement on sedation procedures, and management of clinical protocol violations. Teams were observed so that training could be tailored to departmental strengths and weaknesses. All personnel attended a one-day CRM seminar that explained basic error management, teamwork, and leadership concepts and that used role-play and discussion to reinforce these concepts. Participants used in-house case examples to demonstrate how to improve teamwork. One commented enthusiastically, "I have worked in healthcare for over 20 years and have never spent this much time with a surgeon.... [N]ow I understand better my role in patient care and how to work more collaboratively with others on our team." After the seminar, a senior surgeon exclaimed, "I have never seen a group of people in healthcare so enthusiastic over a training program." Over a period of several months, follow-up included more comprehensive workshops providing information on communication, collaboration, leadership, workload management, and conflict resolution. Trained observers watched teams in action and provided oral and written debriefs to enhance participants' ability to employ newly acquired skills. Selected participants took additional training to become resident CRM experts, to nurture desired behaviors in their department, and to begin a hospital-wide training program.

After approximately a year of CRM training, the percentage of survey participants who felt that their department had a positive safety climate increased from 69 percent to 91 percent. As a result of improved collaboration and service quality, patient volume increased from 17,000 to 18,355 in one year, resulting in a 30 percent increase in revenue. Referring physicians rated the department as one of the best services in the hospital, and practice administrators who were initially skeptical became advocates for extending the program.

Case Analysis

CRM training helps people feel more comfortable about intervening in patient safety matters despite perceived differences in status. An audiologist commented, "Before the CRM training, I would have minded my own business, but I overheard two anesthesiologists discussing dosage and realized they were about to overdose an infant. I decided to speak out as my CRM training taught me, and I know I saved that baby's life." The formal and informal mechanisms specified in the six steps of implementation allow people to train and become confident in approaching patient care in a systematic way that heightens communication, improves teamwork, and reduces the risk of error. Most programs begin after leaders attend conferences or read about CRM in the medical literature. For some institutions, a sentinel event provides the motivation to change, as with aviation during the twentieth century. The six phases of CRM training include organizational assessment, team training, targeted workshops, facilitated debriefs, coaching, and outcomes assessment.

CRM PROGRAM IMPLEMENTATION

Phase 1: Organizational Assessment

The purpose of this phase is to understand the organizational culture, obtain buy-in from leaders and staff, and agree on metrics that define success, such as patient throughput, satisfaction scores, and clinical and financial outcomes. Participants answer the AHRQ safety perception questionnaire, as described in the case history. The data from questionnaires help define team issues that are unique to each organization. The organizational assessment phase is an opportunity to determine the organizational strengths and weaknesses that will influence the design of the next phase. Organizational assessment also allows leaders to gauge readiness to undergo cultural change.

Phase 2: CRM Team Training

The goal of this phase is to introduce the concepts of CRM and specific aviation safety tools, such as briefing, debriefing, and recognition and handling of adverse situations. All personnel participate in an interactive seminar that lasts approximately six hours, as outlined in sidebar 1. Medical error studies and examples of medical successes achieved through CRM help overcome initial skepticism that CRM is a fad. The goal of having everyone present is to stimulate dialogue and reduce the influence of hierarchy in multidisciplinary processes that affect patient safety.

Sidebar 1: CRM Seminar Outline

- Rationale
- History of CRM
- Principles of CRM communication (improving safety by enhancing skill sets in decision making, performance feedback, cross-checking and communication, creating and managing teams, recognizing adverse situations, and managing fatigue)
- Error chains
- Workload management
- Recognition of adverse situations (red flags)
- Role of briefing and debriefing sessions

Phase 3: Targeted Workshops

In this phase, participants build on insights learned during the survey and seminar. The purpose of this phase is to continue the cultural change toward a more teamwork-oriented and safety-conscious organization and address specific unit CRM needs. These two- to four-hour workshops are generally conducted in smaller groups of 10 to 15 people. Typical workshops cover communication strategies, conflict management, checklist design, and leadership development. These workshops become a permanent part of the organization's CRM curriculum, repeated as necessary.

Phase 4: Facilitated Debriefs

The goal of this phase is to observe teams in action and provide feedback to team members and the organization. Briefing and debriefing sessions also can be conducted in association with simulated activities. Briefings clarify who will be leading the team, prepare the team for the flow of the procedure, delineate expectations, and provide opportunities to discuss potential contingency plans.[16] Healthcare team briefings and debriefings take little time to perform, help build shared team mental models, and reduce errors, when performed as indicated in sidebars 2 and 3.[8, 17]

Sidebar 2: Healthcare Team Briefing Format

- Write out team member names.
- Clarify team member roles and responsibilities and state expected outcome.
- Obtain consensus on task to be performed.
- Promote open communication.
  - Encourage team members to ask questions to clear up ambiguities.

- Ask team members to please speak up if uncomfortable with any aspect of a task.
- Identify potential problems.
- Brief team regarding contingencies for potential problems.
- End with, "Any Questions?"

Sidebar 3: Debriefing Format
- Review.
  - What went well?
  - Preferences for amendment based on what could have gone better.
  - Team's communication processes and outcomes.
  - Ability of team to share the same mental model.
- Focus on team, not individual, issues.
- End with, "What did we learn to improve individual and team performance next time?"

Phase 5: CRM Coaching

The purpose of ongoing coaching is to sustain momentum and help teams overcome obstacles. Research in both aviation and healthcare indicates that an organization will revert to old habits if no one reinforces organizational change.[8] After implementation of CRM training in 1994, the U.S. Army realized a 50 percent reduction in accidents. Without ongoing training and coaching, however, the accident rate reverted to preintervention rates within five years.[10] Individual coaching for key leaders and change agents provides the skill set to nurture desired CRM behaviors and embed change throughout organizations.

Phase 6: Outcomes and Assessments

The goal of this phase is to determine the efficacy of the cultural change process using a pretest and posttest model. Results from this phase are used to update and make appropriate changes to the CRM program. The initial program will last 12 to 18 months, depending on organizational size and complexity. True cultural change takes longer, however, and requires ongoing training and feedback, as discussed in Phase 5.

UNIQUE CHALLENGES OF APPLYING CRM TO HEALTHCARE

Adapting aviation safety programs to healthcare requires an understanding of the differences between the professions. Organizations such as the FAA develop and enforce aviation regulations, and the NTSB investigates accidents. Furthermore, in aviation, the Aviation Safety Reporting System (ASRS) reports near misses and errors that impact safety. Widespread use of medical guidelines and acceptance of a process for reporting all medical errors that are not subject to legal discovery have not yet occurred.[18]

Examples of teamwork failure in medical settings include failures to brief teams of plans for operation, speak out regarding potential work overload or patient concerns, discuss alternatives and advocate a course of action, establish leadership and resolve conflicts, debrief actions after performing procedures, and provide adequate team training and supervision for residents and other new healthcare professionals.[19] Barriers to implementing healthcare CRM training include:

- A blaming culture.
- Lack of sustained leadership.
- Limited physician engagement.
- Inadequate funding of safety initiatives.

The trade-offs between safety and productivity create a dynamic tension in a profession that celebrates autonomy. Healthcare professionals face difficult transitions in changing their status from craftsmen to people who value safety and interchangeability.[20]

OVERVIEW OF SAFETY TOOLS THAT HELPED CHANGE AVIATION SAFETY CULTURE

CRM became the cornerstone of most aviation organizations, including the military safety programs during the 1980s. Other aviation safety tools have been developed in conjunction with CRM or as a result of information learned following a major accident. These include checklists, briefings and debriefings, standard operating procedures (SOPs), error-reporting systems, simulation and line observation safety audits (LOSAs). The combination of CRM and effectively using all other aviation tools has helped make aviation one of the safest industries.[4, 21] Next we will describe in depth these aviation safety tools.

Crew Resource Management

CRM is a process for improving safety by enhancing skill sets in decision making, performance feedback, cross-checking and communication, creating and managing teams, recognizing adverse situations (red flags), and managing fatigue.[8, 22] The goal of CRM is to complete a mission safely and efficiently by utilizing all available resources. This leads to accurate, effective decision making by providing the key decision maker with all inputs. Most CRM training programs incorporate the following principles: command, leadership, resource management, workload management, situational awareness, and decision making.[23] Our discussion of these concepts will include both aviation and healthcare examples.

Command

Before we discuss leadership, we address a closely related but significantly different concept: command. We discuss the concept of command first to dispel any misconceptions that CRM weakens the final decision maker's authority. An individual takes command whenever exercising the formal duties of a team leader. So, although CRM does empower all team members to offer their input, the final judgment call remains the prerogative of only one individual.

Command involves a governing authority granting an individual the power to exercise authority in a formal and, oftentimes, impersonal way. Command is prevalently addressed in military, aviation, and some business circles, but it is infrequently discussed in the healthcare setting. However, the mere anointing as the one in command does not automatically ensure that the person so selected will be good at it. It requires formal, stand-alone training, coaching, and follow-up.

Because many different specialties often collaborate on a case, it is common for people of equal rank to compete for final authority. If a team or an organization can formalize who is in command for any given procedure, however, more effective teamwork is possible. Compared to an intensive care unit, the operating room or a cardiac catheterization laboratory are environments in which it is much more evident who will be in command.

Nonetheless, that individual selected to command the procedure must still serve as a good leader by adhering to the behaviors described in the following section on leadership. Even in less formal settings, it is still important for one person to be designated as "in command." Good teamwork is not anarchy; it is not even democracy, "one man, one vote." It is the effective coordination of everyone's insights and efforts by the person in command.

Once the leader chooses a course of action, his or her next responsibility is to get the team to rally around the decision. At the same time, individuals who take command in team situations also must be willing to assume responsibility and accountability for their team's actions. The team should view them as the final authority, and they should ensure that all of the colleagues' efforts are coordinated to provide maximum efficacy. Often team processes break down as a result of nobody being formally in charge of the situation, as in the care of patients with multiple comorbid conditions or the designated commander not fulfilling his or her responsibility.

Again, no direct parallel exists in healthcare, but the federal regulations and company manuals that apply to aviation all state unequivocally that the captain is in command and is responsible for the safety of the passengers, crew, cargo, and aircraft. The captain is accountable for every aspect of a flight. Although we encourage maximum collaboration, for a team to operate effectively there must be one, and only one, final decision maker.

Leadership

Leadership is the most complex principle of CRM because individuals do not realize that everyone involved in patient care has a leadership role. Leadership is defined by the commander's willingness to let team members exercise their rights and responsibilities to ensure a safe and positive outcome. Although there can be only one commander, anyone on the team can exhibit leadership. Leadership is both a right and a responsibility. Team members may have a right to speak up, but they also have a responsibility to do so—a responsibility to the patient, to fellow team members, and to their own conscience.

In our classrooms, we hear from senior surgeons that they often hold their tongue regarding a colleague in the interest of professional courtesy. Team training is designed not to create a perfect world but to improve synergy in an imperfect world. To reduce errors, different individuals will need to be share information with team members to improve outcomes. Leaders promote and maintain a team climate that is conducive to open communication.

Leadership means that: (1) individual team members have a right and responsibility to voice their opinions and concerns and (2) the formally designated team leader must create such an environment. Encouraging and promoting teamwork does not weaken the respect for whoever is in command. Helmreich and Merritt[19] showed that pilots in command who exhibited collaborative leadership styles engendered far more professional respect than those who did not. Indeed, our experience suggests that those who encourage teamwork engender higher levels of respect among peers.[24]

Leadership Characteristics

Teams that have effective leadership are distinguished by the following characteristics: a positive team climate, briefings, and professionalism.

A good leader fosters a positive team climate that allows for a free and synergistic exchange of ideas. Think about the different teams on which you have served. How did the teams with a positive climate differ from those with a poor climate? Which ones functioned better? Healthcare research shows that positive team climate can speed up team learning for new procedures.[12]

Ginnett[25] showed that the long-term outcome of a team's performance could be determined within their first 90 seconds together. A team with a leader who gathers the team together to discuss the procedure beforehand generally performed better than a team that skipped the preflight briefing. Briefings allow the team to review the case and set expectations. They also include discussion of contingency plans in the event of complications. Ginnett's study also showed that teams that conducted briefings performed better when faced with an unexpected situation, even if the contingency plan discussed was not the one actually used.

Time-outs are already used in the operating room, but we recommend taking this process one step further and expanding them into more comprehensive briefings. A briefing does not have to be exhaustive. An exchange of first names, a brief synopsis of the case, and anticipated outcomes in both normal conditions and abnormal conditions are all that are necessary. People respect strength and humanity. It is a very powerful combination, and briefings provide an opportunity for the person in command to project these traits. A study at Concord Hospital in Concord, New Hampshire, showed that briefings were either time neutral or even saved time because of better understanding of expectations.[11] Briefings are an effective means of building loyal, highly functioning teams, and they establish the attending surgeon as the leader.

Leadership is also defined by professionalism. Interestingly, the first definition of a *profession* in the dictionary centers on the act of taking of vows in a religious community. Like religious leaders, professionals in other fields typically have high regard for their calling and will strive to meet the toughest standards. Although it is important that we have these expectations of ourselves, leaders also seek to draw excellence from their team members.

Communication

Communication is the single most important component of CRM. A pilot or doctor can have the best technical skills, finely tuned situational awareness (i.e., understanding what is happening in the external environment), advanced equipment, and excellent decision-making abilities, but without the ability to communicate effectively, all other attributes are diminished. Communication is the glue that holds teams together. When high-performance teams interact effectively, everything else falls into place. Conversely, teams that fail to communicate have suboptimal outcomes.

Communication in CRM involves the effective and timely exchange of ideas, information, and instruction. Such interactions ensure that messages are clearly received and understood, are two-way, and are of benefit to both parties. The exchange must occur in a timely and effective way to ensure a positive outcome. For example, if during a deep-lobe parotidectomy for a recurrent tumor the assistant notices that the surgeon is about to cut a main branch of the facial nerve, she should issue an assertive and confident warning to prevent the patient suffering facial paralysis. Saying, "Stop. I believe that is a branch of the facial nerve," would be more effective than saying, "Shouldn't we be trying to identify the branches of the nerve?" Many accidents in aviation and healthcare occur because the communication is not sufficiently direct to change behavior.

Inquiry

Team members need to be sensitive to the information that is being relayed. Not all are effective advocates of their position. An effective communicator will understand that good communication involves being receptive and seeking meaning. For instance, in the previous example of the parotidectomy, a surgeon who is an effective communicator, upon hearing the vague statement, "Shouldn't we be trying to identify the branches of the nerve," would be hearing alarm bells and ask, "What are you trying to tell me?" or "Are you seeing something I'm not?" Inquiry is an open process to foster the exchange of ideas.[26]

Advocacy

Advocacy is the ability to offer information in a way that is tactful, timely, and effective, ensuring that a free flow of information will continue. Inquiry and advocacy are both used to develop a shared mental model of a situation. They differ in that inquiry utilizes questions to understand someone else's mental model and advocacy uses statements to share our mental model of the situation with someone else.

The Assertiveness Continuum

Advocacy must be accomplished in a respectful way. Assertiveness is a learned skill and must be practiced. People may make their point in a passive way, thinking they may be inoffensive, but passivity is inefficient and leads to suboptimal outcomes. Asking a tentative question at a critical moment is putting too much responsibility for the receiver to correctly interpret the intent.

Aggressiveness is at the other end of the assertiveness continuum and also has problems. Saying something like "HEY STUPID! STOP!" raises barriers and limits future communication.

Properly assertive behavior is respectful but also aware of the criticality of the moment. It is properly assertive to exclaim "WAIT! STOP!" if an irreversible mistake is imminent. Properly assertive behavior adjusts the sense of urgency and volume accordingly. CRM training is designed to help people know the difference.

Timeliness

Many a time as a copilot, we have sat in the cockpit not saying anything, exchanging glances with other crew members and watching the captain go down a questionable path. Error chains that lead to an accident usually take some time to play themselves out. Advocating a concern should be done as soon as possible, before it becomes a crisis, and early enough so that measures can be taken place to counter the initial error that do not interfere with teamwork and camaraderie. If a problem is not identified in a timely manner, then often it is either too late to correct the error or the error can only be avoided or mitigated by crisis measures. Even if a person is unsure, he or she should voice his or her uneasiness. This can facilitate good communication, helping the team understand the problem.

Effectiveness

Effective advocacy requires one to succinctly state information to others. Indirect communication is not effective when advocating. In both aviation and healthcare mishaps, indirect or poor communications have been a causal factor in the mishap. If you see the problem clearly, then state it. Be assertive. Be polite, but be assertive. Effective advocacy relates to leadership that if you are aware of some information that can improve patient safety, you have both the right and the responsibility to speak up and communicate clearly, assertively, and respectfully.

Barriers

Barriers to effective communication can be physical or interpersonal. Common physical barriers are physical distance, facing away from one another while at respective stations, surgical masks, and the inability to read nonverbal clues.

Interpersonal and environmental barriers are more subtle and therefore more dangerous. These barriers include fatigue, stress, cultural differences (both corporate and national cultures), status differences, age, and gender.

These barriers are overcome by emphasis on protocols, checklists, team briefings, leadership, and a strong team dynamic. Overcoming these barriers creates an environment of psychological safety for the team that can improve performance.[12]

Situational Awareness

Situational awareness (SA) is an understanding of what is happening in the external environment. To achieve optimal SA, everyone on the team must remain attentive and continually seek out information. If one is unaware or has incomplete understanding of the situation, the team member cannot make effective decisions.

No one is omniscient. An effective leader relies on the team to promote SA through effective communication about what is occurring. An effective team will support one another by cross-checking information and admitting when team members are confused about the situation. Complacency leads to a loss of SA and team effectiveness.

A key to SA is judgment from reviewing the past and using that knowledge to draw conclusions about the present scenario. Individuals who have good SA go on to monitor the current circumstances, accurately predict what is likely to happen next, and prepare the team for the anticipated outcome. One never knows exactly when one begins losing SA. One usually comes to the realization of something being amiss well after the error chain has progressed into a dangerous spiral of decreasing SA and increasing mistakes. The best way to prevent loss of SA is by adhering to protocols and having a strong team and cross-checking work as it progresses.

Workload Management

Workload management involves organizing tasks in such a way that tasks are distributed equitably among team members. An effective team is ready for contingencies and prevents individuals from becoming overwhelmed while others have fewer tasks. Effective team leaders plan the work and work the plan. A comprehensive briefing before a procedure ensures that everyone is doing the right job at the right time. Effective communication and SA throughout the procedure allow everyone to stay on task. Effective leaders also know how to delegate to make certain neither they nor anyone else on the team is overtaxed. When people become overloaded, important work may get missed and people may become fixated on one particular thing and begin losing overall SA.

One of the greatest detriments to effective workload management is people's reluctance to speak up when overloaded. In both the aviation and healthcare environments, people do not want to appear as incompetent and, therefore, are hesitant to show weakness. A positive team climate can reduce this resistance and improve the team's overall workload management.

Resource Management

Resource management is the optimal use of all assistance available to the team. Resources include supplies, equipment, training, and individual and group expertise. Like workload management, resource management calls for making maximal use of what is available to create a positive outcome.

During the preprocedure briefing, the team should spend time discussing potential needs and identifying the resources available to satisfy those demands. If a resource is not immediately available, the team should determine how to access it. The team leader should think ahead about which resources will be of greatest necessity and make sure that the people using supplies and equipment understand their functions and how to use them.

Decision Making

Decision making is the process of determining and implementing a course of action and evaluating the outcome. If communication is the glue that holds a team together, good decision making is the desired end product of healthcare team training.

There are three approaches to decision making, each of which has its place and its advantages and disadvantages:

- Collaborative: The method under which every person has a say. The goal is to reach team consensus. This process takes time and should be avoided if the situation requires a quick decision.
- Unilateral: One person makes the decisions. This method is fast and effective, but problems arise when team members are not fully trained to step in should something prevent the leader from completing the mission; over time, it inhibits group cohesion, creativity, and ownership. In the unilateral model, effective teamwork begins to break down.
- Consultative: The leader establishes a collegial rapport with the team members and captures their collective wisdom. The leader must know when and how to stop gathering data and avoid letting perfection be the enemy of good.

Ultimately, we have found that the consultative approach is most effective in coordinating high-performance teams of intelligent, skilled professionals.

CRM Training

Now that we have explained the basic concepts of CRM, we will discuss how to integrate these principles in a typical training program. Most training programs incorporate the CRM principles explained earlier along with other aspects of team training. These other areas may include understanding error chains and how to break them, stress management, understanding and learning to control hazardous attitudes and behaviors, risk management,[8] and interpersonal skills.[27] The training methods used for CRM training include didactic instruction, role-playing, case studies, and simulation.[28] There is a wide variation among both aviation and healthcare CRM programs. This variation is important so that team-training programs can be customized to the organization's culture. Many organizations are performing some components of teamwork well, and training should build upon what is working well to minimize resistance to learning.

A one-day healthcare CRM training program might include the following modules:

- Motivation/introduction: Identify the need for team training.
- CRM history: How the safety culture in aviation changed.
- Principles of healthcare team training.
- Error chains: Define and understand how to break error chains.
- Communication: Understand tools and barriers to effective communication.
- Leadership.
- Situational awareness.
- Workload management.
- Briefing and debriefing.
- Summary.

Checklists

Checklists are communication tools that ensure attention to mission-critical items that need to get done. For the most safety-critical items, the concept of dual concurrence is used. Two people must independently verify an item is completed to satisfaction and report that fact to each other. The person charged with completing an item does it and subsequently the item is verified completed by the checklist.

Checklists open a two-way flow of communication between the team leader and members. Most checklists use the challenge-and-response method. Typically, junior team members are charged with the responsibility of challenging the team leader, and the team leader or other appropriate person replies that the item is completed to satisfaction. This allows junior members a system-designed way of questioning a leader without making a personal affront or seeming insubordinate. The following is an example of a checklist that would be used before an operation:

Checklist

Challenge	Reply
Attending physician confirmed	I am Dr. Smith and I am the attending
Patient name and procedure	Ms. Jones for a LEFT hip replacement
Operative site verified	Verified
Lab data	Reviewed
Informed consent form	Completed
Family counseling	Completed
Operator personal factors	Briefed and noted
Team briefing	Completed

If the proper response is not given, the junior team member is given a system-designed way to challenge the response and ensure that it is completed correctly. In the previous example, the team member reading the checklist challenge also has the responsibility to check to see if, in fact, the reply is correct or has been done satisfactorily. It is this dual concurrence that is another system design used to catch any errors by the person replying. Checklists are an aid to reducing errors, but even the best checklist is useless if it is not used. Many individuals might refuse to use a checklist or only partially follow the checklist because they feel they do not need it.[29] An organization with a mature safety culture mandates that checklists are used all the times and followed completely. The experience in aviation is that a complacent safety culture that leaves the checklist unused is the culture more prone to error.[7]

Briefings and Debriefings

According to J. Richard Hackman, in his book *Leading Teams:*

Ginnett observed this inability (or unwillingness) to self-correct among those captains in his study who had been nominated by their peers as marginal team leaders. Although there was as much variation in briefing style among the marginal captains as among those who were viewed as excellent team leaders, there were two major differences between the two groups. First, no matter what style they used in conducting their crew briefings, the marginal captains failed to establish the conditions needed for a good team launch. Second, all of them, again in their own ways, exhibited significant problems with control that made it nearly impossible for them to use their experiences to become more effective. Some of these captains were persistently overcontrolling, not asking for input from other team members and ignoring or diverting any suggestions that members did manage to make. Others were persistently undercontrolling, so democratic or laissez-faire in conducting their briefings that crew members were left uncertain about how the team was supposed to operate. Worst of all were captains who vacillated between overcontrolling and undercontrolling in ways and at times that could not be anticipated, which in some cases nearly incapacitated team members in carrying out their own parts of the work. Ginnett's observations documented that even though these captains' briefings did not go well, they either did not recognize the dysfunctional effects of their style or they were unable (or unwilling) to alter it. How they led was how they led, no matter what consequences ensued.[30]

Briefings are a powerful skill in building a team dynamic that will allow different types of people to work together during normal duties and unexpected when unexpected problems arise. Briefings:

1. Establish the leader of the team, so that other team members know whom to look to for guidance.
2. Open lines of communication among team members to take advantage of team members' knowledge. They set the tone for the upcoming procedure. Protocols are discussed, and learning is reinforced. Responsibilities and expected behaviors are discussed. Misconceptions can be cleared up before they interfere with the accomplishment of the mission.
3. Prepare the team to better understand what is expected to happen and when in the flow of the procedure.
4. Discuss possible contingencies and how to deal with those contingencies. Teams that discuss potential problems ahead of time perform better even when an unexpected, unbriefed problem occurs because briefings create a culture within the team that facilitates exchange of communication and ideas.[25]

In aviation, briefings are conducted at different times among teams and sub-teams. Upon arrival at the airplane, the pilots and flight attendants discuss issues such as potential delays, turbulence, and security issues. Before takeoff, the pilots and flight attendants, separately, discuss issues specific to their duties. Whenever a new crew member enters the dynamic, that person is briefed, so she fully understands the situation solidifying her place on the team. Healthcare team briefings should be used during critical junctures of a patient's care, such as prior to the start of any procedure, handoffs, change in patient status, or discharge.

In summary, briefings are effective in creating a strong team. They open lines of communication. They allow everyone on the team to know his or her role on the team, understand the procedure, and clear up misconceptions. They can prevent errors due to misconceptions long before the misunderstanding becomes critical.

Standard Operating Procedures

Standard operating procedures (SOPs) are the so-called painted lines of teamwork. The painted lines a driver sees that delineate individual lanes were designed by traffic engineers to give drivers the safest path to a destination. So it is with SOPs in a particular operation. Engineers, researchers, and analysts have studied the data and have come up with procedures and best practices to give the best possible outcome. When we follow SOPs, we achieve success more often then when we do not use a proven system.[29,31]

Do SOPs require slavish and rote movement? Absolutely not. As tacticians practicing in the real world every day, we are still expected to draw on all our knowledge, expertise, and judgment, but following SOPs makes our lives easier. We follow a well-delineated path, reserving our limited cognitive resources to coordinate the efforts of our team and resolve contingencies.

An additional and very important benefit of SOPs is that the entire team is expected to follow these well-defined procedures. Everyone has a well-defined expectation so that when a person deviates from the expected path and ventures into potentially unsafe territory, others can note the protocol violation and be able to advocate a return to the expected SOP.

Error Reporting Systems

Adverse events do not happen without warning. Usually, a series of errors lead up to the event. Referred to colloquially as "the holes in the Swiss cheese lining up," this concept applies at the individual level and at the macro level.[32] Error reporting systems are nonpunitive mechanisms that allow for the identification of undesirable trends or safety problems visible only to those at the front line. In aviation, these reports go to a committee comprised of FAA inspectors and members of airlines and union safety committees. The system is nonpunitive as long as people self-disclose and the error was unintentional; there has been a tremendous amount of valuable data that has resulted from this system.

If trends are recognized and dealt with, an accident can be averted. For example, in the late 1980s, United Airlines noticed a trend of airplanes making navigational errors at night or in bad weather and coming dangerously close to mountains while descending into airports. They changed their navigation protocols and saw the trend recede. Another airline noticed the same trend but took no action and lost two airplanes over the next five years due to collision with high terrain. In a more recent example, trend monitoring over the past few years predicted that the next major accident would involve a runway intrusion. The recent Comair crash in Lexington, Kentucky, in July 2006 was an instance of the pilot losing situational awareness while taxiing, being confused about the runway assignment and position on the airport, and taking off on the incorrect and too-short runway.[33]

Simulation

Aviation has been using simulators since the mid-1950s. At first, they were used to practice crisis-type emergencies that were too dangerous to do in the airplane, such as engine failure or a tire failure on landing. Since the early 1990s, they have been used to train and evaluate leadership skills. Oftentimes, training and check rides will consist of virtually normal flight, so that the crew can learn how to work together in normal environments, deal with small problems, and learn how to stop them before they turn into a crisis.

Line Observation Safety Audits (LOSAs)

In line observation safety audits (LOSAs), neutral third-party observers ride in the cockpit and observe the crews for compliance with protocols and any danger-ous trends. Because major accidents are a rare event (see figure 4.3), they are only the tip of the iceberg. Organizations that commit more errors than others are more likely to have a catastrophic event. By analyzing the LOSA data, an organiza-tion can make system changes to avert major events.[34]

Research Questions

Although we have mentioned several successes involving healthcare organiza-tions adapting aviation safety tools and concepts, many unanswered questions remain. What are the specific tools, and how should they be implemented in a healthcare system? Are there any interventions that might induce system errors? Often in healthcare we find institutional changes that are meant to reduce errors actually increase errors in unexpected ways by distracting professionals from es-tablished routines.[35] Previously in this chapter, we discussed how a one-time team training intervention may cause some initial outcome improvements, but with-out any follow-up or continuation training the effect will diminish over time.[17] What type and frequency of continuation training will maintain and improve an organization's safety culture?

Figure 4.3 Accidents Are Only the Tip of the Iceberg

CONCLUSION

Many authorities have suggested aviation safety concepts can help reduce errors.[17,36] In the 1970s, the aviation industry realized that technical proficiency alone could not prevent accidents. Mishap investigations suggested that a breakdown in communication and teamwork was a causal factor in many accidents. Aviation embarked on a quest to change its culture of safety by implementing CRM programs, improving checklists and standard operating procedures, implementing safety-reporting systems, and continuously developing aviation safety tools. Autocratic behaviors in the cockpit that were considered acceptable, even lauded, twenty years ago would now make one an outcast among peers. Today, even the most hardened, grizzled veteran would say, without equivocation, that these modern human behavior standards, despite the initial cultural and sometimes visceral resistance, have made aviation a more progressive and safer industry. The culture of safety has changed in aviation.

Multiple healthcare organizations have implemented aviation safety concepts with successful outcomes. The safety culture of our medical community is often equated to the safety culture that existed prior to CRM's introduction to aviation. It has been almost thirty years since the first CRM programs were developed and implemented in the airlines. The process of culture change is difficult and requires time. The medical community has begun the long process of changing its safety culture, which may take decades to complete.

Key Concepts

- Aviation successfully changed its culture of safety by developing and implementing Crew Resource Management (CRM) programs and other aviation safety tools.
- CRM and selected aviation safety tools have been successfully adapted to healthcare, demonstrating potential for improving outcomes by building a culture that emphasizes safety.
- Effective communication pays dividends in many areas of healthcare by:
  - Improving outcome and cutting expenses associated with preventable medical errors.
  - Facilitating recruitment, retention, and competitive positioning.

REFERENCES

1. National Transportation Safety Board. 1979. *Aircraft Accident Report No. AAR-79–7*. Washington, D.C.: NTSB Bureau of Accident Investigation.

2. Stone, R. B., and G. L. Babcock. 1988. "Airline Pilot's Perspective." In *Human Factors in Aviation*, ed. Earl L. Wiener and David C. Nagel, 529–60. San Diego: Academic Press.

3. Cooper, G. E., M. D. White, and J. K. Lauber. 1979. "Resource Management the Flight Deck." Paper presented at the NASA/Industry Workshop, San Francisco. NASA Conference Publication 2120.

4.   Helmreich, R. L., and H. C. Foushee. 1993. "Why Crew Resource Management? Empirical and Theoretical Bases of Human Factors Training in Aviation." In *Cockpit Resource Management,* ed. E. L. Wiener, B. G. Kanki, and R. L. Helmreich, 3–43. San Diego: Academic Press.

5.   Helmreich, R. L., A. C. Merritt, and J. A. Wilhelm. 1991. "The Evolution of Crew Resource Management Training in Commercial Aviation." *International Journal of Aviation Psychology* 1 (4): 287–300.

6.   Helmreich, R. L., and J. A. Wilhelm. 1991. "Outcomes of Crew Resource Management Training." *International Journal of Aviation Psychology* 9 (1): 19–32.

7.   National Transportation Safety Board. 2006. *U.S. Air Carrier Operations, Calendar Year 2001. Annual Review of Aircraft Accident Data NTSB/ARC-04/01.* Washington, D.C.: NTSB Bureau of Accident Investigation.

8.   Diehl, A. 2001. "Does CRM Really Work?" In *Culture, Environment, and CRM,* ed. Tony Kern, 33–51. New York: McGraw-Hill.

9.   National Transportation Safety Board. 1990. *Aircraft Accident Report—United Airlines Flight 232, McDonnell Douglas DC-10-10, Sioux Gateway Airport, Sioux City, Iowa, July 19, 1989, Report No. NTSB/AAR-90106.* Washington, D.C.: NTSB Bureau of Accident Investigation.

10.   Grubb, G., J. C. Morey, and R. Simon. 2001. "Sustaining and Advancing Performance Improvements Achieved by Crew Resource Management Training." In *Proceedings of the 11th International Symposium on Aviation Psychology.* Columbus: Ohio State University.

11.   Uhlig, P. N., J. Brown, A. K. Nason, et al. 2002. "M. Eisenberg Patient Safety Awards. System Innovation: Concord Hospital." *Joint Commission Journal of Quality Improvement* 12 (12): 666–72.

12.   Edmondson, A., R. Bohmer, and G. Pisan. 2001. "Speeding Up Team Training." *Harvard Business Review* 79 (10): 125–32.

13.   Pronovost, P., S. Berenholtz, T. Dorman, et al. 2003. "Improving Communication in the ICU Using Daily Goals." *Journal of Critical Care* 18 (2): 71–75.

14.   "Ob-Gyns Investigating Model Reforms to Avoid Medical Error." 2004. *Managed Care Weekly Digest,* May 24.

15.   Agency for Healthcare and Research Quality. "Safety Climate Survey." Available at: http://www.ihi.org/NR/rdonlyres/145C099B-5FB4-46EA-8CFD D08D3CE9082C/1704/SafetyClimateSurvey1.pdf. Accessed March 25, 2005.

16.   Healy, G. B., J. M. Barker, and G. G. Madonna. 2006. "Error Reduction through Team Leadership: Applying Aviation's Team Model in the OR." *Bulletin of the American College of Surgeons* 91 (2): 10–15.

17.   Musson, D. M., and R. L. Helmreich. 2004. "Team Training and Resource Management in Healthcare: Current Issues and Future Directions." *Harvard Health Policy Review* 5 (1): 25–35.

18.   Gallagher, T. H., and W. Levinson. 2005. "Disclosing Harmful Medical Errors to Patients: A Time for Professional Action." *Archives of Internal Medicine* 165 (16): 1819–24.

19.   Helmreich, R. L., and A. C. Merritt. 1998. *Culture at Work in Aviation and Medicine: National, Organizational, and Professional Influences.* Aldershot, UK: Ashgate.

20. Amalberti, R., Y. Auroy, D. Berwick, and P. Barach. 2005. "Five System Barriers to Achieving Ultrasafe Health Care." *Annals of Internal Medicine* 142 (9): 756–64.

21. Baker, D. P., S. Gustafson, and J. Beaubien. 2003. "Medical Teamwork and Patient Safety: The Evidence-Based Relation." Report prepared for Center for Quality Improvement and Patient Safety Agency for Healthcare Research and Quality. Washington, D.C.: American Institute for Research.

22. Grogan, E., R. Stiles, D. France, et al. 2004. "The Impact of Aviation-Based Teamwork Training on the Attitudes of Health-Care Professionals." *Journal of the American College of Surgeons* 199 (6): 843–48.

23. United Airlines. 1998. *Command/Leadership/Resource Management Reference Manual.* Denver: United Airlines C/L/R Department.

24. Cohn, K. H., and J. Barker. 2006. "Improving Communication, Collaboration, and Safety Using Crew Resource Management." In *Collaborate for Success! Breakthrough Strategies for Engaging Physicians, Nurses, and Hospital Executives,* ed. K. H. Cohn, 33–44. Chicago: Health Administration Press.

25. Ginnett, R. C. 1987. "First Encounters of the Close Kind: The Formation Process of Airline Flight Crews." PhD dissertation, Yale University.

26. Garvin, D. A., and M. A. Roberto. 2001. "What You Don't Know about Making Decisions." *Harvard Business Review* 9 (9): 108–16.

27. Kanki, B. G., and M. T. Palmer. 1993. "Communication and Crew Resource Management." In *Cockpit Resource Management,* ed. E. L. Wiener, B. G. Kanki, and R. L. Helmreich, 99–136. San Diego: Academic Press.

28. Jensen, R. S. 1995. "Crew Resource Management." In *Pilot Judgment and Crew Resource Management,* 115–49. Aldershot, UK: Ashgate.

29. Wachter, R. M., and K. G. Shojania. 2004. "A Culture of Safety." In *Internal Bleeding: The Truth behind America's Terrifying Epidemic of Medical Mistakes,* 347–53. New York: Rugged Land.

30. Hackman, J. R. 2002. *Leading Teams: Setting the Stage for Great Performance.* Boston: Harvard Business School Press, 221.

31. National Transportation Safety Board. 1994. *Safety Study: A Review of Flight Crew-Involved Major Accidents of U.S. Air Carriers, 1978 through 1990, Report No. NTSB/.* Washington, D.C.: NTSB Bureau of Accident Investigation.

32. Reason, J. 1990. *Human Error.* Cambridge: Cambridge University Press.

33. Associated Press. 2006. "Kentucky Plane Crash Kills 49; Crew Member Is Only Survivor." Available at: http://www.foxnews.com/story/0,2933,210650,00. html. Accessed January 13, 2007.

34. Helmreich, R. L., and J. A. Wilhelm. 2001. "System Safety and Threat and Error Management: The Line Operations Safety Audit (LOSA)." In *Proceedings of the 11th International Symposium on Aviation Psychology.* Columbus: Ohio State University, 1–6.

35. Wachter, R. M., and K. G. Shojania. 2004. "The Forgotten Half of Medication Errors." In *Internal Bleeding: The Truth Behind America's Terrifying Epidemic of Medical Mistakes,* 83–98. New York: Rugged Land.

36. Kohn, L. T., J. M. Corrigan, and M. S. Donaldson, eds. 2000. *To Err Is Human: Building a Safer Health System.* Washington, D.C.: National Academy Press.

CHAPTER 5

Healthcare IT Solutions

Barry P. Chaiken

Information technology (IT) greatly impacts quality and cost in industries from automobiles to banking. With the recent significant investment in healthcare information technology by both public and private sectors, corporations, government, and citizens maintain high hopes that healthcare will soon experience the same advances secured by other industries.

The path to success is not expected to be easy. Stories of failed system implementations, limited clinician adoption and worsened patient safety fill many pages of industry journals. That said, many of us in the informatics world believe that one day, clinical information technology will dramatically improve healthcare clinical and financial outcomes; and that day is soon to be here.

In this chapter, we explore some of the foundations of the medical informatics world. This includes electronic medical records (and its various siblings), clinician portals that leverage Web technology, the medication management process, computerized practitioner order entry, the National Health Information Network, clinical decision support, and some simple tips on how to purchase a clinical information system.

PHASES OF TECHNOLOGY IN HEALTHCARE

The first phase of modern technology-driven medicine began with the discovery of penicillin in 1928. Although technology such as X-rays was used for imaging many decades before, the discovery and industrial production of antibiotics offered real cures that greatly reduced the impact of diseases that ravaged previous generations.

The invention of various imaging modalities, such as computerized tomography (CT) and magnetic resonance imaging (MRI), coupled with the building of new medical machines (e.g., laparoscopes, artificial joints) in the 1980s signaled the second phase of modern medicine. In this era, technology offered advances in diagnosis and treatment of disease, reducing both morbidity and mortality.

The development and deployment of clinical information technology today ushers in the third phase of modern medicine in which life science technology merges with information technology to revolutionize the roles and responsibilities of physicians, nurses, and other healthcare professionals.

For the purposes of this chapter, the focus is on clinical information technology and its impact on quality, patient safety, and healthcare costs. Administrative tools such as practice management systems, coding tools, and financial systems are not included.

DEFINING CLINICAL INFORMATION TECHNOLOGY

Clinical information technology tools encompass a rather large and diverse set of applications. The release of the 1999 Institute of Medicine (IOM) report on patient safety, titled *To Err Is Human,* focused most healthcare providers on software products that regularly impact care delivered by physicians, nurses, pharmacists, and other healthcare professionals.[1] These systems include electronic medical records, computerized practitioner order entry, pharmacy systems, medication administration systems, and imaging storage and retrieval systems.

To foster patient safety and reduce medical errors, organizations implement a variety of clinical information technology tools to achieve specific results. These systems include applications that address accessibility of clinical patient information, medication management, and support of the clinical decision-making processes.

ELECTRONIC RECORDS OF PATIENT MEDICAL INFORMATION

Electronic health records (EHRs) form the basis of the movement to a paperless healthcare delivery and management system. Multiple definitions exist for EHRs and related items such as electronic medical records (EMRs). Experts differ on definitions. The Health Information Management Systems Society (HIMSS), a nonprofit association that brings together all stakeholders in healthcare information technology issues, defines EHRs as follows:

> The Electronic Health Record (EHR) is a longitudinal electronic record of patient health information generated by one or more encounters in any care delivery setting. Included in this information are patient demographics, progress notes, problems, medications, vital signs, past medical history, immunizations, laboratory data and radiology reports. The EHR automates and streamlines the clinician's workflow. The EHR has the ability to generate a complete record of a clinical patient encounter, as well as supporting other care-related activities directly or indirectly via interface—including evidence-based decision support, quality management, and outcomes reporting.[2]

Personal health records (PHRs) are similar to EHRs, although they are usually referenced in this manner when they are in the possession of or owned by the consumer or patient.

Additionally, the continuity of care record (CCR) is defined as an electronic document standard for the summary of personal health information. Clinicians and patients can use it to help promote continuity of care, quality, and patient safety. The standard was developed jointly by the American Society of Testing and Materials International (ASTM), the Massachusetts Medical Society, HIMSS, the American Academy of Family Physicians, and the American Academy of Pediatrics.

INTERNET PORTALS FOR CLINICIANS TO ACCESS PATIENT DATA

Clinicians also access clinical information via Internet portals. These portals aggregate patient information from multiple data sources generated in a variety of care venues (e.g., hospital, clinic, physician's office) and present it in a single-viewer application. Often, single sign-on and authentication is used to facilitate use and reduce the work flow burden on clinician users. (Work flow is defined as the sequence of activities required of one or more participants in the healthcare delivery process [e.g., clinicians and patients] to accomplish a patient care task or group of tasks.[3])

In addition, these portals use off-the-shelf Web technology, such as Internet browsers and the multitude of available plug-ins. This offers clinicians easy-to-use interfaces that are similar to applications commonly used by the general public. Utilizing familiar technology reduces the training necessary to use these systems and allows for personalization of the working environment. Customization of interfaces by users, allowing them to be personalized to the needs of the clinician, greatly facilitates clinician adoption.

MEDICATION MANAGEMENT PROCESS AND INFORMATION TECHNOLOGY

The focus on medication management promoted the deployment of a variety of interrelated systems. Generally, the medication management system encompasses four key areas: prescription, transcription, dispensing, and administration. Prescription covers the writing of patient medication orders. Transcription includes the transfer of orders to generate review and formulation activities in the pharmacy. Dispensing encompasses the preparation of the medication for delivery to the patient. Medication administration covers activities related to giving a medication to a patient.

Prescription

Electronic prescription occurs through the use of computerized practitioner order entry (CPOE) systems. The functionality inherent in these systems varies greatly depending upon the intended user (e.g., physicians, ward clerks). CPOE often includes clinical decision support (CDS). CDS during medication management regularly utilizes medication databases that provide drug-drug interaction and allergy and dose checking information during the phase of medication prescription.

Transcription

Transcription utilizes pharmacy systems that help pharmacists process medication orders and assist in pharmacy management. In addition, these systems often offer medication order checking through the use of medication databases similar to those used during the prescription phase of medication management.

Dispensing

Dispensing of medications can occur through the use a variety of hardware devices that are tied to the pharmacy system. These include robots that pick single-dose medications and package them together for delivery to patients and dispensing cabinets located in inpatient areas that facilitate the accurate picking of medications. These cabinets, containing the most frequently administered medications, use a visual cue, such as an automatically lighted tray or a single opened drawer, to indicate to the nurse the location of the correct patient medication. The cabinets use patient information, obtained manually from the nurse and entered into a computer linked to the cabinet or, more accurately, obtained electronically from the pharmacy system, to drive the cabinet logic.

Administration

Administration works to ensure the five rights of medication administration: right patient, right drug, right dose, right route, and right time. Systems employed during this phase often utilize bar coding of both patients and medications to ensure accuracy and tracking of medication administration.

In addition to bar codes, radio frequency identification (RFID) tags are currently being deployed to assist in medication management. The tags consist of a microchip with an antenna that interacts with electromagnetic waves to exchange information. The capabilities of these tags vary from passive fixed data devices to self-powered data modifiable chips. RFID is also used for tracking of both people and supplies.

PATIENT ORDERS: COMPUTERIZED PRACTITIONER ORDER ENTRY

CPOE systems (sometimes the word *practitioner* is substituted with the word *physician* or *provider*) offer those entering patient orders, usually in an inpatient setting, the ability to place those orders directly into a clinical information technology system. These applications assist practitioners in creating and managing medical orders and include such functionality as electronic signature and clinical decision support (CDS), a sequence of activities required of one or more participants in the healthcare delivery process to accomplish a patient care task.[4] CPOE systems eliminate the need to transcribe written orders thereby avoiding handwriting recognition errors and ensuring a higher level of order accuracy.

CPOE systems are often paired with CDS modules. Broadly speaking, CDS refers to applications that provide clinicians with targeted patient-specific medical knowledge at the point of care by intelligently utilizing all available patient information. CDS utilizes clinical guidelines and databases to identify and present this patient-relevant and circumscribed medical information and advice to the clinician during diagnostic and therapeutic decision making. Clinical decision support systems work to encourage the use of evidence-based medicine (those methodologies that have been proved through scientific rigor to be of value) and care activities that support organizational strategies of patient safety, quality, and care efficiency. The clinical content embedded in clinical decision support systems comes from both commercial sources as well as from institutional committees of experts.

Alerts and reminders form a subset of clinical decision support. Although clinicians use CPOE, alerts inform the practitioner of items that may require evaluation or review. These include such things as unexpected out-of-range lab results and the monitoring of specific blood parameters. Implementation of alerts and reminders regularly proves challenging for organizations. Experts struggle to identify the proper balance between too many and too few alerts and reminders.[5] In addition, patient variability greatly impacts the value of each alert and reminder, thereby making the process of identifying when to fire an alert very complicated. For example, elevated creatinine levels in a young, healthy patient may be very significant, whereas the same levels in a patient with end-stage renal disease may not.

STORAGE OF MEDICAL DIGITAL IMAGES

During the second phase of medical technology innovation, imaging systems became commonplace during both diagnostic and therapeutic interventions. These imaging systems advanced to embrace higher resolution, use of color and 3-D images, and video. In addition, the morbidity and costs associated with these procedures dropped dramatically. The consequence of these advances is not only an increase in the number of imaging studies completed but also the number of images and sizes of files for each study. Organizations providing access to these procedures saw exponential growth in the need for storage space for all these images.

With cost of storing images threatening to make these procedures economically prohibitive, organizations began turning to digital storage of images and videos in what are called picturing archiving and communication systems (PACS). These storage systems allow radiologists, pathologists, and other clinicians to quickly store, search for, and retrieve images for evaluation, documentation, and review.

PACS store images from a variety of generating sources including radiography, CT, MRI, ultrasonography, endoscopy, positron emission tomography (PET), and a number of instruments used in the pathology lab (e.g., microscopes). Computer networks allow these images to be shared throughout an organization as well as remotely with both consulting and attending physicians. Limitations on the quality of the images viewed are a function of the equipment utilized at the viewing site.

EXCHANGING PATIENT DATA VIA A NATIONAL NETWORK

Prompted by the IOM report *To Err Is Human*[6] as well as other previously published studies that outlined problems with quality of care and medical errors, the National Committee on Vital and Health Statistics (NCVHS) advanced a series of recommendations to the U.S. Department of Health and Human Services (DHHS) to develop an "effective, comprehensive health information infrastructure that links all health decision makers, including the public."[7]

The 2001 report, *Information for Health: A Strategy for Building the National Health Information Infrastructure,* detailed the positive impact of clinical information technology on both quality of care and costs.[8] Acting on these recommendations, the DHHS began to form the National Health Information Infrastructure (NHII).

In 2004, President George W. Bush established, by executive order, the Office of the National Coordinator for Health Information Technology (ONCHIT) to work toward facilitating the use of information technology throughout healthcare. The coordinator led the federal effort to create interoperable health information systems able to seamlessly share individual health information.

A nationwide health information network (NHIN) would link disparate healthcare information systems to allow patients, physicians, hospitals, public health agencies and other authorized users across the nation to share clinical information in real-time under stringent security, privacy and other protections. The NHIN is described in greater detail in the framework for strategic action: *The Decade of Health Information Technology: Delivering Consumer-Centric and Information-Rich Health Care.*[9]

Mounting evidence suggests that interoperable health information systems will generate considerable quality of care, patient safety, and financially responsible spending gains by reducing the payment for duplicate and lost healthcare information (tests, radiographs, clinical evaluations, etc.). The January 2005 issue of *Health Affairs* consolidated policy positions, a preliminary business case, and field-based perspectives on interoperable healthcare systems. The article by Jan Walker and colleagues articulated a $77.8 billion net savings per year attributable to provider, laboratory, hospital, free-standing clinic, radiology center, pharmacy, and payer connectivity.[10] Although the magnitude of the projected savings may be challenged, the contributing authors agree that health information technology has the potential to redefine how healthcare is delivered, managed, and used to inform decision making.

Within the DHHS, the Centers for Disease Control and Prevention (CDC) are developing an interoperable health information systems strategy through the creation of the Public Health Information Network (PHIN) initiative. The objectives of the PHIN are to support detection and monitoring efforts, analytic needs for real-time and aggregate information, information resource and knowledge management, alerts and communications for public health professionals and their partners, and response to community health needs and policy recommendations.

FOSTERING ELECTRONIC HEALTH RECORDS THROUGH THE U.S. HEALTH INFORMATION COMMUNITY

In 2005, the secretary of the DHHS formed the American Health Information Community (AHIC), bringing together private industry, academia, payers, consumers, and government leaders to achieve the president's goal of having most Americans using EHRs within 10 years.

Certification of Software for Interoperability

In addition to the AHIC, other organizations were formed to work on the interoperability challenge. The Certification Commission for Health Information Technology (CCHIT), a private nonprofit organization, develops criteria for the "efficient, credible and sustainable mechanism" for certifying healthcare information technology products.[11] The CCHIT evaluates both ambulatory and hospital EHR products submitted by vendors for compliance with its established standards. For its criteria, the CCHIT obtains input from all stakeholders while focusing on the key areas of software functionality, interoperability, and security.

Setting Standards for Interoperability

With a $3.3 million contract from the DHHS in 2005, the American National Standards Institute (ANSI), a nonprofit organization that administers and coordinates voluntary standardization activities in the United States, convened the Health Information Technology Standards Panel (HITSP) to develop, prototype, and evaluate a harmonization process for achieving widely acceptable health information technology standards.[12] Establishment of credible standards assists in supporting interoperability among all healthcare software applications.

Establishing Privacy and Security Rules for Interoperability

In addition to the HITSP, the DHHS awarded an $11.5 million contract to the Health Information Security and Privacy Collaboration (HISPC), a partnership consisting of a multidisciplinary team of experts and the National Governors' Association.[13] The HISPC works with state and territorial governments to assess and develop plans to address variations in business policies and state laws that impact privacy and security. This work is framed to address challenges to health information interoperability.

Regional Efforts to Build Electronic Patient Records

On a local level, regional health information organizations (RHIO) are being formed to allow the interchange of health information among all stakeholders while allowing secure access to all patients. Although RHIOs form an important foundation for the building of comprehensive EHRs, experts continue to work through the various issues of information exchange architecture, security, privacy, and funding. Currently, two major models exist for the formation of RHIOs: a distributed database model—often referred to as the federated model—and the centralized model.

RHIO Models

The distributed model assumes that all patient information resides in the computer systems of the provider that collected the information. In effect, each piece of data that makes up the electronic health record of each patient is stored separately. Formation of a comprehensive medical record requires access to each system in which each piece of information is stored.

In some variations of this model, a centralized database maintains an index of all the systems in which data for a given patient resides, allowing each provider system to be polled only for existing information on a particular patient during the effort to build a complete electronic medical record. In other models, every provider system is polled for information on a patient for every search utilizing a patient identifier.

Availability of patient information is dependent upon the reliability of each independent provider system and its level of compliance with interoperability standards. Access to patient information, including the use of polling for data, is not limited to a region but would need to occur nationally.

The centralized model establishes a regional, centralized database for storage of all patient information. Providers, irrespective of their location, submit patient information utilizing interoperability standards to a centralized health record bank, where it is securely stored. Access to this comprehensive electronic health record by other providers, family members, and others is completely and securely controlled by each patient. As patient information is submitted to the health record bank soon after each patient encounter, future polling of provider systems for patient data is not necessary. Most versions of the centralized model use principles established by financial institutions in the formation of credit reporting agencies, in which reporting of a financial encounter to a centralized entity eliminates the need for a response to future query requests.

LEVERAGING INFORMATION TECHNOLOGY THROUGH PATH INNOVATION

In a study published in the *Journal of the American Medical Association*, Koppel and colleagues reported how a CPOE system installed at an academic medical institution increased medication errors.[14] The authors attributed many of the 22 types of errors to a variety of factors, including poor system design coupled with incompatible care delivery processes. These results highlight the importance of processes in the delivery of expected outcomes (see table 5.1).

It is well known that the application of best practices and evidence-based medicine can significantly improve clinical and financial outcomes. Many informatics experts have long thought that the implementation of clinical information technology systems would bring these best practices more effectively to the physician, thereby reducing unnecessary variation in care, accelerating the adoption of new, proved diagnostic and therapeutic approaches, and decreasing costs associated with ineffectual or inappropriate care. What we are finding is that the results delivered by this new technology are falling far short of the promise.

The failure of these clinical information technology tools to deliver safer, more efficient care is due to many factors, yet all of them have origin in the concept inherent in the phrase *path innovation*. Although the theories and expertise that form the basis of path innovation are not new, their interaction with and subsequent impact on clinical information technology is.

Three Key Factors of Path Innovation

Path innovation is dependent upon three key factors: (1) process improvement or reengineering; (2) clinical guidelines, clinical paths, and evidence-based medicine; and (3) information technology system design. Although subject matter experts exist in all these areas, it is unclear how well these experts historically worked together in the design and implementation of clinical information technology systems.

Process improvement experts understand how processes impact outcomes and what analytical steps are needed to evaluate processes. They are able to suggest changes in processes and predict the potential improvements such changes will deliver.

Experts in clinical content understand what various clinical paths deliver as outcomes. They are able to link various interventions with probabilistic results.

Designers of information technology systems understand the flow of digital information within computer systems and the user interfaces that receive and deliver data to users. They are able to conceptualize how a data point can be stored or reformatted with other data points.

Independent Experts Share Knowledge

Almost universally, these experts work and apply their expertise independently of one another. Information technology system designers develop these systems

Table 5.1
Examples of the Facilitation of Medical Errors through CPOE

Description	Event	Impact
Information errors: Fragmentation and systems integration failure		
Medication discontinuation failures	Change in the dose of a medication from every 4 hours to every 6 hours	Overdose of medication as it is then administered ever 4 hours and every 6 hours
Antibiotic renewal failure	House staff use computer system to enter antibiotic orders while alert to the automatic discontinuation of some antibiotics after three days placed as a sticker in paper chart	Antibiotic inadvertently discontinued
Allergy information delay	Alerts related to drug allergies only appear after drug is ordered	Drug allergies missed due to clinician user scrolling to other parts of the online record before the allergy alert appears
Human-machine interface flaws: Machine rules that do not correspond to work organization or usual behaviors		
Patient selection	Choose the wrong drug and patient	Small font and location of patients and drugs near one another on computer screen leads to clinician users ordering the wrong medications for patients
Wrong medication selection	Clinician users choose incorrect medications for patients	Poorly designed medication screens that require scrolling to other screens for medication information prove confusing and lead to medication and drug dosing errors
Late-in-day orders lost for 24 hours	Newly admitted patients experience a 24-hour delay in receiving care from orders	Patients admitted late in the day (e.g., near midnight) might have their orders entered into the system the next day so that any orders written for "tomorrow" will not occur until more than 24 hours later, whereas the intent was to have the order delivered the next morning
Inflexible ordering screens, incorrect medications	Nonformulary medications entered on screens located in a separate section of the CPOE module	Orders lost, ignored by nursing, and failed to be dispatched to the pharmacy (e.g., nonformulary organ rejection medications)

Source: Adapted from Koppel, R., J. P. Metlay, A. Cohen, et al. 2005. "Physician Order Entry Systems in Facilitating Medication Errors." *Journal of the American Medical Association* 293 (10): 1197–1203.

using specifications developed by product managers who attempt to bridge information technology with healthcare. These product managers are rarely experts in clinical medicine or clinical processes.

Clinical content experts develop clinical content focused solely on clinical issues, rarely incorporating information technology system design or clinical process considerations in their work. This is evident in the effort invested by many organizations to modify existing guidelines to fit their newly implemented clinical information technology systems. Their reported struggles are indicative of the difficulty of this type of work.

Process redesigners often appear on the scene late in implementations, if at all. Working within the environment as presented to them, they try to change existing processes without the advantage of being able to change the inputs (e.g., clinical path) or tools (e.g., system functionality) of the processes.

To implement and effectively leverage clinical information technology systems, a new approach in the use of experts is required. Path innovation integrates different subject matter experts in unique ways to leverage their expertise throughout the design and implementation of clinical information technology systems. Even for systems already built, path innovation can be used to leverage existing functionality in these clinical information technology systems. It can help enhance outcomes while reducing the probability of unacceptable results such as system-related medical and medication errors.

Teams Necessary to Achieve Path Innovation

Path innovation requires the formation of a team of subject matter experts who apply their skills during an entire clinical information technology system project. During the system design phase, clinical and process design experts share their understanding of their discipline with the information technology system developer.

During the implementation phase, the information technology system designer and the clinical content expert act as consultants to the process redesigner to develop new processes that are both radically different from existing processes and that could only be implemented utilizing functionality made available by the new clinical information technology system. In addition, the clinical content expert can use this functionality to conceive of clinical paths impossible without this digital healthcare capability.

Although path innovation builds upon existing approaches, it reflects a new way of thinking and approaching problems. Instead of looking at how an existing process could be modified, path innovation gives birth to brand new processes, formerly impossible in the institution before the installation of the new clinical information technology system. To accomplish this, organizations need to identify subject matter experts who are also able to achieve a basic understanding of the disciplines of their expert colleagues. Then together, these experts work to create new processes that incorporate the needs of the institution with the promise of new information technology systems and clinical content.

Don Berwick, MD, founder of the Institute for Healthcare Improvement, once said, "[E]very system is perfectly designed to achieve exactly the results it achieves."[15] Assuming this to be true, only through the creation of truly new systems (e.g., processes and information technology) using path innovation can we expect to impact results to achieve the safer and higher quality healthcare that we all desire.

CLINICAL DECISION SUPPORT

For more than two decades, clinicians struggled to use evidence-based guidelines. Ever since Wennberg's work back in the 1970s demonstrating the huge practice variation seen even in relatively small geographic areas, quality experts have worked to promote guideline use among physicians to ensure that interventions on patients actually did them some good.[16]

Throughout the 1980s, managed care organizations did everything possible to get physicians to use guidelines in an effort to enhance quality and control costs. Their efforts included education, guideline distribution, economic incentives, and patient education.

Unfortunately, the evidence on guideline use shows poor acceptance.[17,18] In addition, physician adoption of new clinical knowledge tends to be inconsistent and unpredictable In the meantime, patients receive inappropriate, unhelpful, or even harmful care while valuable resources are wasted.

Difficult to Remain Up-to-Date

The rapid advancement of medicine makes it nearly impossible for any physician to remain completely up-to-date on clinical progress. Also, with such rapid change, it is difficult for physicians to separate the valuable information from the less valuable or even suspect medical knowledge that deserves little attention. Last, the structure in which medical information normally comes, journal articles and medical reports, is in the wrong information format to be integrated into a typical medical practice. For example, it requires a huge effort for a physician to evaluate a single peer-reviewed article on a specific aspect of a disease process and then apply that single bit of knowledge to a small subset of patients within a practice panel.

Clinicians who previously worked on guideline development generally find that about 80 percent of the guideline is developed quickly, whereas the remaining portion is labored over for weeks, months, or even years. Often, the guidelines are never completed or, if completed and disseminated, rarely used. Researchers know that it is easy to develop guidelines but very hard to develop high-quality, respected, and, most important, usable ones. In addition, upkeep of the guidelines usually never gets done to include clinical evidence available in new studies.

With the advent of CPOE and high-capacity personal digital assistants (PDAs), there is technology that can effectively deliver guidelines. The challenge exists to develop high-quality, effective, and easy-to-use guidelines that can be deployed intelligently, consistent with work flow, and at the point of care.

Clinical Evidence

Through an effort begun in 1995 by the United Kingdom's National Health Service and the British Medical Journal (BMJ) Publishing Group, there now exists a formulary of evidence-based medical knowledge. The current iteration of the guidelines, named *Clinical Evidence,* covers more than 180 clinical conditions and evaluates more than 2,500 treatments.[19,20] Major disease categories covered are listed in table 5.2.

Clinical Evidence is available in two print versions, full and concise. The release of each version is staggered so that any changes in the guidelines can be included in the next version. It is also available online via a Web-based interface (http://www.clinicalevidence.org) as well as through a synchronized PDA device.

Guidelines are updated continuously with full literature searches on each topic every 12 months. As new information becomes available, it is incorporated into the Web-based version of *Clinical Evidence* and subsequently the next print version.

Clinical Evidence focuses on outcomes that matter to the patient and the physician, such as severity of illness, quality of life, disability, and survival. Guidelines include a list of outcomes and how they are measured. Proxy outcomes such as decreased lipid levels or blood pressure are of lesser interest to the researchers as they are less clear on their true impact on the individual.

Guideline developers mainly utilize the Cochrane Library, Medline, and Embase, looking for high-quality reviews of randomized clinical trials. The evidence is then summarized and peer-reviewed by the section advisors, at least two external expert clinicians, and an editorial committee that includes both

Table 5.2
Major Disease Categories Covered in Clinical Evidence

Blood and lymph disorders
Cardiovascular disorders
Child health
Digestive system disorders
Ear, nose and throat disorders
Endocrine disorders
Eye disorders
HIV and AIDS
Infectious diseases
Kidney disorders
Men's health
Mental health
Musculoskeletal disorders
Neurological disorders
Oral health
Perioperative care
Poisoning
Pregnancy and childbirth
Respiratory disorders (acute)
Respiratory disorders (chronic)
Sexual health
Skin disorders
Sleep disorders
Women's health
Wounds

expert clinicians and epidemiologists. A standardized process allows for collection of comments by *Clinical Evidence* users.

Through the generous support of the United Healthcare Foundation, *Clinical Evidence* is available free to all physicians in the United States. Additionally, through other supporting organizations, it is free to physicians in England, Wales, Italy, and developing countries. It regularly is translated into French, Spanish, Italian, Japanese, and German.

The National Guideline Clearinghouse

The National Guideline Clearinghouse (NGC), an initiative of the DHHS, is a comprehensive database of evidence-based clinical practice guidelines and related documents (http://www.guideline.gov). The NGC was originally created in conjunction with the American Medical Association and the American Association of Health Plans (now America's Health Insurance Plans, or AHIP).

The NGC works to provide clinicians and their organizations with objective, detailed information on clinical practice guidelines and to further their dissemination, implementation, and use. This clinical content comes in the form of structured abstracts (summaries) and links to full-text guidelines or their sources. A guideline comparison utility gives users the ability to generate side-by-side comparisons of guidelines. In addition, the NGC staff produces comparisons called Guideline Synthesis that compare guidelines on similar topics, noting the areas of similarity and difference. The NGC also provides an annotated bibliography database in which users can search for citations on guideline development, methodology, evaluation, and implementation.

Unlike *Clinical Evidence,* guidelines included in the NGC database are submitted by outside professional organizations. After a high-level review of corroborating documentation, the guideline is included in the database. Therefore, the NGC database has multiple versions of guidelines on specific topics. As are the guidelines for *Clinical Evidence,* these guidelines are not specifically developed for use in computerized clinical decision support systems and, therefore, will need extensive modification to fit the new work flow dictated by clinical information technology systems.

SECURING CLINICIAN ADOPTION

Nothing is more critical to obtaining value from a clinical information technology system than the securing of adoption of the new system by clinicians. Deployment of clinical information technology is inherently disruptive, especially when patient care cannot cease to allow the unfettered deployment of the new technology. Often, parallel systems must run for a short period of time to allow the transition to the new system. This, in every instance, places additional burdens and work flow challenges on the clinicians asked to use the new technology.

Successful deployment of new information technology systems requires clinicians to be involved early in the planning process. As these clinicians are experts in the work flow critical to care delivery, their input into the required, newly designed work flow increases the probability that the new processes will be embraced by other clinicians. This, in turn, helps ensure the delivery of quality and cost benefits expected from using the new system.

Deployment plans must first focus on initiatives that deliver value to the clinicians using the system rather than solely on the needs of the institution. By offering this value to these new users, the organization is able to secure their support for the new technology early in the deployment process. In addition, it establishes a level of dialogue that can be used to refine the deployment of additional functionality to maximize the benefit to the institution and patient. Organizations that have included clinicians early in the deployment process and secured their involvement throughout deployment more often struggle trying to keep up with the demands of the clinicians for additional functionality rather than trying to force clinicians to use the system.

In summary, successful deployment of clinical information technology systems requires the early and continued involvement of clinicians throughout the design and implementation phases. Such involvement helps ensure a high probability of a successful implementation and deployment with the expected significant financial and quality of care benefits.

BUYING A CLINICAL INFORMATION TECHNOLOGY SYSTEM

Buying a clinical information technology system challenges every organization's senior management team. Unlike other administrative applications that help manage a facility, the clinical information technology system touches directly the lives of patients and the work flow of physicians, nurses, and other clinicians. Careers and entire organizations can be ruined by poor vendor choices and botched implementations (i.e., installation of the software and hardware) and deployments (i.e., introduction of applications to end users). Poorly chosen clinical information technology systems can drive physicians to competitor institutions, impact facility accreditation, and in some cases invite litigation due to unexpected morbidity or mortality.

As frightening as this task is, the best way to be successful is to be humble. Senior executives must accept the fact that full investigation of the features and functionality of clinical information technology systems before purchase is impossible. No individual or committee has the technical expertise and available time to effectively evaluate and fully review the capabilities of a comprehensive clinical information technology system. Therefore, organizations must base their decision to purchase systems on factors that function as surrogates for the usefulness and appropriateness of the systems in its institutions. These may include such items as the source of clinical content included with the system, list of organizations using the system, and perceived ease of use of the application.

Evaluate Live Systems

Although information technology vendors utilize demonstrations of their software to educate clients about their products, viewing working systems deployed in patient care areas offers the most valuable information. Unfortunately for both vendors and purchasers, the competitiveness of the healthcare information technology marketplace, coupled with the complexity of these systems, encourages vendors to showcase software products during demonstrations that are either partially completed or are in a beta version.

Therefore, often what is seen in these demonstrations does not accurately represent the features and functionality currently available. It is important to take vendors at their word when they declare that the demonstrated software is representative of features and functionality under development.

Focus on Deployed Working Systems Only

To increase the probability of purchasing a product that will satisfy the needs of an organization, institutions must focus on existing, working, deployed, and implemented versions of the applications being considered for purchase. The best way to evaluate current-state versions of applications is to visit current clients of each vendor and to witness the daily use of the various applications.

Organizations must be patient and allocate adequate time to see the systems working under all conditions. This includes visiting multiple hospitals and various patient care areas throughout each hospital.

Forge Solid Vendor Relationships

For most organizations, it is more prudent to engage in relationships with vendors that have established working applications that can be immediately deployed and utilized. Although working, released software will have its inevitable share of problems, it is likely there will be fewer problems and solutions will be readily found.

In some cases, it may be advantageous to engage in relationships with vendors that are offering software that has just been released or is under development. In these instances, organizations must enter the agreement recognizing the potential benefits from such arrangements but also the problems and delays in the software that may be associated with purchasing new, untested information technology products. Organizations that do not have extensive information technology infrastructure and departments should be wary of entering into these types of arrangements.

The following sections outline a recommended process for choosing clinical information technology for an institution.

Review and Embrace Strategic Vision

The purchase of all clinical information technology tools must be driven by the clinical strategic vision of the organization. The strategic vision represents the views and aspirations of the board of directors, the medical staff, and other clinical professionals in the organization. Clearly, cost control is always a consideration, but the importance of patient safety and quality healthcare overwhelmingly drives decision making.

Broadly Explore Options

A high level of evaluation of your organization will quickly identify the potential suppliers of the application software required. In almost all cases, there will be a relatively small number of vendors who provide software that meets the needs of an organization. Identification of these vendors can be done through a request for information process (RFI), searching the Internet, and contacting colleagues at institutions similar to one's own.

Understand the Vendor

As relationships with application vendors extend far beyond the implementation phase, a strong, open, and trusting relationship is necessary to be able to ensure that implemented software will deliver the expected results to an organization. Because problems will arise, a positive relationship is required to ensure that problems are resolved. A good working relationship with a vendor, as exhibited by respectful and honest interactions with all representatives of the organization, unequivocally trumps perceived advantages in features and functionality that might be seen in other products.

Evaluate the Product

The best way to evaluate clinical information technology applications is to actually see them functioning in a real working environment. Unless an organization is working as a development partner with a vendor, various client organizations, comparable to the purchasing institution, should be available to be visited to observe the applications being used by clinical professionals.

Purchasing organizations must budget more than one day to visit these client organizations and see the applications being used at a variety of times during the day. Workloads vary, with morning physician rounds often presenting the greatest demands upon systems because of their high number of new patient orders and the need for patient care documentation. In addition, evening use represents a time when information technology staffing may be low or system maintenance may occur.

Organizations should request that their representatives be allowed to visit patient care areas unencumbered and be able to ask questions of the various users of the applications. The more institutions visited, the better the information that can be collected to evaluate the applications and the vendor.

Understand Pricing

Vendor pricing is greatly influenced by the level of ongoing maintenance payments, the strategic value of the organization to the vendor, and market forces.

Therefore, in negotiating contracts with vendors, be sure to take a very broad and considered view of the products, services, and support being provided.

Cost of ownership includes not only the purchase price of the software but also the ongoing maintenance fee to the vendor and the cost of implementing, deploying, and maintaining the system during its life. Finally, the importance of the quality of the relationship with the vendor cannot be overemphasized, as it will have the greatest impact on the success of implementation and, eventually, clinician adoption.

Secure Adoption

Implementing clinical information technology without broad involvement and support by the clinical staff—requiring focus on all stakeholders, including physicians, nurses, pharmacists, therapists, and other health professionals—all but guarantees a failed and wasteful deployment. Clinical information technology systems alone do not fix clinical problems, advance safety, or reduce costs by themselves. These systems provide tools that can be used by clinicians to change how they deliver care. Only with clinician creativity, insight, and experience molding the implementation can new processes deployed with these tools deliver acceptable work flows and generate good outcomes.

If deployment is poor and disruptive, clinicians will create work-arounds to these failing system processes, a development that guarantees medical errors and unacceptable waste. By securing adoption, organizations can be assured of usable systems that are embraced by clinicians and that are able to deliver expected and much-needed clinical and financial outcomes.

Case Study

In 2003, Vinnez Valley Hospital (VVH, a pseudonym), a 345-bed nonprofit community hospital embraced a five-year strategic plan to enhance quality, improve patient safety, and increase efficiency in all its inpatient and outpatient areas. Recognizing that information technology plays a key role in improving patient care while offering opportunities to streamline work flow, the chief executive officer of the hospital hired a board-certified physician trained in informatics at a leading academic medical center to lead the information technology purchase, implementation, and deployment processes as chief medical informatics officer (CMIO).

Understanding the huge task ahead, the CMIO identified several overriding activities to realize a successful information technology purchase. They included:

1. Completing a comprehensive inventory of existing information technology systems that documented current functionality, cost of ownership, role in patient care delivery, and planned upgrades of the software.
2. Identifying with the hospital's senior management team and clinical leadership the information technology needs of the organization.

3. Reviewing the current thought leadership on information technology systems and its role in enhancing patient safety, improving quality, and increasing efficiency.
4. Prioritizing the needs of the organization based upon review of items 1 through 3.
5. Developing a budget and implementation plan for the purchase of information technology systems.
6. Researching the currently available commercial applications that offer the capabilities to satisfy the needs of the organization.
7. After choosing the systems, creating a detailed plan for technical implementation, migration of old applications to newer systems, and clinician deployment.
8. After deployment, monitoring the impact of the systems on patient safety, quality, and care efficiency and regularly reporting these results to senior management, the board of trustees, the employees, and the clinicians working in the hospital.

Upon the completion of the evaluation of the existing systems, the CMIO identified the following systems that required replacement either because of limited functionality or the loss of vendor support. These included the order management, pharmacy management, and laboratory management systems.

Robust discussions with clinical leadership helped identify additional needs. Of most interest was nursing documentation and electronic medical record systems. Although physicians, in general, expressed enthusiasm for information technology and its potential positive impact on patient care, they remained concerned about the impact of electronic medical records and computerized physician order entry on the efficiency of their work flow.

After approximately three months of information gathering by the CMIO, next steps required the formation of a diverse advisory committee with members representing varied stakeholders within the hospital. Representatives were chosen from nursing, the medical staff, information technology, finance, laboratory, pharmacy, radiology, and clinical services. The committee met each week to discuss information technology options, decide strategy, and work on action items. At the end of 2003, the committee delivered to the senior management team and the VVH board of trustees a comprehensive information technology wish list prioritized by need, impact on patient care, and estimated cost. In addition, the committee estimated the work flow impact on staff and clinicians for each system.

After review by the senior team and the board, the committee was given a budget and list of systems to work toward implementing. Less than what the committee requested, the hospital purchased in 2004 new laboratory, pharmacy, and electronic medical record systems. The electronic medical record system included a module for provider order entry.

Understanding that implementation and transition to these new systems could take a substantial period of time, the committee developed a three-year implementation and deployment plan that allowed the staggered roll out of the new systems. Laboratory and pharmacy were chosen to be installed first, as they had the least immediate impact on the medical staff. The CMIO recognized that an EMR system, especially with provider order entry, would cause the greatest changes in work flow for admitting physicians.

The laboratory and pharmacy systems were researched with emphasis on user recommendations and visits to live hospital sites. Although labor intensive for the hospital information technology team, the installation of both these systems went smoothly over a period of nine months, with systems live by April 2005.

Choosing and installing the electronic medical record proved considerably more challenging. After researching available systems through requests for proposals, product demonstrations, vendor discussions, and multiple visits to similar hospitals running the various vendor systems, a single system was deemed to offer the best fit for the needs of the hospital. Approved by the committee and the senior management team, the committee then focused on securing support from the medical staff. The committee realized that the implementation of the electronic medical record without adoption by the medical staff would end in failure.

To achieve this end, the committee identified the leaders of the medical staff, including all specialties, and key physicians who admitted large numbers of patients to the hospital. Over a period of three months, representatives of the committee met with 27 of the 32 influencers identified as key opinion makers. During these one-hour sessions, each committee member: (1) presented an overview of the clinical information technology strategy for the hospital, including the process followed to develop the strategy; (2) reviewed the high-level features of the chosen clinical information products; and (3) explored deployment issues important to the opinion leader. At the conclusion of these meetings the committee felt comfortable that they had identified the most important issues concerning deployment of the system.

Deployment of the electronic medical record system began with a pilot project on one ward in the hospital. After this two-month pilot in which implementation and deployment issues germane to the hospital were identified, the system was then rolled out to the rest of the hospital at a pace of one ward per week. At the end of four months, every inpatient unit had the system live.

To support system users, committee members provided 24-7 help line coverage to address any clinical issues that arose because of the new system. In addition, hospital information technology staff provided around-the-clock user support for technical and usability issues.

Short of the usual struggles that occur in any major system installation, the information technology work with its concurrent clinical work flow change went relatively smoothly. At present, the organization is collecting both process and outcome measures to calculate the impact of the clinical information technology on patient safety, quality of care, and costs. In the meantime, the organization believes that it has improved its competitiveness in the marketplace, as its success rate in attracting young, well-trained specialists to the hospital has improved with several important recruitment wins over its crosstown rival.

CONCLUSION

Clinical information technology offers healthcare a powerful but complex tool to address issues of patient safety, quality of care, and cost. Although requiring significant changes in a clinician's approach to treating patients, it offers opportunities for enhancement of care that cannot be achieved without the technology. Clinical information technology alone will not solve healthcare's current challenges, but combined with a creative mindset of embracing new ways of doing things, it does offer the means to radically transform medical care both in the United States and around the world.

Key Concepts

- Information technology offers healthcare a powerful tool to address issues of patient safety, quality of care, and cost.
- Interoperability, the foundation of regional health information organizations and the National Health Information Network, allows the sharing of patient data across care settings, thereby offering the means to construct a complete electronic health record.
- The formation of multidisciplinary teams of experts that follow the principles of path innovation offers the best approach to developing, implementing, and deploying clinical information technology systems.
- Clinical decision support provides clinicians with a powerful tool to improve quality of care, reduce medical errors, and decrease unnecessary care by supplying evidence-based, patient-specific, relevant information at the point of patient care.

NOTES

1. Kohn, L. T., J. M. Corrigan, and M. S. Donaldson, eds. 1999. *To Err Is Human: Building a Safer Health System.* Washington, D.C.: Institute of Medicine, National Academy Press.

2. Health Information Management Systems Society. 2006. *HIMSS Dictionary of Healthcare Information Technology Terms, Acronyms and Organizations.* Chicago: Health Information Management Systems Society.

3. Osheroff, J. A., E. A. Pifer, J. M. Teich, et al. 2005. *Improving Outcomes with Clinical Decision Support: An Implementer's Guide.* Chicago: Health Information Management Systems Society.

4. Ibid.

5. Ibid.

6. Kohn, Corrigan, Donaldson, *To Err Is Human*.

7. Lumpkin, J. R., NCVHS Workgroup on the National Health Information In-
frastructure. 2001. *Information for Health: A Strategy for Building the National Health
Information Infrastructure.* Washington, D.C.: National Committee on Vital and
Health Statistics, U.S. Department of Health and Human Services.

8. Ibid.

9. Thompson, T. G., and D. J. Brailer. 2004. *The Decade of Health Information
Technology: Delivering Consumer-Centric and Information-Rich Health Care.* Available at:
http://www.hhs.gov/healthit/documents/hitframework.pdf. Accessed July 30, 2007.

10. Walker, J., E. Pan, D. Johnston, et al. 2005. "The Value of Health Care Information Exchange and Interoperability." *Health Affairs Web Exclusive,* January 19:
W5-10–W5-18.

11. Certification Commission for Healthcare Information Technology. 2007. Available at: http://www.cchit.org. Accessed February 20, 2007.

12. American National Standards Institute. n.d. *Healthcare Information Technology
Standards Panel.* Available at: http://www.ansi.org/standards_activities/standards_
boards_panels/hisb/hitsp.aspx?menuid=3. Accessed July 30, 2007.

13. Health Information and Privacy Collaboration (HISPC). 2007. "Health Information Security and Privacy Collaboration Hosts National Meeting to Discuss
Stakeholder Concerns." *RTI International.* Available at: http://www.rti.org/page.
cfm?objectid=09E8D494-C491-42FC-BA13EAD1217245C0. Accessed February 20,
2007.

14. Koppel, R., J. P. Metlay, A. Cohen, et al. 2005. "Physician Order Entry Systems in Facilitating Medication Errors." *Journal of the American Medical Association*
293 (10): 1197–1203.

15. Berwick, D. M. 1996. "Education and Debate: A Primer on Leading the Improvement of Systems." *British Medical Journal* 312: 619–22. Available at: http://
www.bmj.com/cgi/content/full/312/7031/619. Accessed July 30, 2007.

16. Wennberg, J., and A. Gittelsohn. 1973. "Small Area Variations in Health Care
Delivery." *Science* 182: 1102–8.

17. Lomas, J., G. M. Anderson, and K. Domnick-Pierre. 1989. "Do Practice
Guidelines Guide Practice: The Effect of a Consensus Statement on the Practice of
Physicians." *New England Journal of Medicine* 321: 1306–11.

18. Kosecoff, J., D. E. Kanouse, and W. H. Rogers. 1987. "Effects of a National
Institutes of Health Consensus Development Program on Physician Practice." *Journal
of the American Medical Association* 258: 2708–13.

19. *BMJ Clinical Evidence.* 2007. Available at: http://www.clinicalevidence.com.
Accessed December 15, 2006.

20. Godlee, F., and D. Tovey, eds. 2004. *Clinical Evidence Concise*, 11. *British
Medical Journal.*

FURTHER READING

Chaiken, B. P. 2001. "Evidence-Based Medicine: A Tool at the Point of Care." *Nursing Economics* 19 (5): 234–35.

Chaiken, B. P. 2002. "Clinical Decision Support: Success through Smart Deployment." *Journal of Quality Health Care* 1 (4): 15–16.

Chaiken, B. P. 2002. "Opinion: Clinical Guidelines at Point of Care Needed to Improve Quality, Safety." *iHealthbeat, California Healthcare Foundation*. Available at: http://www.ihealthbeat.org/articles/2002/10/11/Clinical-guidelines-at-point-of-care-needed-to-improve-quality-safety.aspx. Accessed July 30, 2007.

Chaiken, B. P. 2004. "Useable Clinical Evidence-Based Guidelines . . . For Real." *Patient Safety and Quality Healthcare* 2 (1): 14–16.

eHealthTrust. Available at: http://www.ehealthtrust.com.

Garg, A. X., N. K. Adhikari, and H. McDonald. 2005. "Effect of Computerized Clinical Decision Support Systems on Practitioner Performance and Patient Outcomes." *Journal of the American Medical Association* 293: 1223–38.

Healthcare Information and Management Systems Society. Available at: http://www.himss.org.

National Guideline Clearinghouse. Available at: http://www.guidelines.gov.

Slawson, D. C., A. F. Shaughnessy, and J. H. Bennett. 1994. "Becoming a Medical Information Master: Feeling Good about Not Knowing Everything." *Journal of Family Practice* 38: 505–13.

U.S. Department of Health and Human Services, Health Information Technology. Available at: http://www.hhs.gov/healthit.

Wears, R. L., and M. Berg. 2005. "Computer Technology and Clinical Work." *Journal of the American Medical Association* 293: 1261–63.

CHAPTER 6

Market Dynamics and Financing Strategies in the Development of Medical Technologies

Jonathan Gertler

Although issues of access and resources remain in the forefront in the delivery of clinical care, many technical product innovations may change the method by which care is delivered and facilitate a quality-cost paradigm shift that is critical in many disease states. The moves to minimally invasive surgery, greater diagnostic and therapeutic accuracy, and personalized medicine are but a few of the aspects of clinical care that technical innovation can influence. Many individual physicians may contribute significantly to this through the generation of the primary idea or through a more direct contribution on an entrepreneurial level by assuming a role of advisor or central part of the management team. In order to facilitate this contribution, a thorough understanding of the market and financing dynamics critical to the success of these ventures is necessary. This chapter will discuss the evolution of medical technology, financing medical innovations, and errors made in company development.

THE EVOLUTION OF MEDICAL TECHNOLOGY

Traditionally, medical devices have been viewed as implantables, disposables, or capital equipment assuming a permanent place in the delivery network. Examples of these include fixed items such as MRIs, CT scanners, laser devices, as well as disposables or implantables such as catheters, pacemakers, defibrillators, ventricular assist devices, ablation devices, biopsy devices, and diagnostic and imaging adjunctive reagents, IT infrastructures, or film. Although therapeutics or more biologically or chemically derived compounds often are considered separate from the engineering solutions listed, in fact the mechanistic conversion of biology and engineering into biomedical device and technology products is increasing. For example, antiproliferatives, biomaterials, sensing feedback, tissue stimulation, and cell-based molecular diagnostics and therapeutics have had significant impact on cardiovascular, orthopedic, cancer, and diabetes management as well as an increasing role in drug discovery and acceleration of drug development. With this in mind, it is helpful to attempt to separate invention or innovation into several categories that, in turn, may drive some of the regulatory, investment, and market development risk associated with innovation.

As depicted in the figure 6.1, medical technology development may be subdivided into three major categories: category 1, a disruptive technology with huge technology value; category 2, a paradigm shift based on established clinical principles; and category 3, variations on existing clinical themes.

Significant disruptive technology values are often characterized by a large and unmet clinical need, new clinical principles applied, a complete shift of patient control, or significant behavioral shifts of care delivery. Examples of this on the medical-device level can include the progression of angioplasty versus surgery during the era in which angioplasty was first introduced, the aggressive monitoring and control of diabetes that gave birth to significant changes in the development of glucose monitoring devices once the Diabetes Control and Complications Trial (DCCT) was published in 1994, as well as endoscopy for gastrointestinal therapy and diagnosis during the early days of this development.

Category 2, which entails a paradigm shift based on established clinical principles, more commonly involves the conversion of well-established techniques to a minimally invasive method, ease of use with improved outcomes, or extensions of established techniques to new indications. Category 2 extensions may emanate from category 1 disruptions. For instance, endovascular ancillary interventions including atherectomy and even stent placement can be thought of as disruptive at their onset but ultimately represent a paradigm shift based on established clinical principles once these techniques had taken hold. Similarly, the advent of endovascular aneurysm repair techniques, which were an

Figure 6.1 Categories of Medical Technology Development

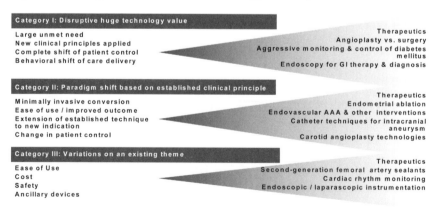

extension of early endovascular angioplasty techniques, are supplanting open surgical interventions. In like manner, treatment of intracranial aneurysms and intracranial arterial interventions has advanced with both biomaterials and engineering solutions for vascular malformations, carotid angioplasty has extended coronary angioplasty to a new territory, and endometrial ablation for hemorrhagic dysfunctional menstrual bleeding was an extension of established gynecologic surgical techniques.

Category 3 encompasses variations on an existing theme; they simply invoke incremental improvements that can still have an impact on ease of use, cost, and safety. In addition, improvements in ancillary devices associated with category 1 and category 2 developments after they are long adopted can have an impact. Examples in this category include second- and third-generation femoral artery closure devices, improvements in cardiac rhythm monitoring, and the ever-changing extension and ergonomic improvements in endoscopic and laparoscopic instrumentation.

FINANCING MEDICAL INNOVATIONS

Utilizing the previous categorization criteria, this chapter will now review the aspects of financing that are critical to the development of any new enterprise. Although frequently not thought of as a core or primary strategy for the development of new companies, financial support and proper capitalization are the lifeblood of any new technology development. This section will outline the sources of capital and how they relate to the stage of company development, delve more deeply into the diligence process by which companies are funded and value is created, discuss the means by which invested capital gains liquidity (i.e., is able to return capital to the primary investors), and review some of the more common mistakes committed by inexperienced entrepreneurs.

Stage of Corporate Development

Stages of corporate development can be also arbitrarily divided into four general areas as depicted in figure 6.2. The seed or start-up stage is the initial stage of corporate development. In this circumstance, the company has a concept or product under development but is probably not fully operational. It is often in existence less than 18 months as a corporate entity.

In the early stage, the company may have a product or service in preclinical testing. It is unlikely that the company will have advanced to either the development or capitalization stage in which actual testing in humans has been established. It is also not likely to be generating revenues, although strategic partnerships with more developed companies may be providing financial support that does not entail partial ownership in the company but does contribute financially to the company's cash position. Although usually in business less than three years, depending on financing strategy, many such companies may languish for extensive periods of time in this stage.

Figure 6.2 Stages of Company Development

Seed/Start-Up Stage

- The initial stage. The company has a concept or product under development, but is probably not fully operational. Usually in existence less than 18 months.

Early Stage

- The company has a product or service in preclinical testing. May or may not be generating revenues based on strategic partnerships. Usually in businesss less than three years.

Expansion Stage

- Later stage clinical trials. The company demonstrates significant potential with promising trial(s), and has stable financing Usually in business more than three years.

Later Stage

- Nearing launch, partnering of new drug with other trials coming up the pipeline of development. Company has established investors, a public market, strategic partnerships. May includes pine-outs of product from existing private companies.

In the expansion stage, the company is often in clinical trials and moving toward definitive abilities to bring a product to approval and therefore to commercialization. Financing is often stable and well established, and the management team is usually mature and experienced and able to marshal the company through such development.

Later-stage companies are often nearing launch or have launched their product or products in the commercial markets and often have a pipeline of new development behind the established or lead product. Investors are professional and have significant funds available. The company may or may not have a public market presence and may have well-defined strategic partnerships with larger companies. This stage may also include products from existing private or public companies with a much larger portfolio of offerings that have been sold to a management team or investors to fill a stand-alone developing company.

Funding Options at Each Stage

It is critically important for the stage of capital to be matched to the stage of the company life cycle. This is further depicted in figure 6.3. Angel investment capital has primarily been designed for the start-up, preclinical, and early stages of clinical development of a seed or early-stage company. Angel investment by definition is noninstitutional private money invested in companies either by

Figure 6.3 Stages of Company and Correlating Capital Sources

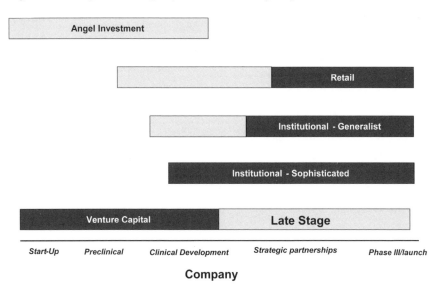

high net worth individuals or consortia of high net worth individuals. Although some companies have attempted to use angel capital through the later stages of development, this can pose significant problems. Given that the capital needed to bring a medical-device company to maturity may extend into the hundreds of millions of dollars, and pharmacological solutions or convergence technologies involving biological or chemical entities regulated through a drug rather than device method may run close to a billion dollars, angel investment clearly will not have the sustainable sources of funds to bring a company through to maturity. Although it may be appropriate for less capital-intensive, single-product development through the late clinical stage, angel investment can frequently jump-start a company but also can undermine a company through inadequate capitalization should the company require greater support to prove its value and therefore develop liquidity for investors. Therefore, angel investment is traditionally limited to the earlier stage, both of corporate and clinical development.

Venture capital is an institutional supply of money that may be embedded in very large funds with deep pockets. Venture capital, however, may also involve smaller funds that seek to return capital to institutional investors through emphasis on the early stage. Therefore, depending on the size of the fund and the expertise of the investors associated, venture capital may run the route from the start-up through the clinically mature company and increasingly may be seen investing in public companies of a smaller stature and nature that require long-term and dedicated investment to either reposition or relaunch product lines or corporate strategies.

Public invested capital is usually relegated to the late stage of clinical development. It is very difficult for a medical-device company to become a public entity offered to the general investing retail and institutional public until it is either at a late stage of clinical development with a highly innovative and disruptive category 1 platform or generating significant revenues based on either a category 1 or category 2 innovation. Category 3 innovations as stand-alone single-product companies tend not to be able to mount a public invested capital base unless they are part of a significantly larger and more diversified product portfolio or platform of development.

The growth drivers for life-science funding are primarily driven by perceived adoption cycles. Although the risks of the separate categories of development were outlined in the first section of this chapter, a review of the diligence criteria is helpful to the inventor or would-be entrepreneur to define clearly the criteria by which any idea or business plan will be judged. The following list is not complete, as each circumstance drives specific and individualized diligence efforts by investors; certain basic principles, however, need to be followed.

Due Diligence Issues

For the development of an idea into an investable proposition and, therefore, one that will be capitalized through its proper development, it is critical to understand the method by which new medical devices are evaluated by the investment community. The previously mentioned categories can be utilized to assess the risk of several critical aspects of diligence done by investors or strategic acquirers of a new technology. The criteria by which these categories are judged include the clinical and scientific principle on which the device is based, the market size and unmet need, reimbursement hurdles, regulatory hurdles, the quality of the intellectual property, development time, manufacturability, and impediments to sales into the adopting clinical community. Inevitably, category 1 technologies are higher risk in all of these categories than are those characterized by category 2 and category 3 definitions. These issues are summarized in figure 6.4.

The process includes but is not limited to the following:

- Technology and products.
- Comparison to current existing therapies.
- Proprietary defensible conditions (i.e., intellectual property).
- Scientific review.
- Regulatory challenges and expectations.
- Manufacturability and cost of goods.
- Management capability, experience, and integrity.

The first step in identifying whether your product can be a serious and credible entry into the marketplace rests with the technology base itself. The technology must have a credible clinical application in which an unmet need is clearly present. It may be incremental, additive, or disruptive; that is, category 3, 2, or 1. Although engineering solutions can be arrived at in the production or design of a new medical device, these solutions often are severely limited by a misunderstanding of the clinical scenario at which they are directed. Invention in search of an application or market leads either to increasing cost in our healthcare system without the benefit

Figure 6.4 Diligence Issue, Risk, and Category of Technology

Criteria	Category I	Category II	Category III
Clinical / Scientific Principle	High Risk	Medium Risk	Low Risk
Market Size / Unmet Need	Variable	Variable	Variable
Adoption Hurdles/ Reimbursement	High Risk	Medium Risk	Low Risk
Regulatory Pathways	High Risk	Medium Risk - High Risk	Variable
IP Landscape	Variable	Variable	Variable
Development Time	Long	Long	Variable
Manufacturability	Medium Risk - High Risk	Medium Risk - High Risk	Variable
Sales Impediments (as stand alone)	LARGE	LARGE	LARGE

of improved quality or safety, or it leads to investment failure either financially or ethically with regard to promotion of an inappropriately supported device.

Products need to address a real clinical need. In addition, drivers of adoption are multiple and varied and need to be considered alongside the immediate clinical question:

- Acceptance of gold standard therapies and clinical community view as to their effectiveness.
- Epidemiology of target population including projected growth of the clinical problem or the population itself.
- Opinion leader commitments and biases.
- Patient advocacy forces.
- New competitive development.
- Reimbursement and distribution channels.
- Historical failures and successes.

Intellectual property is the core competitive issue in most device-based solutions. Patent filings with regard to earliest proof of concept, date of provisional filings, date of final filing, breadth of claims, and type of patent (design, materials, manufacturing, use, method, etc.) are all critical in an area in which intellectual property rights will allow market dominance. Clear delineation of academic parent institution rights or prenegotiated licensing arrangements, early filings with the patent office, and thorough notebook validation of times of concept and date of invention are cornerstones of protection in an increasingly litigious space.

Current competitive or accepted therapies need to be compared to any proposed innovation using randomized studies or meta-analyses when feasible. As much of medicine is still not evidence based, the literature may reflect long-standing clinical assumptions rather than demonstrated effectiveness. Adoption is driven by numerous factors, including but not limited to the therapeutic window for existing and new approaches, ease of use, learning curve, quality of life, discomfort level, required ancillary services, and the specialty controlling the patient flow. The due diligence process for any investor will examine the data generated to date by the founding scientist, clinician, company, or early investors. These will need to demonstrate logical mechanical, physiological, and engineering support for the concept that may be derived from several sources, including computer modeling, prototype development with in vitro testing, early animal validation, and later-stage clinical trials.

Determination of the class of device is critical to the time to market launch. The regulatory classification is critical given the length of time and complexity for different classes of devices to reach approval, thus driving valuation assessment. By the time the medical device has reached the maturity to attract outside investors, experienced business development personnel assume management of the project. Inventors, scientists, and clinicians responsible for the original development of the device or technology and question often have been relegated to the role of either chief scientific officer, director of research and development, or head of a scientific advisory board. The structure of companies even at an early stage will therefore involve people well schooled and experienced in the process of fund-raising, human resource management, overall company vision, engineering, and the core, driving clinical or scientific competence that initiated the company in the beginning. Therefore, a long track record should be available for all the involved personnel, and this must be examined to determine the capability for execution, work ethic, behavioral code, management and scientific integrity, and previous successes and failures of the assembled team. Direct meetings, review of previous accomplishments, and interviews can accomplish this diligence with both identified and unidentified referees for the individuals in question.

New products must be physician and patient enabling to merit adoption; that is, they must fit an unmet need. This can take the form of increasing capability of a physician or medical center for complex interventions in therapies that lower the skill level because of the innovation's attributes, improvement of outcomes, increasing access for patients, and addressing problems heretofore untreated. Similarly, for medical centers to adopt a physician- or patient-enabling product, the product may be considered attractive if it increases market share because of innovation, increases throughput for diagnostic and therapeutic processes, reduces the per-procedure cost, and improves patient safety and other clinical outcomes. Finally, for strategic partners to invest or codevelop a technology, the presence of state-of-the-art materials, new therapies, synergies, and the ability for the partner to develop new platforms must all be attractive.

Liquidity and Exits as Drivers of Investment

Once the diligence process is understood, it is more easily tied to the chain of funding; that is, tied to the type and stage of investors appropriate to the company stage, who in turn are driven by the need to return their invested dollars at a multiple either to themselves or to the people for whom they are investing. The chain of funding ultimately has many sources as well as many drivers and goals. Many physicians think of policy makers as sources of funding for scientific development, much as businesspeople think of various sources of capital as funding for business and development. Each of these sources of funding has an end result they are attempting to accomplish. For instance, policy makers and sources of scientific grants such as the National Institutes of Health, National Science Foundation, and NASA are driven by a desire to improve social and scientific programs by addressing unmet needs with economically sensible and technologically advanced solutions. Although the end result or exit is not a financial reward, these sources of funding view the end result of scientific insight and disseminated knowledge as the exit or the goal of their grant making. Similarly, institutions such as universities, medical centers, and consortia of multidisciplinary scientists seek as their drivers institutional revenues and grants to fuel intellectual as well as institutional passion for the development of chosen fields of study. The exits for these groups include institutional revenues and recognition, as well as the potential for departmental and individual clinician scientist return.

At a later stage of technology funding, investors ranging from private angel investors to public market institutional investors seek opportunities by which to grow the capital that they either possess individually or have been entrusted by consortia of financial sources. In this setting, the exit driver is a return of the investment that can be accomplished through several mechanisms. These drivers of investment at both the public and private level are depicted in figure 6.5.

We will discuss two primary exit modalities: the sale of a company to a larger company or to another group of investors and the emergence of the company into the public markets with the ability for the shares of the company to trade openly among public investors. Each of the categories that have served as the basis for the discussion so far can also be viewed as having significant implications for the way a company is valued and the means by which it can exit. Although it is axiomatic that it is very difficult for small companies without significant development to be attractive to institutional investors in the public markets as there are certain hurdles that must be met before an initial public offering can be contemplated and successful, there is no restriction whatsoever as to the stage of a company at the time of its sale. Thus, category 1, 2, and 3 companies may find themselves sought after by larger acquiring companies for different reasons.

Category 3 companies that are often single-product-focused companies with incremental improvement are able to enter the public markets only if the technology is approaching such a large clinical and economic opportunity that revenues are being generated with great certainty and at a high level. This is rare. For the most part, this category of company is acquired by a larger company with a well-established sales force that in turn seeks to integrate the product offering into its platform to enhance revenues as well as enhance the productivity of individual salespeople approaching the clinician community.

Figure 6.5 Drivers of Funding in Private, Academic, and Public Sectors

Sources	Drivers
Surveillance/Vision **Policy Makers** • Institute of Medicine • National Institute of Health • National Science Foundation • NASA • IDN's/Academic Consortiums	• Unmet need • Mandated solutions • Quality/Cost
Vision/Execution **Technology Initiators** • Technology transfer • Institutional venture • Institutional Consortiums (e.g. CMIT) • Incubators • Entrepreneurs • Inventive clinicians/scientists	• Institutional revenues • Grant renewal • Individual returns
Execution/Portfolio Management **Traditional Partners** • Venture allies • Ongoing concerns • Limited/Strategic partners • Entrepreneurial network	• ROI • Business Leadership • Innovation

NASA: National Aeronautics and Space Administration
ROI: Return on Investment
CMIT: Center for Minimally Invasive Technologies
IDN: Integrated Delivery Networks

Category 2 companies in which development is expensive and adoption hurdles may be more profound are also likely drivers of acquisition activity. Given the relative regulatory and adoption risks associated in this category, however, it is likely that the company will need to be significantly more mature to demonstrate that it will be a long-term attractive investment for any acquiring company. Similarly, as these companies are much more expensive to take through development than are category 3 companies, the expectations for return on investment by the investors will be higher, the price to be paid will therefore be higher, and the proof of market acceptance and wisdom of investment will necessitate the company being more mature before it is embedded in a larger entity.

Category 1 companies are high risk/high return. Because the failure rates of trying to change medical and scientific paradigms are high and the rate of adoption of new technologies is low, it is the rare company in this category that returns invested capital. However, it is also this category of company that creates so-called home runs for the investor community when things do work right. The category 1 company that has demonstrated clinical success even in a preapproved mode, and certainly one that has achieved regulatory status that allows commercialization, may represent such a huge potential market shift that both public and private investors (e.g., the public company exit or the acquiring large company) may be willing to take a chance and provide an exit for the company in question. Examples of successful companies in this category include drug-eluting stent companies that have entered the public market and sold as public entities to even larger companies and diabetes-monitoring companies with radical new methods of improving glucose control that have been acquired at huge premiums to their last stated value.

As investors determine where to place their bets, the observations on return of capital usually create a mindset of portfolio management. Some will mix categories to hedge against the high-risk/high-reward events that dominate category 1 companies, others will emphasize only the high risk, whereas others will be inclined to emphasize a slow, steady approach to investing that supports incremental improvement but does not risk capital on highly speculative ventures. Finding the right investor philosophy is as much a process of network and advice as it is understanding the type of company that is being offered at the various stages of development.

ERRORS MADE IN COMPANY DEVELOPMENT

Now let us look at classic entrepreneurial mistakes. These mistakes emanate from clinical and scientific supposition to financing strategy errors. All can be damaging, sometimes fatal mistakes.

From a clinical or development perspective, understanding the diligence process can help avoid the following red flags:

- Technology in search of an indication, rather than an attempt to fill an unmet clinical need.
- The proposed intervention driven by an unexplained phenomenon (i.e., those engineering technologies that appear to have a clinical effect, the cause of which is not fully understood).
- The diagnostic in search of a therapeutic (e.g., an ability to diagnose a genetic trait that is not understood with regard to either its prognosis or the need to develop or apply a specific clinical therapy).
- The improvement that requires salesmanship to prove value (i.e., the platform that flies in the face of current clinical practice without a rational plan for developing data to displace the gold standard).

Similarly, financing errors that can be fatal to a business plan include:

- A lack of understanding of the milestones that will create value in a company and not linking them to expected rounds of financing; a lack of honest self-appraisal of a company's technology and commercial worth at any given time in the investment cycle.

- An investment management approach that overspends or undercapitalizes, thus preventing an opportunistic exit or the preservation of an investment position while value is accruing. The return on investment sought and the tolerance for risk balanced against potential gain is an independent portfolio management decision, but a consistent philosophy should be adhered to.
- Unreasonable valuation expectations. A better return on investment is provided by giving up a larger piece of the company in exchange for having sufficient capital to drive high exit returns. Holding onto greater equity share while preventing the company from having sufficient funds to grow and develop is deleterious to investors and management in the long run.
- Lack of a clear use of proceeds for any projected investment round:

  - Unattainable milestones.
  - Poorly focused effort.
  - Inadequate personnel to achieve goals.

- Not being open in any plan to changes in the business model or the technology platform.
- Lack of realism about adoption rate or regulatory hurdles to overcome.

CONCLUSION

Medical-device development is driven by numerous factors: entrepreneurial zeal, clinical insight, investor desire for significant returns, government policies that reflect unmet needs, and technology opportunities. It is a process unlike many other commercial exercises, in which the marriage of ethical, clinically driven, data-seeking behavior is closely monitored by government agencies and in which adoption is unofficially but completely driven by patients and physicians whose complex needs cannot be fully legislated. Capitalization of these companies, which are predicated on expensive and often difficult-to-prove value propositions, is a critical but frequently underemphasized ingredient for commercial success. As the process of invention, development, regulatory approval, and widespread dissemination by commercial means is the process that reduces good and useful ideas to the bedside, it is imperative for the clinician inventor, healthcare executive, and patient advocate, among others, to be cognizant of the dynamics that drive ideas into the market.

Key Concepts

- Look for the technology that reflects physiological understanding and a therapeutic approach that is consistent with acceptable standards of medical practice.

- Continually review stage and breadth of company offerings as you plan your investment and exit-management strategy.
- Build the company's resources (technology, management, board of directors, strategy), continually reassessing progress within the company and alignment to the clinical and financial needs of the targeted market.
- Never forget that financing strategy is critical to a company's success; technology and management are the engines for great investor returns, but financing provides the fuel.

FURTHER READING

Blowers, Stephen C., Peter H. Griffith, and Thomas L. Milan. 1999. *The Ernst and Young LLP Guide to the IPO Value Journey.* New York: Wiley.

Gertler, Jonathan, and James Garvey. 2001. "From Idea to Product: Financing and Regulatory Issues in Product Development." In *Surgical Research,* ed. Wiley W. Souba and Douglas W. Wilmore, 1405–14. San Diego: Academic Press.

Higgins, Robert C. 2004. *Analysis for Financial Management.* New York: McGraw-Hill.

Lajoux, Alexandra Reed. 1998. *The Art of M&A Integration: A Guide to Resources, Processes, and Responsibilities.* New York: McGraw-Hill.

Moore, Geoffrey A. 1995. *Inside the Tornado: Marketing Strategies from Silicon Valley's Cutting Edge.* New York: HarperCollins.

APPENDIX 1: GLOSSARY

- **Angel investment:** High net worth individual investors.
- **Dilution:** Equity-reducing investment.
- **Exits:** Liquidity events either by merger/acquisition/public offering.
- **IP:** Intellectual property.
- **IPO:** Initial public offering.
- **Nondilutive financing:** Non-equity-affecting inflow of funds.
- **Private equity:** Late-stage, usually growth capital/leveraged-buyout investors.
- **Public equity:** Public company investment.
- **Strategic partnership:** Marketing, development, and financing relationship with a larger company.
- **Valuation:**

  - Premoney: Value of company before investment dollars.
  - Postmoney: Value of company including new investment.

- **Venture capital:** Professional, private investors.

CHAPTER 7

Improving Outcomes and Reimbursement: Outpatient Management of Pediatric Diabetes and the Implications for Chronic Illness

Karen Rubin, Jayne Oliva, and Debi Croes

Delivering care to youth with diabetes in an outpatient setting promotes prevention and self-management and generally results in improved outcomes and fewer complications and hospitalizations. Connecticut Children's Medical Center (CCMC), like institutions nationwide, however, found that delivering quality outpatient care to children was simply not profitable. In fact, if near-term profitability was the organization's sole goal, children would be managed as inpatients where care was more favorably reimbursed.

What a vexing and at times heartbreaking medical conundrum for providers and patients alike, given the alarming escalation of diabetes in the United States and the high cost of acute care. Since the early 1990s, the number of people in the United States with diagnosed diabetes has more than doubled, and an estimated 175,000 people aged 20 years or younger have diabetes. One in three U.S. children born in 2000 could develop diabetes during their lifetime.[1] Studies prove that dollars invested wisely in prevention can pay big dividends in health and cost savings. The estimated annual cost for ongoing outpatient care of the child with diabetes is $2,021, whereas a single hospitalization averages $5,915.[2] Despite this and other similar studies, most insurers are far more inclined to cover the cost of complications but skimp on the prevention.

Unwilling to deliver anything less than the best care from the most appropriate provider and determined to more closely involve patients and their families, CCMC set out to challenge the status quo. Staff embarked on a mission to make a case to payers for a different reimbursement structure by developing an outpatient model that demonstrated cost-effective care delivery and improved outcomes. Additionally, in light of burgeoning costs for chronic illness nationwide, the authors raise what we believe is a compelling case for applying the lessons learned in managing and recouping costs for diabetes to other chronic illnesses as well.

This chapter outlines the process CCMC used for converting childhood diabetes coverage from an unprofitable fee-for-service (FFS) structure to a model that addresses, at a more favorable reimbursement rate, the chronic, continuous requirements for youth with this debilitating chronic illness.

CCMC'S INITIAL OUTPATIENT MODEL

Motivated by the goal of doing right by its youngsters with diabetes, CCMC set out to build an outpatient pediatric diabetes program that:

- Improved care quality and patient outcomes.
- Empowered patients and families for enhanced self-management and compliance.
- Reconfigured staff performance expectations to provide the right care at the right time.
- Delivered profitable reimbursement.

CCMC's approach to care capitalized on findings from the 1993 diabetes control and complications trial (DCCT), embraced by the medical community as the gold standard for treating youth with type 1 diabetes mellitus (T1DM).[3] This trial showed that intensive insulin regimens for adolescents and adults dramatically reduced A1C levels—a marker of improved metabolic control—which in turn slowed the progression of microvascular complications. Hailing the value of a multidisciplinary team, the trial proved that intense care, together with focused consultation, educational services, and family involvement, could reduce complications and dramatically improve patients' quality of life.

Children Are Unique

Unlike most adults, children with newly diagnosed T1DM (and some with type 2 diabetes) require immediate initiation of insulin treatment. Additionally, youngsters and their families need intense individualized instruction in diabetes management skills. After about three months, patients are generally medically stable and families sufficiently comfortable and competent to handle the routine associated with daily diabetes management.

Nationwide, approximately 25 percent of children with newly diagnosed diabetes present with ketoacidosis and require stabilization in the hospital, often in an intensive care unit. The remaining 75 percent of newly diagnosed children are medically stable enough to be safely managed in an ambulatory care setting, provided the diabetes care team has the resources it needs to provide intense outpatient management.[4]

A Phalanx of Support at CCMC

Connecticut Children's Medical Center, combining the pediatric services from three separate institutions, opened its doors in a brand-new building in 1996.

The only freestanding independent hospital in Connecticut that exclusively serves children, it is also the home of the University of Connecticut School of Medicine Department of Pediatrics and its pediatric residency program. Outpatient services include a primary care practice that serves nearly 15,000 children from the greater Hartford area and a wide array of pediatric specialties.

The endocrinology practice at CCMC had the resources it needed to deliver high-quality outpatient multidisciplinary care. Team based and focused, CCMC's intense proactive and multilayered approach helped shorten or prevent the inpatient stay for hospitalized youths and shifted care to the ambulatory setting as soon as patients were medically stable.

Patients benefited from a team of specialists that included endocrinologists, advanced practice registered nurses (APRNs), registered nurses (RNs), nurse/nutrition educators, registered dietitians (RDs), psychological support specialists, and medical assistants. Additionally, all nonphysician team members were certified diabetes educators (CDEs).

Patient Management

Newly diagnosed patients received close medical supervision, delivered face-to-face or non-face-to-face, depending on the services required, as follows:

- Face-to-face visits included the initial comprehensive team assessment at diagnosis, laboratory confirmation of diabetes with glucose and A1C level, and four subsequent scheduled visits with team members. Postdiagnosis visits were necessary so the team could extend and reinforce the initial education in diabetes self-management skills and provide psychosocial support to the patient and family.
- Non-face-to-face care included initial phone contacts with the endocrinologist on call for daily insulin doses for three or more days, followed by at least weekly phone contact with the case manager preceding a two-week postdiagnosis visit with the team. Frequent phone contacts to adjust insulin dose, answer diabetes management questions, respond to acute metabolic changes, and assist with sick-day management represented most of the non-face-to-face care the team dispensed during the initial three months of treatment.

Meeting American Diabetes Association Guidelines

CCMC structured its ongoing care for established patients to meet American Diabetes Association guidelines for pediatric diabetes treatment:

- Comprehensive diabetes visits every three months with on-site, point-of-care A1C testing. These visits encompassed ongoing diabetes self-management education, nutrition counseling, and psychological support as needed. Psychosocial support helped address, among other things, the increased incidence of depression and eating disorders in adolescents and the additional stressors that the disease imposed on the family. Team members scheduled additional visits with patients who fared poorly, used continuous home glucose monitoring with a sensor, or switched from conventional insulin therapy to an intensive insulin regimen using multiple injections.

- Twenty-four-hour phone availability so the team could immediately address insulin dose adjustment, sick-day, and perioperative insulin management; hypoglycemia and early diabetic ketoacidosis (a life-threatening medical condition); insulin pump failures; and other emergencies as required.
- Coordinated team outreach to the staff of schools, day-care centers, and residential settings to enable them to better meet patient healthcare needs.

Insulin Pumps

An important part of the diabetes care the team delivered was pump therapy. The insulin pump is intensive treatment that offers youth with diabetes and their families greater lifestyle flexibility. Children on insulin pumps typically have more stable blood glucose levels with less hypoglycemia because the pump delivers a steadier dose of insulin matched more precisely to food. It was not surprising that many children with diabetes found the pump liberating, as did their parents.

Pump therapy was not without its pitfalls, however. Because the pump uses only short-acting insulin, there was an increased danger that users could develop diabetic ketoacidosis. Therefore, the team carefully screened all pump candidates and their families for motivation and skill readiness and then taught those who qualified how to manage any potential medical complications. The three-pronged process included:

1. Pump therapy option: The CCMC pediatric endocrinologists discussed pump therapy with each established patient as a possible option and provided a team-designed pump information packet.
2. Pump information/education session: Interested patients and their families attended an educational program to help them decide if they wanted, and were able, to pursue pump therapy.
3. Insulin pump initiation program: Candidates who qualified received:

   - The individual pump assessment visit.
   - Pump nutrition visit.
   - Practice pump start with saline.
   - Actual insulin pump start.
   - Daily non-face-to-face contact via phone, fax, or e-mail for up to one week.

- Follow-up visits at two and six weeks.
- A three-month visit with an endocrinologist.

The increasing sophistication and features of recent pumps led the CCMC team to incorporate patient and family attendance at an advanced pump class during the three-month insulin pump initiation period.

Service Glitches

As the diabetes program grew over the years to meet demand, CCMC identified several issues that affected service delivery:

- Provider resources were not clearly or consistently allocated to services in the best way possible to meet patient needs.
- The existing diabetes care delivery model placed conflicting demands on providers and staff, resulting in significant stress and inefficient operations.
- Although staff estimated volume growth for the service to be relatively slow (4 percent annually), new-onset diabetes patient referrals required sufficient resource allocation to manage an unpredictable but urgent need.
- Wait times on insulin pump starts for T1DM patients were longer than desirable, sometimes as much as a year.

A NEW WAY OF DOING BUSINESS

Delivered by competent and credentialed professionals—not all of whom were physicians—outpatient services included urgent and scheduled care, phone contacts, response to e-mails and faxes, diabetes and nutrition self-management counseling, and educational materials. Herein was the reimbursement hitch: Many of the diabetes-related services the team provided, crucial to better outcomes, fell into the payer-defined category of nonphysician or noncovered care. Patients continued to receive the finest treatment from a team of dedicated professionals, but the program itself was sinking financially. Either nonphysician providers delivered care that was not reimbursed or physicians stepped in; either way costs escalated. Initially, the resulting deficits were covered by hospital funding and/or indirectly through research dollars. CCMC could not continue to absorb these costs, however, posing a real threat to the sustainability of the pediatric diabetes program. Could CCMC make care delivery profitable in order for its program to be self-sustaining?

The answer was yes, but not without a lot of soul searching and elbow grease. With hard work and gritty determination, physicians and staff, with assistance from consultants, redesigned operations and staffing to meet patient needs more effectively and profitably, use provider resources efficiently, actively involve patients and families and caregivers to boost compliance, and track resource utilization and measure outcomes. Accomplishing these goals required creation of:

- An efficient, patient-focused service delivery model that reorganized existing services into business lines and allocated providers and resources effectively to maximize productivity.
- Physician and nonphysician provider capacity and commitment agreements to detail provider resource allocation to services, thus ensuring delivery of quality patient care by the most appropriate provider resource, allot provider clinical time, and delineate performance expectations.
- Financial and volume projections to identify associated costs and revenue.
- Outcomes and cost tracking by all multidisciplinary diabetes team members, to monitor the continuous care provided (both face-to-face and non-face-to-face), associated costs, and disease outcomes.

Three Business Lines

The first step in the process to reconfigure care delivery was to parse existing services for all of its patients into three distinct business lines:

- Urgent new-onset diabetes care.
- Established care of diabetes patients.
- Insulin pump initiation.

Working as a team, and aided by consultants, staff then undertook the at-times arduous task of meticulously documenting the type of service and patient visit that took place within each business component.

As staff documented the services currently provided, discussions also centered on the team's opinion as to what was, in truth, the very best way to manage patient care in each of the three areas, without forgetting how visit predictability figured into the equation. For example, new patients presenting with diabetes required that staff complete an immediate overall patient evaluation, develop a care plan, educate patients and families, and organize supporting services. The team had no control over when new patient referrals would arrive at the door. But they knew they had to see these T1DM patients immediately, and it required an average of two days of on-site evaluation and care plan development to do so.

Naming Names

After describing actual and desired services within each business line, the next step in the process was to determine which team member delivered the actual care. Was it the physician, registered nurse, or dietitian? It was critical that CCMC clearly understand everyone's role in order to ensure correct staffing, bill for its services, and collect payment.

In the case of the new, emergent T1DM patient, team-based care was the preferred approach. Rather than a physician taking a lead on the team, however, an APRN organized and coordinated team-based care with on-call physician oversight. This arrangement brought a whole new approach to managing and delivering care in this business line that, although treating a relatively small number of patients, was both urgent and unpredictable. Now instead of interrupting a physician from a very busy schedule, which also tended to upend the equilibrium in the clinic, the APRN managed the emergent patients with a team of caregivers that included a certified diabetes educator, social worker, and nutritionist, seeking physician guidance only when necessary.

The same APRN-led configuration applied to insulin pump initiation. To best deliver this service, the APRN assembled a team that included a certified diabetes educator, social worker, dietitian, and nurse—no physician needed. And in terms of predictability, all insulin pump visits could be scheduled.

These team assignments left the physicians more uninterrupted time for care oversight and management of the scheduled medical visits for established patients, which helped streamline clinic operations and improve service predictability for patients.

The clinical pathways for each business line, with team assignments, are delineated in figures 7.1, 7.2, and 7.3.

Capacity and Commitment Agreements

Staff now had a comprehensive, written, and consistent understanding of what service was delivered and by whom. Now it was time to commit more formally to performance expectations, assign clinical roles, and allot provider time for every member of the team.

The diabetes team at CCMC started by examining the current and future service and staffing agreements, and determining how many physicians, nurses, registered dietitians or others it took to deliver on those care delivery promises. For example, the team committed to assigning each patient a designated primary physician, as well as a CDE for both visits and phone support. To tackle the challenge of responsiveness to fax and telephone referrals from community physicians, the team reassigned an APRN to manage initial feedback.

Physician Buy-In

Physicians at the endocrinology practice agreed to adhere to the faculty practice plan's norm of allocating 70 percent of their time to clinical activity and 30 percent to teaching, research, and administration. They then helped create, and thus support, productivity expectations during diabetes clinic time (of two visits per hour) and agreed that a standard ambulatory session would be three-and-a-half to four hours long. Operational redesign increased access—each endocrinologist had 30 percent more available slots—and an additional physician was added to manage increased volume.

Figure 7.1 New-onset Care: Clinical Care Pathway

Service	Team Provider(s)
• History/physical/assessment • Confirmation of diagnosis with glucose, A1c • initiation of insulin therapy ⇩	APRN, MD
• Diabetes self-management education / survival skills, training • Psychosocial assessment of patient/family ⇩	APRN, RN, RD, MHS
• Daily phone contact for insulin dose adjustment followed by phone contact as needed ⇩	MD, CM
• Phone contact as needed ⇩	CM, MD
• 2-week visit – extension of initial education ⇩	APRN RD, MHS as needed
• 6-week visit – extension of initial education ⇩	APRN RD, MHS as needed
• 12-week visit – extension of initial education ⇩	APRN RD, MHS as needed

• All required point of care lab testing:
  ○ glucose
  ○ ketones
  ○ A1c (at baseline and at 3 months)
⇩
	MA

• Download of glucose meters at each visit ⇩	MA
• Database entry	DM

Key:

MA: Medical Assistant

RD: Registered dietician

APRN: Advanced practice registered nurse

RN: Registered nurse

MHS: Mental health specialist (i.e., Social Worker)

CM: Case manager (APRN, RD, or RN)

DM: Database Manager

On the nonphysician side, CCMC defined specific roles and the expected time required to complete each task. APRNs, for example, were responsible for new T1DM patients, pump starts, and initial management of new referral calls. The APRNs had no regularly scheduled visit sessions, but they could be assigned other clinical tasks, such as when they were not tied up with urgent new patients.

The team completed the same analysis for every service in each of the business lines within diabetes care. CDEs agreed to reconfigure their responsibilities to spend half their time responding to telephone calls and half their time conducting on-site patient education. Registered dietitians expanded their duties so they had

Figure 7.2 Established Care: Clinical Care Pathway

Service	Team Provider(s)	Key:
• Comprehensive diabetes visits every 3 months ⬇	MD – 3 visits/year RD – 1 visit/yr	**MA:** Medical Assistant
• Additional diabetes visits with one or more team members as needed ⬇	MD, APRN, RD, MHS	**RD:** Registered dietician
• At each visit, all required point of care lab testing: o Glucose o Ketones o A1c (at baseline and at 3 months) ⬇	MA	**APRN:** Advanced practice registered nurse
• At each visit, download of glucose meter /teaching of new meter as needed ⬇	MA	**RN:** Registered nurse
24 hour phone availability for: • Insulin dose adjustment • Sick day management • Insulin pump malfunction • Perioperative management • Pharmacy • Management of diabetic emergencies; severe hypoglycemia/diabetic ketoacidocis (DKA) ⬇	MD, APRN, RD, RN	**MHS:** Mental health specialist **CM:** Case manager (APRN, RD, or RN)
• education/support to staff at schools, day care center, residential settings ⬇	APRN, RD, RN	**DM:** Database Manager
• letters for travel, schools, field trips ⬇	DM	
• crisis management including involvement of Department of Child and Family Services (DCF) as needed ⬇	MD, APRN, RN, RD, CDE, MHS	
• database entry	DM	

time to see scheduled diabetes and endocrine patients, coordinate lipid disorder patients, and help with scheduled insulin pump starts. Again, this task assessment was critical when the team moved forward to negotiate reimbursement for care delivered by staff other than physicians.

Financial and Volume Projections

Armed with a clear understanding of how to deliver care in each business line, financial and volume projections were developed to identify associated costs and revenues and to be certain CCMC had enough staff to meet current and future demand.

Figure 7.3 Insulin Pump Initiation: Clinical Care Pathway

Service	Team Provider(s)
Individual Pump assessment Interview ⬇	APRN
Pump Nutrition Visit if needed ⬇	RD
Pump Saline Start (average 4 hours) ⬇	APRN
Insulin Pump Start (average 6 hours) ⬇	APRN
Non face-to-face contact (phone/fax) for 3-6 days post insulin pump start followed by contact as needed ⬇	APRN/MD
2 week follow up visit post insulin pump start, glucose meter & pump download ⬇	APRN/MA
6 week follow up visit post insulin pump start, glucose meter & pump download ⬇	APRN/MA
Advanced pump class (between 8-12 wks post insulin pump start) ⬇	Given by certified insulin pump trainer from pump company with oversight of program content/ coordination by APRN
12 week visit	MD
Meter & pump download	MA
All required point-of-care lab testing: glucose ketones A1c ⬇	MA
Database entry	DM

Key:

MA: Medical Assistant

RD: Registered dietician

APRN: Advanced practice registered nurse

RN: Registered nurse

MHS: Mental health specialist (i.e. SW)

CM: Case manager (APRN, RD, or RN)

DM: Database Manager

An Operational Turnaround

The reconfigured operational model, developed with and welcomed by the endocrinology physicians and staff, significantly improved practice operations, specifically:

- Physicians' weekly schedules were more predictable and their on-call duties more efficiently configured.
- Routine scheduling decisions were managed by support staff because appointment availability was built into normal weekly schedules rather

than determined by individual physicians on a case-by-case basis, as was previously done.

- Assigning T1DM patient referrals to APRNs utilized a more cost-efficient provider resource for a significant portion of an unpredictable but urgent patient care service, yet retained care oversight by the on-call physician.
- Separation of ambulatory referral management from other traditional on-call duties improved the ability of on-call physicians to respond to true urgencies and inpatient needs.
- Assignment of designated physicians for all patients and availability of ancillary providers, particularly CDEs, improved patient service.
- Patient access and service improved, due to elimination of specialty clinics and opening of all sessions to all types of patients.
- Allocation of adequate and appropriate resources to insulin pump starts significantly reduced the excessive backlog, and growing demand eventually stabilized.

Improved Outcomes

Having accomplished the considerable challenge of retooling for operational efficiency, CCMC now had to demonstrate improvement in pediatric diabetes outcomes and assemble the data needed to approach payers with a persuasive argument for rethinking reimbursements, rewarding and compensating CCMC and its providers for the use of proven treatment protocols that resulted in improved outcomes.

The CCMC pediatric diabetes team built a clinical database to provide staff with immediate access to a variety of patient outcomes, including episodes of hypoglycemia, diabetic ketoacidosis, hospitalizations, emergency department visits, and A1C levels. Team members checked the database frequently to assess outcomes and continue to improve patient care.

At the core of data collection was a system to track *all* diabetes care provided by *all* team members for both patient visits and non-face-to-face contacts. The tracking system required team members to complete contact sheets, which were filed in the patient's medical record and entered into the database during the next medical visit. Meticulous record keeping allowed the team to accurately track staff time for any patient encounter and then correlate time spent to outcome.

But getting everyone to be consistent about reporting took a fair amount of effort. It required constant monitoring and reinforcement about the importance of gathering the information. Indeed, once staff understood the patient benefits of having this data readily available for quality improvement purposes, they became more invested in the collection process.

This storehouse of data, compiled without the benefit of an electronic medical record, demonstrated sustained improvement of all outcomes over the prior five years in the context of steady increases in patient volume. Furthermore, analysis of trends in metabolic control in various patient subsets had resulted in patient, family-, and friend-centered improvement initiatives for both adolescents and minorities. For instance, to address the disparities in metabolic control observed in adolescents and Medicaid T1DM patients, CCMC undertook two performance improvement initiatives: First, the team's psychological support specialist provided coping skills training for adolescents; second, all diabetes team members enhanced their outreach to Medicaid patients and families for implementation of more intensive insulin regimens and insulin pump therapy. Figures 7.4, 7.5, and 7.6 demonstrate the improvement achieved.

NEGOTIATING A GLOBAL RATE

CCMC wanted a pay-for-performance, global rate model that appropriately reimbursed the team for the quality care it provided. The database proved crucial in that quest for two reasons. In capturing outcomes, it was a highly effective tool for continuous quality improvement. And it also provided payers with a snapshot of their covered patients, showing low A1C levels coupled with low rates of emergency department visits and hospitalizations. Compared to the national average of 13 hospitalizations and 29 emergency department visits of diabetic children per 100 person-years,[5] the CCMC averaged 2.3 and 15, respectively, in 2006.

Referencing its business lines and services, CCMC could explain the continuous care children with diabetes required. And the team could back up the benefits of

Figure 7.4 Trends in Metabolic Control in Adolescents with T1DM

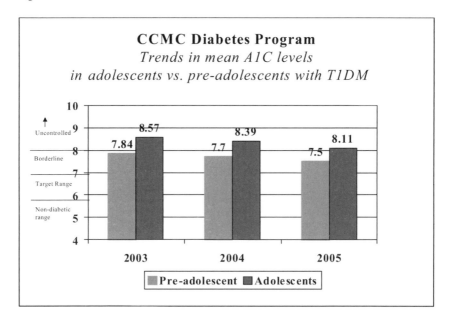

Figure 7.5 Trends in Metabolic Control in Medicaid Patients with T1DM

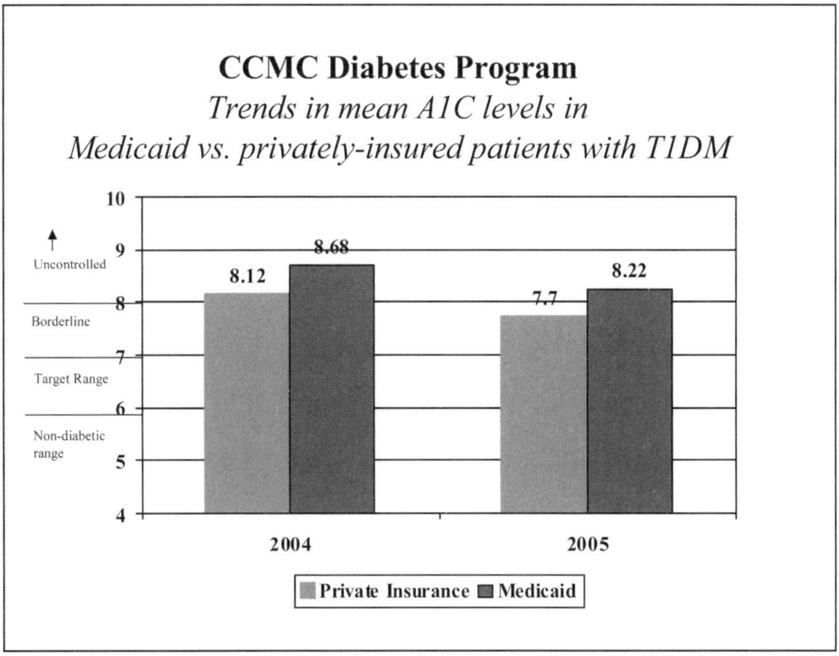

CCMC Diabetes Program
Trends in mean A1C levels in
Medicaid vs. privately-insured patients with T1DM

8.68

8.12

8.22

7.7

Uncontrolled

Borderline

Target Range

Non-diabetic range

2004   2005

■ Private Insurance ■ Medicaid

such care with demonstrated outcome improvements. The result? Payers were open to replacing the fee-for-service structure with a viable alternative: a global rate model that would be a better fit for the continuous care requirements of youth with diabetes.

Pitching the Argument

Armed with a model of care that demonstrated improved outcomes for pediatric diabetes patients, the CCMC team was ready to take its case for a global rate structure to Connecticut's major insurers. Using contacts it made in the Connecticut State Legislature, CCMC gained access to insurance industry connections and an attorney specializing in managed care lobbying. Through these efforts, CCMC held a statewide forum to educate the major payers about pediatric diabetes care and the proposed global rate reimbursement model. CCMC's presentation gave all payers baseline information about the impact of pediatric diabetes and laid the groundwork for the individual contract negotiations that followed.

Citing its clinical database, CCMC was able to show how intensive diabetes management on an outpatient basis would decrease hospitalization rates and emergency department visits. Additionally, by referencing the growing trend in outpatient volume for patients with T1DM, the team provided the rationale for a

Figure 7.6 Trends in Metabolic Control for Pump Therapy Patients

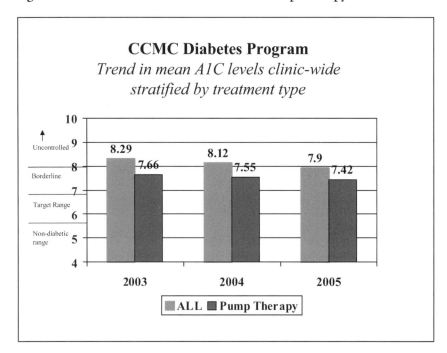

shift in care from inpatient to an ambulatory setting for the majority of new-onset patients. This rationale was the first step in making a case for a global rate reimbursement model that would reallocate dollars accordingly.

Negotiating the Contract

The CCMC team developed specific global rate dollar amounts for each of the three business lines, based on the true cost of delivering multidisciplinary care and demonstrating the cost savings for each insurer's enrolled patients. CCMC then negotiated the actual global rate for each business line with individual payers, settling on an amount that was proprietary between each payer and CCMC. During annual contract negotiations, the intention is for CCMC to share outcome data with insurers and request that rates be adjusted accordingly.

The CCMC team developed a process for negotiations that helped keep their eyes on the desired end result:

- Understood their go and no-go rate. CCMC approached the process with patience and flexibility, but the team had a specific goal in mind when it sat down to bargain. They aimed high in their initial rate request but allowed sufficient wiggle room to negotiate. They knew where they could be flexible with their counteroffers and where they had to stand firm to make the new reimbursement system work.

- Transacted with the power players. CCMC brought its decision makers to the negotiations and requested that each payer do the same. The nature of CCMC's unique provider-payer agreement demanded that only the key decision leaders should sit at the table in order to hammer out the details of the contract then and there.

- Focused on the right picture. The team kept discussions focused on the strategic reasons for a reimbursement change (e.g., cost savings and improved outcomes) rather than on the operational issues that could stand in the way of implementing a new rate structure. Once agreement was reached in principle to change the payment model, both sides worked to resolve the operational hurdles of implementing a new system.

A New Dynamic

Even as CCMC lobbied to change the reimbursement model, it sought to transform the dynamic among all parties in the process—providers, patients, and payers—by establishing a truly collaborative relationship. CCMC's multidisciplinary team approach to care provided the clinical, educational, and support services necessary to teach and empower patients and families to be more involved in—and responsible for—improving their health. By transitioning to a global rate, the team could continue to provide these services, project revenues more accurately, and improve program quality to further enhance patient care. The new reimbursement structure allowed CCMC to maintain and improve a cost-effective model of quality care, which in turn ensured fewer health problems for diabetes patients and decreased costs for payers.

Smoothing the Way

Payers responded positively to CCMC's proposal for a global reimbursement rate, but there were also some concerns. The insurers understood the strategic reasons and the logic for changing the payment process. The snags centered on the mechanisms required to implement the change. Specifically, the insurers felt that they could not easily manage global rate billing within their current systems.

To sidestep the barriers, CCMC worked out a five-step process to ensure a seamless interface with each insurer's current billing systems. First, recognizing that the diabetes care providers could easily revert to old habits, CCMC put internal safeguards in place to prevent team members from submitting fee-for-service bills for services covered under the global fee.

Second, although the diabetes program was under the auspices of the endocrinology service, a private practice division of CCMC's faculty practice plan, a hospital-based global rate program was preferable to a physician practice-based global rate program. The new model required an automated, recurring billing system that generated monthly bills, and the hospital had such a structure in place. This involved:

- Only the initial referral from the primary care provider.
- No co-payment.
- A global rate program that was an addendum to the annual hospital contract with the payer so that renegotiation of contract was unnecessary.

Third, the model, designed as a monthly rate for each covered patient in each of the three business lines (new onset, established care, and insulin pump start), simplified the following operational issues:

- It avoided need to prorate charges if a patient left the program.
- It was easy for patients to transition from one type of care to another (e.g., new onset patients moving to established care).
- It identified a dedicated staff person to verify and submit the monthly global bills.

Fourth, the hospital bill was unitized, or showed a recurring charge with start and end date versus a daily accounting of episodic visits. As a result, the patient does not need to reregister at each office visit. (For any services not covered under the global rate [e.g., lab, radiology], however, the patient does need to reregister, and bills are submitted.)

Fifth, Level II Healthcare Common Procedure Coding System (HCPCS) codes were the best fit for interfacing the global rate model with the insurers' current systems, specifically:

- New onset care: G-9001 (coordinated care fee, initial rate).
- Established care: G-9002 (coordinated care fee, maintenance rate).
- Insulin pump initiation: G-9003 (coordinated care fee, risk adjusted high, initial).

A Win-Win for All

CCMC has now successfully negotiated several global rate contracts, with enough improvement in the revenue stream to ensure the viability of its diabetes care program. Global rates proved to be a win-win for all concerned: for CCMC's patients and its bottom line and for payers. CCMC can continue to provide evidence-based care, which means a healthier life with fewer complications for youngsters with diabetes. And healthier patients mean significant reimbursement savings for insurers. On average, it costs more than $5,000 to hospitalize a patient with diabetes,[6] compared to an average cost of $1,500 per patient for new onset, established, and pump infusion phases of the CCMC diabetes care program.

Learning Curve

As with any new initiative, the work to change from established fee-for-service reimbursement to a global rate model was a learning exercise. CCMC gleaned several important lessons:

- Hold annual meetings with the insurers. Reviewing outcome data should be part of the agreement. A yearly reassessment binds both parties to track and report outcomes, reaffirms the program's success, and provides an opportunity to make any needed adjustments in the care or reimbursement model.
- Protect the global rate from deductibles, co-pays, or other allowances that could affect the revenue stream. Decision leaders on both sides should understand that a global fee is based on the cost of service delivery and is already efficient and streamlined.
- Set up revenue tracking systems to correlate to the clinical database.
- Recalculate the global fee on a regular basis. Costs and service delivery can change. Although it may not be necessary to renegotiate annually, there should be a clause in the contract that allows for a reevaluation at specified periods.

APPLYING LESSONS LEARNED: A PRIMER FOR RETHINKING CHRONIC CARE DELIVERY

CCMC succeeded where others had failed in creating a new model of care for diabetes, one of the most debilitating and chronic illnesses facing the United States. Clinicians redesigned service delivery, empowered patients, and convinced insurers to manage and pay for care in an entirely different fashion.

Can the lessons CCMC learned for improving profitability, productivity, patient access, care coordination, outcomes, and reimbursements—in the outpatient setting—resonate for other chronic illnesses as well? In truth, the care model, operational improvements, and reimbursement structure that CCMC undertook to create a profitable service, with outstanding patient outcomes, could be replicated in other settings. Specifically, the model is applicable for any chronic illness or disease that requires:

- Intensive face-to-face services delivered in an ambulatory setting.
- Non-face-to-face services for maintenance, support, or management of acute episodes.
- Services that could be delivered by either physician or nonphysician providers.

Chronic illnesses that meet these criteria include the care and treatment of cystic fibrosis, obesity, and early metabolic syndrome (prediabetes).

Here are five lessons learned at CCMC that could be applied in the chronic illness outpatient realm:

1. Develop categories of care. CCMC created three business lines—new onset, established, and insulin pump care—to describe its patient panel. Other organizations have sorted care into chronic, complex, and episodic treatment. Create the categories that work best for the type of patients served and the care delivered. Classifying care delivery is important because it provides the framework for assembling the right operational and staffing support by patient type to ensure high-quality care, a smooth patient encounter, and maximum provider productivity.

2. Determine who and when. For each category created, determine who delivers what, when, and for how long. Does the physician need to deliver the service, or can the APRN better manage the care? Is the visit scheduled or on an emergent basis? And is the patient treated within the hour or in the clinic for a two-day evaluation? Knowing the flow and approximate duration of the patient's visit is critical to this process. Have all the providers in the practice, from physicians to nutritionists, estimate what it takes to care for patients in each of the respective care categories.

3. Set performance expectations. Delineate and, if necessary, realign tasks for each category of care to be sure the right clinician delivers the right treatment at the right time. This information is crucial to understanding staffing and capacity requirements. Remember also to keep the physicians' time pure, so when doctors are with patients they provide care and treatment and do not get distracted by tasks that support staff could easily handle, such as finding the medical chart or chasing lab results.

4. Capture and analyze outcomes. Put data management systems in place to capture statistics that demonstrate improved outcomes. Readily accessible outcome data allow clinicians to continually monitor care quality and adjust care plans as needed for better results. And this is precisely the information that leadership takes to the table when it comes time to negotiate with insurers over reimbursement fees.

5. Lobby for a global rate. The traditional fee-for-service reimbursement structure may not be the best model for managing chronic illness. The very nature of these debilitating conditions requires preventive care before complications set in, regular and/or continuous attention, and oftentimes care delivery from staff other than physicians (that is, noncovered providers). Educate insurers about the nuances of care delivery for the chronic illness that are managed and then work together with decision makers to advance a more equitable reimbursement structure.

CONCLUSION: NO SHRINKING VIOLETS

Completely reorganizing and overhauling patient management is tough work, but the rewards are sweet for providers (improved care and revenue), patients (better health), and payers (decreased costs) alike. Organizations that challenge assumptions and aim high can succeed. CCMC believed in the quality of diabetes care it delivered. Even as other outpatient programs struggled and sank, CCMC persisted on its path to improved performance. When others said it could not be done, CCMC took on the insurance giants and won their support for an entirely different reimbursement system.

Sweeping change requires commitment to common ground and common goals, for the greater good. Who can quibble with improving care, relieving suffering, maintaining good health, and decreasing costs? Proving it, as CCMC was able to do in the outcome data it captured, brought payers on board to reward demonstrated performance. CCMC united providers, patients, and payers in a new patient-responsive dynamic to manage and pay for chronic diabetes care with a process that could shed better light on caring for chronic illness nationwide.

NOTES

1.   National Center for Chronic Disease Prevention and Health Promotion. 2006. "Diabetes: Disabling, Deadly, and on the Rise 2006." *Centers for Disease Control and Prevention*. Available at: http://www.cdc.gov/nccdphp/publications/aag/ddt.htm. Accessed July 30, 2007.

2.   Klingensmith, G. J., and H. F. Allen. 2001. "The Cost of Providing Care to the Pediatric Patient with Diabetes." *The Endocrinologist* 11 (1): 41–47.

3.   Diabetes Control and Complications Trail Research Group. 1993. "The Effect of Intensive Treatment of Diabetes on the Development and Progression of Long-Term Complications in Insulin-Dependent Diabetes Mellitus." *New England Journal of Medicine* 329: 977–86.

4.   Klingensmith and Allen, 41–47.

5.   Levine, B. S., B. J. Anderson, D. A. Butler, J. E. Antisdel, et al. 2001. "Predictors of Glycemic Control and Short-Term Adverse Outcomes in Youth with Type 1 Diabetes." *Journal of Pediatrics* 139 (2): 197–203.

6.   Klingensmith and Allen, 41–47.

CHAPTER 8

Healthcare as an Economic Engine

R. Donald McDaniel Jr., Anirban Basu,
David I. Kovel, and Ian Batstone

The purpose of this chapter is twofold: to describe the key components of the U.S. healthcare system in an economic context and to define the economic magnitude of the industry and its critical importance to the overall U.S. economy. It will provide an overview of the key economic units that participate in healthcare delivery and financing in the United States and how they are organized. Second, it will describe the interdependence of the various actors and provide an overview of the collective economic impact of the industry. This chapter will present the factors that lead people to refer to healthcare as an "economic engine of growth."

THE CHALLENGE AND THE OPPORTUNITY

But the very real problems with the health care system mask a simple fact: Without it the nation's labor market would be in a deep coma. Since 2001, 1.7 million new jobs have been added in the health care sector, which includes related industries such as pharmaceuticals and health insurance. Meanwhile, the number of private-sector jobs outside of health care is no higher than it was five years ago.[1]

Healthcare in the United States is a conundrum, and one's perspective of its virtues or pitfalls may depend solely on the lens through which one views it; a highly compensated practitioner, administrator, or therapist may be quite happy with their profession and industry, whereas a policy maker, employer, or consumer may be quite concerned about growing costs, sometimes substandard care, and general inconsistency in delivery of health services. The system is widely viewed as the best for specialty, tertiary, and quaternary care, yet it also is the only system in a developed country that does not provide health insurance to all its citizens. In fact, between 2000 and 2005, some 7 million Americans lost their health insurance coverage, according to the U.S. Census Bureau. At the end of 2005, Americans without health insurance totaled 47 million.

So it seems that the predominant problem with the current U.S. healthcare system is that there is too much spending and too little productive output. As a study by IBM, titled "Healthcare 2015: Win-Win or Lose-Lose?" states, the "U.S. spends 22% more than second-ranked Luxembourg ... and 2.4 times the OECD [Organization for Economic Cooperation and Development] average. Yet the World Health Organization (WHO) ranks it 37th in overall health system performance."[2] Specifically, the WHO ranking refers to measures used to indicate comparable health status performance and trends among different countries. Comparably, the OECD collects data on different aspects of the performance of health systems among its member countries, including data on life expectancy, mortality from specific diseases (e.g., cardiovascular diseases and cancer), external causes of death, infant mortality, infant birth weight, and dental health among children. The United States performs poorly in almost every indicator measured relative to the amount of spending on healthcare, which would lead one to believe that the investment in health services does not generate a commensurate return. The exploration of this discussion is beyond the scope of this chapter but is an important concept to garner: that the consumption of health services in the United States is not really value driven.

Fixing the paradox that is the U.S. healthcare system is not easy, however, principally because tinkering comes at a risk. A major reason that larger-scale reform attempts to date have not been effective is the concern about the one big potential unintended consequence: that somehow such reform could severely harm the healthcare economy, possibly the major industry contributor to the overall health of the U.S. economy.

The health industry in the United States contributes mightily to the overall health of its economy on many levels. On a direct basis, the health sector makes major contributions to U.S. income and employment. For example, the U.S. Bureau of Labor Statistics predicted that 16 percent of all new jobs created by 2012 will be in the health services arena and that until 2012, 10 of the 20 fastest growing occupations will be in a health services industry, including job growth of almost 60 percent in the home healthcare services industry.[3]

Further, because of the interconnectedness of the economy as a whole, continued growth in the healthcare sector creates an economic ripple effect; that is to say, a dollar of revenue in the healthcare industry creates something more than a dollar of activity in the community that surrounds various healthcare entities. In many smaller communities, for example, healthcare institutions (predominantly hospitals) are typically the largest employer. Interestingly enough, they are often the largest exporter to other nearby communities. Many hospital systems, particularly academic medical centers, expand with an outpatient center expansion strategy, branding freestanding health centers in proximate communities. Additionally, health institutions might simultaneously employ both the best and brightest among us as well as the least-educated workers, making it an exceptionally attractive industry for many constituents, including workforce development advocates and policy makers. For example, although hospitals engage a great many high-income physicians, nurses, technical staff, allied health professionals, and administrators, the modern hospital also requires health assistants and technicians, nursing support personnel, janitorial staff, and a bevy of clerical and lower-level administrative support resources. On any given day, even a suburban hospital in the most affluent area will simultaneously house an employee parking area with expensive cars and a series of bus stops that facilitate transportation for the lower-wage earners, often coming from geographically proximate urban areas.

From 1990, annual growth in healthcare and related spending of more than 9 percent has outstripped the overall economic growth of approximately 3.5 percent, meaning that in every budget year a larger portion of scarce resources are being applied to the health industry, at the expense of resource allocations to other industries. This has many impacts. Federal, state, and local governments are faced with an ever-increasing cost of healthcare in the face of modest revenue growth. Specifically, the Medicare and Medicaid programs are growing quite aggressively. During federal fiscal year 2005, the Medicare program generated benefit payments to participants of more than $330 billion, and the Medicaid program, a joint federal-state-funded initiative, generated federal benefit payments of more than $170 billion. All told in fiscal 2005, spending on healthcare initiatives constituted 20 percent of total federal spending.[4]

In the private sector, companies, especially those with fewer than 100 employees, are faced with tough decisions about how to deal with health insurance premium increases. Strategies include cutting other expenses, reducing wages, reducing or eliminating health and other benefits, and shifting increasing costs to employees in the form of larger health co-payments and deductibles. Regardless, all of these approaches may be problematic for employers, and such forced austerity in the face of potential growth opportunities could be recessionary. Additionally, rapidly rising healthcare costs and insurance premiums are generally thought to depress wage growth and overall employment, simultaneously retarding gross domestic product (GDP) growth and raising inflation. On the other hand, many view increased healthcare spending as at worst neutral and sometimes positive; one individual's medical spending is another's personal income.

Finally, there are many qualitative reasons why healthcare is important to communities beyond its economic impact. Leading healthcare organizations and a strong healthcare infrastructure enhance a community's attractiveness as a home, a place to locate a business, or as a place to retire. Healthcare is clearly one item on everyone's checklist when contemplating where to live. Further, a powerful healthcare presence in a community is important to businesses because of the industry's economic stability. Healthcare has often been referred to as recession proof because the volume of health services is not very dependent upon exogenous factors and patients who have acute health needs are not dissuaded during economic downturns.

The Industry

The healthcare industry is complex and unique among other U.S. industries in terms of its organization, the actors that shape the industry, the role that nonprofit entities play, and the seemingly disparate economic incentives in place. It employs a paradoxical mix of the latest in medical technology and the necessary human touch, corporate formalization and cottage-industry inefficiency, high quality and low quality, and sophistication and naïveté. As stated already, the industry is a major jobs creator and provides the economic anchor for many communities throughout the United States.

The actors in U.S. healthcare are numerous: providers (including hospitals, solo physicians and physician group practices, dental practices, nursing and residential care facilities, diagnostic, ancillary and other service providers), payers (including health insurers, employers, and government), policy makers and regulators, and consumers. Current estimates peg healthcare spending at 15 percent of GDP, which is the highest in the world. Healthcare's concentration of the U.S. economy is projected to grow to almost 20 percent by 2016.[5] In 2004, the healthcare industry provided 13.5 million jobs, making it the largest industry in the United States. According to the Bureau of Labor Statistics, the industry will create about 19 percent, or 3.6 million, of the new jobs between 2004 and 2014, which does not fully account for its impact, as this projection does not include consulting and independent contracting fees.

Table 8.1 presents the various healthcare entities and their relative distribution by organization type and employment. Of the 545,000 firms operating in the healthcare industry, approximately 76 percent are offices of physicians, dentists, or other health practitioners. Many of these practices are small groups of practitioners. In some cases, the groups are one singular economic entity, such as a professional association, but in many cases several individual practitioners physically aggregate their respective practices to share expenses and pool staff support. Conversely, hospitals constitute only 1.9 percent of total healthcare establishments, but

Table 8.1
Percentage Distribution of Wage and Salary Employment and Establishments in Healthcare, 2004

Establishment Type	Establishments	Employment
Hospitals, public and private	1.9%	41.3%
Nursing and residential care facilities	11.6%	21.3%
Offices of physicians	37.0%	15.5%
Offices of dentists	21.0%	5.7%
Home healthcare services	3.0%	5.8%
Offices of other health practitioners	18.7%	4.0%
Outpatient care centers	3.2%	3.4%
Other ambulatory healthcare services	1.5%	1.5%
Medical and diagnostic laboratories	2.1%	1.4%

Source: Bureau of Labor Statistics.

employment in hospitals equals more than 41 percent of the employment base for all health workers.

The United States is the only industrialized country that does not offer universal health insurance coverage but offers certain publicly funded programs to provide healthcare for the elderly, disabled, and poor. This leaves more than 45 million people currently uninsured, according to the U.S. Census Bureau (see figure 8.1).

Currently, about 85 percent of U.S. citizens have health insurance, either through their employers or purchased individually. Access to health insurance in the United States is uniquely tied to employment; many U.S. citizens are offered health insurance through their employer, and employers negotiate with health insurers to secure coverage for their employees. Additionally, health insurance purchased through an employer is tax advantaged, utilizing pretax dollars, whereas individual purchases are not. This tax subsidy creates another incentive to purchase insurance and demand more medical services, as eloquently described by Duke University professor Clark C. Havighurst:

> The tax subsidy thus introduces new "moral hazards" into health care decision-making. Not only are employers, union leaders, legislators, and courts happy to commit employee-voters' money in ways that make themselves appear to care about health above all things, but their stake in not having to say "no" to more and better health care also coincides perfectly with the preferences of the politically powerful health care industry. For these reasons, the tax subsidy

Figure 8.1 Number of Uninsured Americans

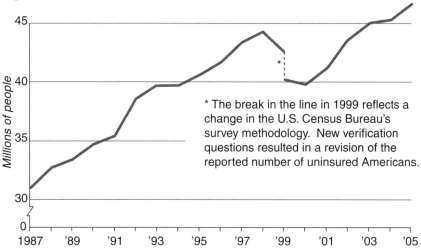

The number of uninsured Americans rose from 31 million in 1987 (13 percent of the population) to 46.6 million in 2005 (16 percent). During that time period, the U.S. population grew from 242 million to 296 million.

Source: U.S. Census Bureau, *Current Population Survey, 1988 to 2006 Annual Social and Economic Supplements.*

has survived through political thick and thin even though every policy wonk knows that it is a principal cause of wasteful spending on health services. Liberals, of course, resist proposals to fix this glaring defect in the incentive system that drives health care spending. Why fix incentives to encourage consumers to make more appropriate health care choices when big government stands ready to choose for them?[6]

The Actors

Healthcare organizations include those that provide preventive, diagnostic, therapeutic, rehabilitative, maintenance, or palliative care along with the sale or dispensing of a drug, device, piece of equipment, or other item ordered by a licensed practitioner. Major contributors to the healthcare engine include:

Hospitals

Hospitals provide a broad range of medical care, including diagnostic services, surgery, and continuous nursing care. Some hospitals provide specialty services relating to the mentally ill, cancer patients, or children. Care may be on an inpatient or outpatient basis.

There are several categories of hospitals, but the majority of hospitals are nonprofit, 501(c)3 organizations. They can be classified as community hospitals, religious affiliated, or academic affiliated. Of the more than 5,000 hospitals in the United States, almost 70 percent are owned by nonprofits, 16 percent are owned by state and local governments, and the balance are owned by corporate, for-profit entities. In fact, some 80 percent of all operating hospital beds in the United States are run by nonprofit hospitals or health systems.[7]

Hospital labor needs depend on many factors, including bed size, location, goals, philosophy, organization, and management style of the hospital. Hospitals employ workers with all levels of education and training. This diversification enables hospitals to provide a greater variety of services than is offered in other areas of the healthcare industry; hospitals also have a scale advantage when extending or adding new service lines in that their already-large labor base creates opportunities to leverage incumbent skills and already-developed infrastructure. About 3 in 10 hospital workers are registered nurses who, combined with other service and support occupations in the hospital setting, hold about half of all hospital jobs.[8] Other employees include therapists and social workers.

In recent years, several hospitals have expanded their long-term and home healthcare services as both a service line extension and a risk mitigation strategy. Throughout the 1990s, as hospitals' censuses eroded in the face of aggressive managed care, they were forced to develop lower-cost, lower-acuity services that would be attractive to managed care organizations, organizations whose mantra became "anyplace but the hospital." Arbitrarily moving patients from acute beds into less acute settings was ultimately proved to be shortsighted. Currently, hospitals across the United States are at or near capacity, both in emergency departments and acute care beds, particularly in metropolitan areas. Typically, the leading causes of these capacity issues are staffing shortages (especially in nursing), growing demand for hospital services, increased illness acuity, and insufficient space on the general medical surgical and intensive care floors and in the emergency departments.[9]

Nursing and Residential Care Facilities

These facilities provide inpatient, postacute, skilled nursing, rehabilitation, and health-related personal care to individuals who require continuous nursing care but are not ill enough for hospital services. Nursing aides provide the majority of direct care. Other facilities, such as recuperative homes or assisted living facilities, cater to patients who require less assistance. These residential care centers can provide continuous social and personal care to those who have a limited ability to care for themselves, such as the elderly. These facilities also include alcohol and drug rehabilitation centers, group homes, and halfway houses.

Physicians

The physician marketplace in the United States is dynamic, diverse, and growing, both from domestic and international labor sources. From 1980 to 2004, the total number of physicians in the United States increased from 467,679 to 884,974, whereas the physician-to-population ratio grew from 207 to 296 per 100,000 people.[10] It is expected that similar growth in the physician workforce will continue for a number of years, based on current rates of physician training as well as the announced creation of at least five new medical schools in the United States. The influence of a growing physician workforce on healthcare delivery is somewhat unknown; if history is a guide, continued growth in the physician population should come with continued growth in health expenditures per capita—a cause and effect that flies in the face of the tenets of competitive market supply and demand. However, studies have shown that physician concentration is a key to overall economic performance in an area. This phenomenon derives from several factors, including the revenue generated by the physician's practice, the role the high-income physician plays in the local economy, and the number of jobs created by the typical physician practice. Relative to the latter, the annual Medical Group Management Association Cost Survey presents data that shows that, on average, each practicing full-time equivalent physician in practice in the United States, across all specialties, requires four or more full-time equivalent support personnel.[11]

According to the Bureau of Labor Statistics, approximately 16 percent of all physicians in the United States in 2004 were employed by hospitals.[12] Physician employment is more prevalent in academic medical center settings than in community hospitals. In the case of the former, physicians are often employed by the faculty practice plan of the affiliated medical college. Nonetheless, the predominant current model of physician as free agent in place in most communities creates unique challenges for hospital administrators. There is no industry in the United States in which the leader of the business does not control (i.e., through an employment or ownership arrangement) the principal means of production; in the case of physicians who are voluntary medical staff members of multiple hospitals, physicians are free to use any hospital available to them and their patients, and there is fierce competition among hospitals to woo the physicians who drive more acute patient volume.

Despite the overall growth in physician supply, there is some evidence that the system is at risk for physician shortages, especially in certain specialties, including radiology, anesthesiology, cardiology, and rheumatology.[13] Further, many physician professional associations have expressed concerns about potential shortages, including concerns that potential shortages may negatively affect the mission of medical schools. In an attempt to remedy this problem, the Association of American Medical Colleges (AAMC) has recommended increasing the number of medical graduates in the United States by as much as 30 percent, building new medical schools, and increasing enrollment in existing medical schools.[14] Simply increasing the number of domestic candidates may not suffice, however, which will require continued growth in the number of foreign medical graduates (FMGs) to fill unmet need. FMGs have long been a valuable and reliable resource for U.S. physician workforce deficits, with the American Medical Association indicating that more than 215,928 FMGs were actively practicing in the United States in 2004, constituting almost 24 percent of the total physician workforce.[15] Given projected shortfalls, it seems likely that FMGs will continue to serve the U.S. marketplace.

Health Insurers

Health insurers have become more prevalent in the United States since the close of World War II. It was during that war that the U.S. government limited the ability of businesses to offer higher wages and created a tax advantage to health insurance benefits provided through employers. This advantage and the influence firms came to control over their employees' healthcare decision making had more to do with the growth of insurance than any other single factor in the United States.

Currently, roughly 60 percent of Americans who receive health insurance coverage do so from an employer, and about 9 percent purchase insurance individually. Government programs administer insurance to almost 30 percent of the insured population, predominantly in the Medicare and Medicaid programs and the variety of health insurance programs for active and retired military personnel. In 2004, private insurance paid for 36 percent of personal health expenditures, private out-of-pocket payments were 15 percent, and federal, state, and local governments paid 44 percent.[16] Table 8.2 provides a breakdown of insurance classes, including uninsured, according to the U.S. Census Bureau.

There has been much debate about the growth in health insurance premiums since the beginning of the twenty-first century. According to the Kaiser Family Foundation, hikes in health insurance premiums went from a low of 5 percent from 1998 to 1999 to a high of almost 14 percent from 2002 to 2003.[17] Premiums for the foreseeable future are expected to grow approximately 7 percent per year, ensuring that the health insurance component of the health economy will double in the next 10 years. As one might expect, the growth in premiums

Table 8.2
Number of Non-Elderly Americans by Health Insurance Status, 2001–2005

	Uninsured		Medicaid/ SCHIP	Employer- sponsored insurance	Individually purchased insurance	Medicare	Military healthcare
	Number (millions)	Percentage	Percentage	Percentage	Percentage	Percentage	Percentage
2005	46.6	15.9	13.0	59.5	9.1	13.7	3.8
2004	45.3	15.6	13.0	59.8	9.3	13.6	3.7
2003	45.0	15.6	12.4	60.4	9.2	13.7	3.5
2002	43.6	15.2	11.6	61.3	9.3	13.4	3.5
2001	41.2	14.6	11.2	62.6	9.2	13.5	3.4

Source: U.S. Census Bureau.

has afforded commercial payers a concomitant improvement in profitability; according to Hoover's data from January 2007, each of the Big Four health insurer monoliths—Aetna, Cigna, United Health Group, and WellPoint—experienced operating margins in the 8 percent-plus range for each of the years from 2004 to 2006.[18]

Employers

Every year, human resource directors and benefits consultants work with insurers to limit the growth in increases for employers' health insurance premiums. There are several reasons why premiums continue to increase, not the least of which is the growth in medical costs themselves. Among the various pressures that drive cost inflation in both insurance premiums and medical costs are new treatments, drugs, diagnostic tests, and medical device innovations; increased demand for services; and declining health status. To battle these cost increases, employers and other plan sponsors are increasing the level of cost shifting to employees, some by utilizing consumer-directed health plans that almost completely shift the decision-making burden for the first several thousands of dollars to the employee and his or her family. To date, these activities have not kept pace with increased medical spending trends, but there is an active movement to mitigate increasing expenses.

Why the Economic Engine Will Continue

There are a multitude of reasons why healthcare will continue to be a major growth industry in the United States. They include:

- Healthcare is labor intensive. The healthcare industry is highly labor intensive, especially so because of the industry's historic underspending on information and other technologies that have enhanced labor productivity in other industries. As noted elsewhere, labor requirements in healthcare span from entry-level, low-paid positions that require little formal education to highly technical positions that require a high level of formal education and training, making the industry very attractive to workforce development advocates. Additionally, the third-party reimbursement system creates administrative complexity, particularly in terms of processing medical claims and the tracking and follow-up that occur in the provider's business office related to payment status. Although it is true that the majority of medical claims are now submitted electronically (75 percent were submitted electronically in 2006, as opposed to 44 percent in 2002),[19] it is still a very labor-intensive and costly effort by the provider's business office and the payer's claims departments to accommodate the volume of claims in the current system. As an example, it costs an insurer and a provider office roughly the same to process and track, respectively, a medical claim filed to an insurer in the amount of $200 as it does for a claim for $50,000. The current system that provides first-dollar payments by insurers requires significant administrative staff to manage. If the patient paid for all medical costs less than $500 at the point of service, millions of medical claims would be eliminated, thus significantly reducing administrative costs.

- Employment is domestic. Relative to labor force issues in other industries that require high labor inputs, healthcare is unique in that much of the labor used in healthcare delivery has to be physically proximate to the employer. Although there are ongoing attempts to move certain labor-intensive functions offshore (such as reading radiology films as well as administrative functions such as data entry and medical claims processing), the bulk of healthcare employment needs to be locally based. Therefore, a higher percentage of each new dollar of revenue generated by a healthcare provider organization is kept within the United States than is the case with other industries.

- Healthcare is ubiquitous, and acyclical. Healthcare has a broader impact than other industries because, as a basic staple of life, its presence is inescapable. Every community in the United States, from the most affluent to the poorest, has some healthcare footprint, and planning for the provision of health services is always a top or near-top priority for community resource planners. Additionally, the frequency or intensity of health services is only weakly correlated with economic cycles or other exogenous factors; when healthcare is needed, it is needed, and the more acute the service, the less price sensitive the consumer.

- There is an unwillingness to ration care. Many developed countries have tackled the issue of rationing healthcare, most in explicit ways. The United States has historically approached the issue of rationing with great trepidation, and in cases in which rationing is deployed, it is almost always implicit and often arbitrary. Such an unwillingness to face the obvious resource constraints will only become more problematic in the future, at the intersection of better life-preserving technology and a graying population.

- New clinical and information technology will always be introduced. New medical devices, prescription drugs, and diagnostic technologies will continue to be used and highly valued, and the threat of defensive medicine will ensure that providers will continue to use the latest technology even in circumstances in which there is questionable marginal benefit. Also, the deployment of clinical decision support systems promises to arm providers with tools to ensure better patient compliance with appropriately indicated treatments, which may swell utilization of certain services for underserved populations.

  Another cost-expanding role that technology deployment may play is as a substitute for labor. As healthcare expenditures continue to grow, precipitating the need for ever-greater sources of labor, there will ultimately be a time when the provider sector makes an earnest commitment to replace labor with technology (or to make it more productive by investing more in information technology). "Low productivity in health is mostly a product of low investment," says Harvard economist Dale Jorgenson.[20] Although technology ultimately will greatly improve efficiency and reduce costs, technology deployment in the short run will come at a cost.

- Advancements in medical science will accelerate. Medical spending over the past century has resulted in enormous financial and qualitative return on investment. Healthcare has enabled Americans to enjoy and sustain a very high quality of life, with relatively open access to the best that healthcare can offer. The most significant return on healthcare investment, however, has been the eradication or management of crippling and disabling illnesses (e.g., the discovery of insulin in 1922 or the discovery of the polio vaccine in 1954). More recently, there have been significant advancements in the sequencing of the human genome to identify predispositions to chronic diseases. These have all had a significant impact of the life expectancy of Americans; at the beginning of the twentieth century, life expectancy was 47 years, and by 2004, life expectancy had climbed to 78 years.[21] Regardless of the discovery, however, there is one common theme historically: Advancements in technology and science have almost always driven new or enhanced demand for a series of clinical treatments, driving overall costs in the system.

- There will be demographic pressures. Demographics in the United States will change dramatically during the next 20 years as more people reach their sixties, seventies, and beyond. The U.S. Census Bureau projects that the "number of Americans age 65 or older will swell from 35 million today to more than 62 million by 2025—nearly an 80 percent increase."[22] As people grow older, demand for health services increases dramatically.

Specifically, long-term care is projected to grow very rapidly; a recent study by VHA suggests that between 2020 and 2030, expenditures on long-term care services will grow by more than 42 percent.[23]

- There will be health status pressures. Nonmedical social and behavioral factors such as smoking, obesity, alcohol use, and a sedentary lifestyle are causing nearly half of all annual mortality in the United States.[24] However, a very small portion of the approximately $2 trillion spent annually on healthcare in the United States is devoted to reducing risks posed by these preventable conditions. As chronic disease rates continue to escalate and the social and cultural diversity in the United States continues to grow, the system will be prone to increased costs related to dealing with chronic conditions and increasing complex comorbidities.

- Healthcare is political. As the saying goes, "All politics are local." One could similarly adopt the saying, "All healthcare is local." One of the toughest things to do in the United States is to close a community hospital, because of its importance to the psyche and the economic vibrancy of that community. In fact, in many communities that have suffered economic decline in manufacturing and other tangible-goods industries, healthcare, and specifically hospitals, have become the economic savior and predominant job creator. According to the American Hospital Association, in 2004 community hospitals generated 4.9 million direct healthcare jobs, approximately 8 million ripple-effect jobs created in the local economies that surround the hospitals, and a direct and indirect economic impact of more than $1.6 trillion.[25] As many community hospitals are the community's key local employer, in some markets with otherwise high unemployment the local economy would be crippled if the community hospital were shuttered.

The Economic Impact of a Hospital

An applied economist would measure the economic impacts of a particular hospital or center of healthcare delivery by utilizing a series of multipliers that estimates the effects of hospital operations on a local or regional economy. Metaphorically, the economist strives to measure the cumulative impacts generated by the equivalent of an object falling into the center of a lake, with the initial splash representing the direct impacts and the concentric ripples that invariably follow representing a combination of indirect and induced impacts.

The case of an individual hospital or medical center is instructive. Many hospitals employ hundreds of employees, some thousands. As noted earlier, in many communities the local medical center represents the single largest nongovernmental employer. The jobs at the medical center are classified as direct employment.

The hospital also purchases goods and services from businesses, many of them local. These goods and services range from delivery services and office products to liability insurance and construction services. These business-to-business transactions are termed *indirect effects,* and at least theoretically they could be larger in magnitude than the direct impacts. Businesses conducting transactions with a medical facility will, in turn, have more income with which to purchase goods and services from other businesses, and these businesses, in turn, will have more income to spend and so on. The totality of this succession of business sales constitutes the indirect economic impact of the hospital. To the extent that employment is supported at entities that can trace a portion of their revenue base to the operations of a particular medical institution, that employment is classified as *indirect employment.*

The economic impact does not end there; there are more ripples. Households in the vicinity of the hospital enjoy higher incomes than they would but for the hospital's operations. Some of this augmented income is associated with hospital employees themselves, but another group of households enjoys higher income because of the fact that the entity with which they work generates greater revenue through hospital operations.

A significant share of these incomes is spent among area businesses, including restaurants, movie theaters, dry cleaners, utilities and telecom providers, department stores, barber shops, boutiques, health clubs, contractors, landscapers, and automobile dealerships. The economic activity supported by the household income traceable to the hospital/medical center's operations is termed the *induced effects.* As with direct and indirect effects, induced effects can be measured in terms of jobs, income, and business sales.

Total economic impacts associated with a facility's operations therefore equal the sum of direct, indirect, and induced impacts. The ratio of total impacts to direct impacts represents the multiplier.

But there may be additional economic impacts beyond those described. For instance, many hospitals across the United States are undergoing significant facility upgrades. This investment creates a separate set of construction-related impacts that are above and beyond those associated with operations.

Moreover, hospital operations and physical upgrades generate directly and/or indirectly tax revenues for local taxing entities, including through personal income taxes, retail taxes, residential transactions taxes, amusement taxes, and property taxes. This revenue provides government with a greater capacity to deliver services, which in turn creates a series of economic impacts on a local or regional economy by triggering additional hiring and procurement activity.

An Illustration: The Economic Impact of the Johns Hopkins Medical Institutions in Maryland

Maryland is a relatively small state, with some 5.6 million residents. The state's population concentration, as one would expect, surrounds the major urban areas; the Baltimore region boasts a population of just more than 2.6 million residents, and the Washington, DC, suburbs count almost 2 million residents.

Healthcare and the broader life sciences field is one of the most important industries in Maryland's economy. Among the largest employers in Maryland, 21 of the top 50 are healthcare institutions, including three Johns Hopkins–owned entities, two University of Maryland Medical System–owned entities, two MedStar Health System–owned entities, and the local Blue Cross Blue Shield affiliate, CareFirst BlueChoice. Further, institutions in Maryland are among the largest recipients of U.S. government grants for healthcare-related research; the two major academic institutions in Baltimore, the Johns Hopkins Medical Institutions and the University of Maryland Medical System and Medical School, drive much of that research.

Geography is beneficial to the region; much of the federal government's healthcare apparatus is in Maryland, including the Centers for Medicare and Medicaid Services (CMS) in a Baltimore suburb and the National Institutes of Health, based in the Washington, DC, suburbs. On a combined basis, these two subagencies of the Department of Health and Human Services employ more than 18,000 people, with bright employment prospects for the future; in particular, the CMS in managing the Medicare program and the new Part D drug benefit stands to require more human capital as the percentage of the population eligible for Medicare increases over the indefinite future.

The need to attract the best and the brightest is also important for Maryland's healthcare community. As stated throughout, hospitals are among the largest employers in their communities. "In Maryland alone, community hospitals directly produced approximately 80,672 full and part-time positions in 2002. Almost 8 percent of total employment for the state is supported by hospital employment when multiplier effects are taken into account. Maryland's community hospitals have a yearly payroll of over $3.5 billion."[26]

The Special Role of the Johns Hopkins Medical Institutions

The Johns Hopkins Medical Institutions are a critical component of the Baltimore region and of Maryland's economic health. The Hopkins medical complex consists of the Johns Hopkins University Medical School; the Johns Hopkins Health System, which includes three hospitals (the Johns Hopkins Hospital, Johns Hopkins Bayview Medical Center, and Howard County General Hospital); Johns Hopkins Geriatric Center; Johns Hopkins Home Health; Johns Hopkins Outpatient Center on the main hospital campus; several group practice locations in strategic areas around Baltimore; and 18 locations of Johns Hopkins Community Physicians.

In January 2003, an economic consulting firm, Bay Area Economics (BAE), completed an economic impact analysis of Johns Hopkins's role in the Maryland economy.[27] In its report, BAE identified key economic contributions by Hopkins to the local and regional economy. They included:

- Income: Hopkins institutions generated $7 billion in income to the Maryland economy in 2002—$1 of every $28 in the state's economy.
- Jobs: As the largest private employer in Maryland, the university boasted more than 43,000 employees in 2002, and since 1999 Johns Hopkins has added more than 1,000 jobs a year to its payroll.

- Indirect employment benefit: According to Hopkins, its activities (direct employment and spending on goods and services from other employers) support more than 85,000 Maryland jobs. "More than three of every 100 people drawing paychecks in the state either work for Johns Hopkins or have a job because Johns Hopkins is here spending money."[27]
- Construction activities: As Hopkins embarked on its new cancer research building, the state of Maryland committed $20 million to the project because the state knew the initiative would drive secondary economic development based on the Hopkins track record. That state investment allowed Hopkins to expand cancer research by $23 million a year, which, according to Hopkins, supports 690 new Maryland jobs and $31 million a year in income for other businesses, organizations, and individuals in Maryland. In addition, the Hopkins institutions spent more than $200 million on building or renovation projects in fiscal year 2002 alone, providing work for a variety of skilled tradesmen, drawing support from all areas of the state of Maryland.
- International economic development: Every day Hopkins sees patients from all over the world, totaling some 126 countries to date. These patients bring their spouses, parents, and families with them, spending millions in Maryland restaurants, retail outlets, gas stations, hotels, and other establishments.
- Research and new venture activity: Johns Hopkins attracts more federal research and development funding than any other U.S. university. In 2001 alone, Hopkins faculty won almost 100 patents and submitted more than 400 patent applications. Additionally, technology transfer activities at Hopkins have yielded the formation of more than 20 Maryland-based start-up ventures.
- Workforce development: As a direct result of the development of the Hopkins biotechnology initiative in East Baltimore, the commercial construction industry in Baltimore is booming. In fact, there is currently more than 2 million square feet of commercial construction space being built in the Baltimore metropolitan area, much of which is related to Hopkins's projects. This activity has allowed city and state urban planners to encourage workforce development focused on training people living in the neighborhoods affected by the construction. One such program, JumpStart, has been funded by the Annie E. Casey Foundation, and others to provide preapprenticeship construction craft training to underserved populations, including significant populations of ex-convicts and those formerly addicted to drugs and alcohol. This program is attempting to fill the construction support positions most needed by the industry. JumpStart is expected to birth 40 to 60 new construction industry jobs per year, valued at $30,000 per job per year, for an annual direct compensation impact of approximately $1.5 million. This impact

is from a segment of the population that has not been a positive economic contributor historically.
- Charity care: Finally, Hopkins is also a prominent provider of healthcare
  services in Maryland to the indigent and in 2002 provided more than
  $144 million worth of uncompensated healthcare.

In addition to its role as a major economic actor in Baltimore and surrounds,
the Hopkins institutions serve as a major source of pride for the region and its
residents. The hospital has been recognized for a number of years by *U.S. News
and World Report* as the top-ranked hospital in the United States, with world-
renowned centers of excellence in a variety of clinical areas, including urology,
ophthalmology, cancer, burn care, and pediatric specialty care. The recognition
as a center of excellence serves to attract related industry and other businesses that
want to operate in a city with a world-class medical institution.

CONCLUSION

Despite all of the dysfunction in the current U.S. health system, its role as a major economic engine is without question. The United States is broadly regarded
as an international leader in a variety of health services categories. International
patients with a variety of ailments choose to travel to many of the U.S.-based
healthcare epicenters, such as Boston, Baltimore, New York, or Rochester, Minne-
sota, home of the world-famous Mayo Clinic. Healthcare now constitutes almost
16 percent of the domestic U.S. economy and employees a sizable number of its
citizens. The healthcare sector is one of the fastest-growing segments of the U.S.
economy and employs millions of Americans and foreign nationals.

Many industry leaders bemoan the increasing costs of healthcare as a driver
of anticompetitiveness. One classic example is the auto industry. According to a
recent publication by the Galen Institute, the cost of providing healthcare adds
approximately $1,500 to the cost of each new vehicle General Motors (GM) sold
in 2005, more per car than the cost of the steel used to construct the car.[28] Further,
GM projected spending almost $6 billion on healthcare in 2006. This compares
very unfavorably with the foreign competition, according to Rick Wagoner, chief
executive officer of GM, who said in a recent speech to the Economic Club of
Chicago, "Our foreign domiciled competitors have just a fraction of these costs,
because they have few, if any, U.S. retirees, and in their home countries, their
governments cover a much greater portion of employee and retiree health care
costs."[28]

Those within the industry recognize that health supply, which is composed
overwhelmingly of labor, fuels the consumption activity of health industry workers and those in related industries; one person's expenditure is another's income.
To make wholesale changes to the healthcare landscape would run the risk of
tinkering with the most prominent U.S. job producer and the industry most
able to keep its spin-off economic activity within the borders of the United States.
It is for this reason, along with the strong, entrenched political power of the key
constituents and patrons of the industry, that any major reform initiatives seem

highly unlikely. Regardless, the healthcare industry is a critical resource to the overall U.S. economy and a major factor in its citizens' economic and social quality of life.

NOTES

1. Mandel, M., and J. Weber. 2006. "What's Really Propping Up the Economy." *Business Week Online,* September 25. Available at: http://www.business week.com/magazine/content/06_39/b4002001.htm. Accessed April 22, 2007.

2. Adams, J. 2006. "Healthcare 2015: Win-Win or Lose-Lose?" *IBM Global Business Services.* Available at: https://www-03.ibm.com/industries/healthcare/doc/content/bin/Healthcare2015-Win-win_or_lose-lose72pg.pdf. Accessed April 15, 2007.

3. U.S. Department of Labor, Bureau of Labor Statistics. 2005. "Health Care." Available at: http://www.bls.gov/oco/cg/cgs035.htm#outlook. Accessed May 24, 2007.

4. Centers for Medicare and Medicaid Services, Office of Financial Management. n.d. "Effects of Health Care Spending on the U.S. Economy." Available at: http://aspe.hhs.gov/health/costgrowth/report.pdf. Accessed May 24, 2007.

5. Poisal, J., C. Truffer, S. Smith, et al. 2007. "Health Spending Projections through 2016: Modest Changes Obscure Part D's Impact." *Health Affairs* 26 (2): W242–W253.

6. Kirkendall, T. 2007. "Houston's Clear Thinkers." *blog.kir.com,* July 2. Available at: http://blog.kir.com/archives/cat_health_care_finance.asp. Accessed April 16, 2007.

7. State Health Facts.org. 2005. "Hospital Beds per 1,000 Population by Ownership Type, 1999–2005." *Henry J. Kaiser Foundation.* Available at: http://www.state healthfacts.org/cgi-bin/healthfacts.cgi?action=compare&category=Providers+%26+Service+Use&subcategory=Hospital+Trends&topic=Beds+by+Ownership%2C+1999-2005. Accessed April 10, 2007.

8. Bureau of Labor Statistics, U.S. Department of Labor. 2005. "Career Guide to Industries, 2006–07 Edition: Health Care." Available at: http://www.bls.gov/oco/cg/cgs035.htm. Accessed May 25, 2007.

9. Bazzoli, G., L. R. Brewster, G. Liu, and S. Kuo. 2003. "Does U.S. Hospital Capacity Need to Be Expanded?" *Health Affairs* 22 (6): 40–54.

10. Pasko, T., and D. Smart. 2006. *Physician Characteristics and Distribution in the U.S.* Chicago: American Medical Association.

11. *MGMA.com.* Medical Group Management Association. Available at: www.mgma.org. Accessed April 1, 2007.

12. U.S. Department of Labor, Bureau of Labor Statistics. 2006. "Occupational Outlook Handbook: Physicians and Surgeons." Available at: http://www.bls.gov/oco/ocos074.htm. Accessed May 24, 2007.

13. Akl, E., R. Mustafa, F. Bdair, and H. J. Schünemann. 2007. "The United States Physician Workforce and International Medical Graduates: Trends and Characteristics." *Journal of General Internal Medicine* 22 (2): 264–68.

14. Ibid.

15. Ibid.

16. National Center for Health Statistics. 2006. "Health, United States, 2006." *Department of Health and Human Services, Centers for Disease Control and Prevention.* Available at: http://www.cdc.gov/nchs/data/hus/hus06.pdf. Accessed May 24, 2007.

17. Henry J. Kaiser Family Foundation. 2004. "Trends and Indicators in the Changing Health Care Marketplace." Available at: http://www.kff.org/insurance/7031/print-sec3.cfm. Accessed May 24, 2007.

18. American Hospital Association. 2007. "2007 Health and Hospital Trends." *AHA.org*. Available at: http://www.aha.org/aha/research-and-trends/health-and-hospital-trends/2007.html. Accessed May 24, 2007.

19. America's Health Insurance Plans. 2006. "Electronic Processing of Health Claims Speeds Payments, Cuts Costs." *AHIP.org*. Available at: http://www.ahip.org/content/pressrelease.aspx?docid=16454. Accessed April 28, 2007.

20. Akl, Mustafa, Bdair, and Schunemann, 264–68.

21. *Healthcare 2000: A Strategic Assessment of the Health Care Environment in the United States*. 2000. Irving, Texas: VHA and Deloitte and Touche.

22. Surface Transportation Policy Partnership. n.d. "Aging Americans: Stranded without Options." *Transact.org*. Available at: http://www.transact.org/library/reports_html/seniors/Aging_exec_summ.pdf. Accessed May 24, 2007.

23. *Healthcare 2000: A Strategic Assessment of the Health Care Environment in the United States*. 2000. Irving, Texas: VHA and Deloitte and Touche.

24. Shodell, D. 2006. "Paying for Prevention." *Medscape Public Health and Prevention*. Available at: http://www.medscape.com/viewarticle/544651. Accessed April 18, 2007.

25. American Hospital Association. 2006. "Beyond Health Care: The Economic Contribution of Hospitals." *AHA.org*. Available at: http://www.aha.org/aha/content/2006/pdf/ECONRPT3.pdf. Accessed May 24, 2007.

26. Sage Policy Group. 2004. *An Analysis of the Economic Impacts of Maryland's Medical Liability Environment*. Baltimore: Sage Policy Group, 28.

27. Johns Hopkins University. 2003. "Johns Hopkins Economic Impact in Maryland." *JHU.ed*. Available at: http://www.jhu.edu/news_info/reports/impact/report5.html. Accessed April 18, 2007.

28. Turner, Grace-Marie. 2006. "Rules & Red Tape, Mandates: U.S. Industry Is in the Crosshairs of Bad Tax Policy." Galen Institute. Available at: http://www.galen.org/redtape.asp?docID=859. Accessed May 24, 2007.

CHAPTER 9

Improving Systems of Care:
A Patient's Perspective

Rudy Wilson Galdonik

To try to describe what it means to be a patient, whether through illness or injury, is like summarizing all aspects of parenting in one paragraph. For many people, the word *patient* means nothing more than taking preventive steps or seeking treatment for a minor medical problem—a temporary inconvenience and expense. For others, becoming a patient is the result of a sudden life-changing event or diagnosis. For those living with a chronic condition, being a patient is a journey with varying stages, from routine to earth-shattering. Attempting to identify and examine all the intricacies of being sick is a mammoth if not impossible undertaking, because what is earth-shattering to one person may border on routine for another.

For people working in healthcare, a personal journey into sickness is often the catalyst that enables them to understand issues involving the loss of health more fully. Medical providers look at the healthcare system with new respect and understanding once they have personally experienced the emotions, challenges, and opportunities of being sick.

Susan Keane Baker, author of *Managing Patient Expectations: The Art of Finding and Keeping Loyal Patients,* states, "'[O]ne size fits all' satisfaction strategies cannot work for every patient because preferences are created and altered by individual experiences and influences."[1] Systems of care need to manage the expectations of patients and their caregivers. Walk in the shoes of a patient and his caregiver, and opportunities for improving systems of care will present themselves at every turn.

In his article "A Hospitalization from Hell: A Patient's Perspective on Quality," Paul D. Cleary emphasizes, "Patients are the best source of information about a hospital system's communication, education, and pain-management processes, and they are the only source of information about whether they were treated with dignity and respect."[2] Most improvements that have the greatest value for patients and their supporters are relatively easy and inexpensive to implement. For example, patients and their families need compassion and empathy. The first 60 seconds of every encounter are critical in laying the foundation for the patient's feelings about the experience.[3] A vital first step is for staff to greet patients with care and concern. This can be as simple as greeting patients with a smile and full attention.

ONE PERSON'S JOURNEY

Expertise involves having or displaying special skill or knowledge derived from training or experience and skillfulness by virtue of possessing special knowledge.[4] I have been a patient, the caregiver of a patient, and a worker in hospital human resources. I count myself an expert on being sick. Occasionally, I meet someone who states, "Oh, I'm so sorry for all you've been through." However, I choose to count myself privileged to know what it means to be sick, because with that knowledge and understanding comes a myriad of gifts that I am able to embrace and share. The following will summarize my history as patient, caregiver, and hospital employee. I will then describe key elements that I believe are vital in assuring quality systems of care.

JOURNEY AS PATIENT

I first became a patient in the mid-1950s when an atrial septal defect (ASD) was detected in my heart during my kindergarten medical exam. Open-heart surgery was not a viable option in the mid-1950s, so our family physician, whose practice was located in an extension of his home, gave my parents the best advice he could offer for the time: "Just don't let her overdo it." This translated to a sedentary childhood: no running, bicycling, swimming, or sports of any kind. I learned quickly that physical exertion of any kind would have to be relegated to those moments when I was down the street and around the corner from my mother's watchful eye.

Although exams were few and congenital expertise was almost nonexistent, I clearly remember the day I had my first chest X-ray. As I lay on the gurney, a mammoth machine was rolled into the examining room by a nurse clad from head to toe in starched white. Because this was the same lady who delivered injections, she and the Machine were immediately a threat. No one explained to me what was about to happen. I decided that the machine held no other purpose than to eat me. With childlike determination, I also decided I would not go down without a fight. Screaming, pleading, and thrashing filled the afternoon until finally a frazzled doctor told my mother he had the information he needed. I was alive, intact, and proud of my victory over the Machine. Upon my release, I learned that the doctor simply had wanted to look more closely at my insides. The Machine was nothing more than a camera for people's insides. On the drive home, I pressed my swollen, pink face against the car window and thought, "They wanted to take a picture of my insides? Why didn't they just say so, and save us all a lot of grief?" That experience, as does every experience one has within the healthcare system, laid the groundwork for the expectations I would have later as a patient.

My health remained relatively stable until I turned 24. Then I began to feel arrhythmias: unexplained pounding and skipped heartbeats. I decided to seek a new physician because our family doctor, who was still practicing, was approaching 80. My new family practitioner took a baseline electrocardiogram (EKG). My irregular heartbeats caused the needle tracing the rhythm of my heart to fly off the paper. The doctor, convinced that his EKG machine was at fault, attempted to bring it back to its senses by banging the machine with his fist and then unplugging and realigning the tape, all to no avail. Finally, when the doctor told me his findings, he said open-heart surgery to repair my ASD and prolapsed mitral valve was clearly in my future. "Old age is going to be your worst enemy," he said.

Little did I know that old age would rear its ugly head one year later. As the arrhythmias continued to worsen, I attempted to control my bad beats and my fear by finding a rock that I would hold in the palm of my hand. I would stroke the rock's smooth surface in an effort to calm my nerves, which I believed would reduce, if not eliminate, my arrhythmias. This layperson's primitive form of treatment is called denial.

Then in January 1978, *Good Housekeeping* magazine included an article about identical twin girls born with identical holes in their hearts.[5] It described how open-heart surgery "fixed" the girls. I saw myself in every paragraph. A recent out-of-state job transfer meant I would again need to find a new doctor.

The Yellow Pages led me to a new physician. As I sat in his office, he inquired, "So what brings you here today?" "Sir, I think I need open-heart surgery," was my response. With that, the doctor smiled and said, "Honey, you've just moved away from your mother. You are probably lonely. I would go home and have a baby if I were you." My Yellow Pages doctor dispensed this advice without ever placing a stethoscope to my chest. This advice, had I followed it, would have killed both me and the recommended baby.

Because my arrhythmias continued to worsen, within weeks I found myself at a cardiologist's office. This doctor, an expert, was very intrigued by my EKG, yet his clinical expertise did not outweigh one personal drawback. He had dandruff, a condition that became increasingly apparent as he leaned close to my face to listen with his stethoscope. In my mind, clinical expertise was secondary to a cosmetic issue, and the doctor's hygiene was critical. I decided to launch a quest for the perfect doctor, one who was knowledgeable and someone with whom I could establish a relationship based on respect and trust.

Finally, a coworker who had had bypass surgery suggested her internist, whom I credit with saving my life. The day before my 26th birthday, I had open-heart surgery to patch my ASD and repair my prolapsed mitral valve. One year later, the pronouncement "You're cured" and another move out of state became the catalyst for my dropping out of the healthcare system. For the next 22 years, the only doctor I visited was a gynecologist or a general practitioner for treatment of a specific, superficial complaint. I wanted to see myself as a healthy person, not one living with a chronic health condition.

This changed in 1999 when I developed endocarditis. Following my open-heart surgery in 1978, I had been told clearly of the risks for infection. As a preventive measure, I took oral antibiotics prior to every dental visit. In 1999, despite being on antibiotics, I developed a fever and flu-like symptoms shortly after a dental visit. Because I had had 22 years of uneventful health, endocarditis was never considered when I consulted an internist about my unexplained fever. The doctor ordered a regimen of antibiotics, which reduced the fever, but as soon as the regimen ended the fever returned. This continued for a month.

When he suggested another round of antibiotics, I emphatically replied, "No. Something's not right." I knew in my gut something was very wrong. I insisted that more needed to be done to identify the source of my fevers. I listed every disease I could think of as a possible underlying cause, yet endocarditis was still not even on the radar screen. My physician listened. He saw my frustration and sensed my concern. He ordered a series of tests, and two days later a blood culture showed the growth of bacteria. An echocardiogram at a local cardiology practice confirmed endocarditis. My new cardiologist announced, "We have good news and bad news. We now know what's wrong with you, and you're not going home, you're going straight to the hospital." Ten days of hospitalization and a month of aggressive treatment with IV antibiotics successfully treated the infection in my heart. But four months later, I developed symptoms of heart failure, and tests showed I needed a second open-heart surgery to replace both my mitral and aortic valves with mechanical valves. Twenty-two years of bad blood flow, coupled with the infection, had taken its toll on my heart. Six months later, heart block required the installation of a pacemaker.

Being a lifelong heart patient did not afford immunity from developing other problems. One year later, I was again rushed to the hospital by the same internist who performed the blood culture two years earlier. My complaint was only a random ache on my right side, but his exam suggested infection, and he immediately ordered a CAT scan. Those results suggested possible ovarian cancer or a burst appendix. At our local women's hospital, it was confirmed that my appendix had burst and my body had walled off the infection. Two weeks of aggressive IV antibiotics preceded more surgery, which led to my new norm of living with chronic health issues.

JOURNEY AS CAREGIVER

Significant events such as marriage or the birth of a child bring dreams of a joyous future. Our minds carry pictures of how life will play out. Whenever a person faces a health challenge, it often is accompanied by an innate sense of immunity from additional suffering. We assume there is a system of checks and balances that spreads the suffering around. When a new, unrelated trauma enters the scene, emotions of denial, anger, and sadness can be particularly strong.

In 1975, I married my college sweetheart. We proclaimed our love and commitment "till death do us part." The unspoken belief was that my congenital heart disease would determine the length and course of our life together. Three years after marrying, we faced my first open-heart surgery together. My husband spent countless hours at my side loving and supporting me. As my health returned, we considered ourselves fortunate to have faced this crisis early in our relationship, because it became the platform from which we embraced life. Heart disease had been a challenge we faced as a couple, and in our minds this precluded other hardships from entering our lives. We learned in time that life can be very unfair.

I found myself in the role of caregiver in 1993 when my husband of 18 years woke one morning with a lump on his neck. For the first time, it was my turn to drive the patient to doctors and hospitals, to oversee billing and appointments, and to perform basic nursing duties for my husband's care and comfort. In my role as caregiver, I held my husband's hand as we heard the words, "There is nothing else we can do." My role of caregiver continued as I stood at the edge of my husband's open grave, clutching two children who were too young to understand why their daddy was no longer coming home.

The role of caregiver is often more challenging than that of the patient. Caregiving is fraught with emotional, physical, and mental stress. When the relationship between the caregiver and the patient is positive, the caregiver experiences feelings of fear, sadness, anger, and general uncertainty. Stress from financial burdens is common. If the relationship between caregiver and patient is negative, resentment, anger, and guilt can enter the picture. The caregiver becomes the bridge between the sick world and the outside world. Maintaining balance between these multiple roles is crucial but often very difficult. Physical and mental exhaustion can make the caregiver sick. If caregivers place their own needs over those of the patient, they may feel guilt and remorse.

JOURNEY AS ADMINISTRATOR

My role of hospital human resource professional came quite by accident. After college graduation, I spent several years in corporate human resources. In the years when I first began to notice arrhythmias, I received a promotion to a new job at a medical center campus of a state university. Initially, I walked through hospital corridors holding my breath. The hospital's sights, smells, and sounds were overwhelming. Faces of tired, sick patients lining the clinic walls contributed to an "us" versus "them" attitude. I prided myself in the fact that I was not one of them. I created an invisible barrier between their sickness and my personal reality of relative activity and health.

Then one day all that changed. My journey as patient, which began in a physician's home office, would now take me to the doctor who would walk me through my first open-heart surgery, and late one afternoon I found myself being escorted to an assigned hospital bed. During that first night, I counted myself a prisoner in a place where people die. The system that seemed unfamiliar and frightening became my world.

When I returned to my human resources job after my open-heart surgery, I was a different person with a new mission and passion. I felt privileged to play an administrative role in the business of saving lives. Strolling through hospital corridors afforded me opportunities to reach out, if only with a smile or to hold a door open for the people coming for treatment. Job placement, satisfaction, and personal fulfillment for the employees serving on the front line became critically important to me. I saw individuals working at the medical center as a family on a mission.

LESSONS LEARNED

Have my experiences within the healthcare system been completely smooth sailing? Absolutely not. There have been gaps in care. There have been mistakes, even mistakes that could have cost me my life or justified a malpractice claim. But it was during my first night as an inpatient prior to my first open-heart surgery that I realized I held the ability to choose how I would exist in a terrifying place where people go to die. I decided if I was going to be a patient, I was going to be a good one. I was going to join the team. I evolved from prisoner and victim to survivor and advocate. I credit my transformation to the myriad of doctors, nurses, and medical professionals, even including the transporter who befriended me on my many excursions through hospital corridors. Each individual had a job to do, and it became apparent with each day that they all wanted to use their professional skills and abilities to provide me with the best possible outcome. I credit my transformation to strangers who were committed to saving my life or making their best effort to extend it. Arthur W. Frank states in his book *At the Will of the Body: Reflections on Illness,* "Illness takes away parts of your life, but in doing so it gives you the opportunity to choose the life you will lead, as opposed to living out the one you have simply accumulated over the years."[6] I did not have a choice when it came to the diagnosis of heart disease. I did not have a choice when cancer entered my husband's life. But I do have a choice on how I view those experiences, and I count it a privilege to share some of the lessons I have learned along the way.

LESSON 1: THE TIMES, THEY ARE A CHANGING

In 1990, I purchased a small travel agency in a storefront location. On-time delivery of paper tickets was key to my customers' satisfaction. Today, the travel industry is unrecognizable from 15 years ago. Paper tickets are becoming collectors' items. And the speed with which all this change is occurring can only be described as breakneck.

Healthcare is experiencing its own breakneck evolution. The difference is that in healthcare there is no shortage of sick people; just the opposite. More accurate diagnoses are resulting in new conditions. Improved treatments are keeping patients alive longer, creating whole new populations. For example, I am a member of one of the fastest-growing medical populations: congenital heart patients living into adulthood. Lifestyle issues such as obesity, smoking, and stress are producing patients in unprecedented numbers. In order for healthcare systems to function optimally, they need to embrace constant change.

LESSON 2: PATIENTS, THEY ARE A CHANGING

Days of obedient patients who listen without question to professionals in starched, white uniforms are going the way of storefront travel agents. The white lab coat is no longer the symbol of total, unquestioned authority. Women, who make the vast majority of healthcare decisions, are becoming more empowered. As patients are becoming increasingly tech savvy, they are tapping into a mind-boggling array of healthcare information on the Internet. Technology is creating a standard of instant communication. Immigration is creating whole populations who require additional services, such as translation, to assure proper care and treatment.

Books with titles such as *You, The Smart Patient,*[7] *The Intelligent Patient's Guide to the Doctor-Patient Relationship,*[8] and *Don't Let Your HMO Kill You*[9] carefully spell out what patients and their caregivers can and should do. Patients and caregivers want answers. They are feeling empowered, and they want to step up and become more involved. When healthcare systems embrace individuality and the fact that patients and their caregivers are the ultimate consumers rather than objects of care, then together a team relationship can be formed to better meet and respond to the needs of everyone.

LESSON 3: DESPITE ADVANCES IN HEALTHCARE, LITTLE THINGS STILL MAKE A DIFFERENCE

Despite the impact of science and technology on healthcare, meeting the basic needs of the patient still has the biggest impact on how patients and their caregivers perceive their experiences within a healthcare system. One of the most significant differences between a medical professional who is just doing a job and one who is making a difference is the ability to see the patient and his supporters as complex individuals with unique histories, fears, hopes, questions, and passions that profoundly affect who they are and how they will respond to care. Medical professionals who see the patient as a physical specimen, a sum of lab results and statistics recorded in a file, may get the job done, but the experience will be empty and prone to problems. When I underwent my first chest X-ray as a child, I was treated like an object not worthy of receiving an explanation of what was about to happen and why. Unfortunately, the trauma I experienced was not just the result of a 1950s attitude toward children. Sadly, patients of all ages, especially the aged and infirm, still feel as if they are being treated like children simply because information is not offered.

Healthcare systems that have a policy of explaining every procedure and why it is necessary honor the patient's right to know and solicit his understanding and cooperation. I experienced this during both of my open-heart surgeries. The first hospital had a policy of taking the patient and one caregiver on a tour of the surgical intensive care unit (ICU) prior to surgery. The tour included seeing the room where I would go immediately following surgery. I was introduced to the nursing staff and was shown some of the equipment that would help in my recovery. I was hesitant about taking the tour, but when I woke after surgery I had a clear sense of where I was and what was happening to me. Nurses assigned to my care said, "Hi, I'm Nancy, we've already met."

My second open-heart surgery was at a different hospital that also had a policy of clear communication, even if the patient appeared to be sleeping. I remember hearing nurses explaining why they were suctioning my lungs. The procedure was unpleasant, but because I was included as part of the team, I was able to offer my full cooperation.

Communication is particularly important when a patient complains about his care. He is, at the outset, expressing a need for help to resolve a problem. He is saying, in effect, I want this relationship to continue, but I need you to help me. Patients who complain are actually more loyal to the medical staff than those who are dissatisfied but say nothing.[10] The optimum solution is for patients, their support network, and medical professionals to come together and function as a team. Team players see themselves as united in one purpose: to achieve the best possible outcome for the patient and his caregivers. No one person decides and dictates how the patient's care should be handled.

LESSON 4: LISTEN WITH COMPASSION

Visit any medically oriented online message board such as WomenHeart.org, sponsored by the National Coalition for Women with Heart Disease, and the most common thread is one of communication. "ER says I'm female so problem not heart" and "How do I get my doc to listen?" are typical discussion topics.

Just as patients are the sum of their experiences, medical professionals come to each patient encounter with their own set of notions and expectations. A 25-year-old female patient suggesting a course of treatment as outlined in *Good Housekeeping* magazine is seen by one doctor as suspect and is advised to become pregnant. A patient with flu-like symptoms is given a regimen of antibiotics without exploring the history of congenital heart disease coupled with a recent dental visit.

A gifted professional perfects the art of listening in a way that demonstrates understanding and respect. This results in a rapport that becomes the foundation for effective care.

For example, the internist who oversaw my care during my first open-heart surgery demonstrated this skill through words and actions. He would stroll into the examining room, look directly at me as he spoke, ponder, if only for a moment, what I was saying, and repeat my words to clarify that we understood each other. When our visit included longer discussions, the doctor would make a point to sit in a chair. Independently, these gestures seem small and insignificant, but together they spoke volumes. Thirty years later, I vividly remember how I felt. I knew this highly respected doctor had a full load of patients, yet his style of communication made me believe I was the only patient on his agenda. I believed this doctor cared for me and what was happening to me. I wanted to follow his orders and show the respect I had for him. We functioned as a team, and together I believed we would achieve the most favorable outcome.

Contrast this with the obstetrician who delivered my second child. For nine months, each visit would begin with his rushing into the examining room. He would pause at the door and look at his watch. This entrance told me he had places to go and better things to do. As my ninth month approached, we decided that a Cesarean section would be necessary. Looking at the calendar, I suggested the first Friday after my due date. This would allow my husband to spend the weekend at the hospital. But my doctor said, "That won't work. I play golf on Fridays." If we shared an interest in golf, this comment might have been an opportunity to bond. But, because of the physician's rushed style over the previous months, what I heard was lack of concern and availability on his part. Together, the physician's rushed demeanor and "golf on Fridays" confirmed my earlier suspicions: I was an intrusion and not a priority.

The agreed-upon Thursday delivery date arrived, and as I lay on the gurney waiting for the surgical suite to be made available, I had an anaphylactic reaction to vancomycin, a favorite antibiotic for heart patients, which my obstetrician had added to my IV. Because of my heart history, the doctor's decision to use antibiotics was sound, but his lack of communication resulted in my being unaware that anything had been added to my IV. Precious minutes went by as the medicine entered my system before I realized something was very wrong. Fortunately, a quick response by the healthcare team averted a potential disaster. As the afternoon progressed, it was decided that I was in no condition to deliver a baby. My son was born the next day, Friday. Shortly after my son's birth, I shared my feelings and frustrations with my internist, who had recommended this obstetrician. I suggested he not recommend this obstetrician again.

LESSON 5: EVALUATE SURROUNDINGS WITH CRITICAL EYES

The impact of the physical environment should not be underestimated. Three recent visits to three different clinical settings left me with significantly different experiences based purely on physical settings.

Recently, I was scheduled for the battery to be replaced on my pacemaker. The procedure was scheduled at my local hospital's 10-story outpatient surgical center. Entering the building, I immediately noticed the first floor had recently undergone an impressive renovation. Floors, lighting, furniture, and even layout had been carefully designed with the latest in colors and textures in mind. My instructions were to arrive at admitting promptly at 7:00 A.M. It was apparent that lots of other patients had received the same instructions for their procedures. A long counter, separated by partitions, was available for admitting personnel to begin the requisite paperwork. But there was a problem. Designers included six partitioned areas, but only two people were working. And to make matters worse, patients whose numbers increased by the minute were forced to stand and wait their turn, even though they may have been sick, tired, and afraid. Although designers did their jobs in making the outpatient admitting area pretty, management forgot to ask themselves, "Why are we here, and what do those people need?"

Just weeks earlier, I found myself at another major medical center as a visitor. A distant family member was in intensive care following a stroke. As family members maintained a vigil, they had two places to spend their time. One was a tiny waiting room down the hall from the ICU lined with tattered, straight-back chairs. The room was overflowing with a variety of family members who, I suspected, changed in identity over time but not in number. As hours turned to days, the only other place for people to maintain their vigil was the hospital cafeteria. An elevator ride down to the hospital's basement opened into a dismal cinder-block corridor. One small sign pointed the way to the hospital's cafeteria. As we groped and wove our way around abandoned wheelchairs, gurneys, and supply carts, the wall color changed from chipped gray to stained pastels. A cracked, stained linoleum floor guided us to our destination. A coat of paint, new flooring, equipment organization, and improved lighting would have sent the message, "We care," to both staff and visitors.

My third experience was my admittance to Women and Infants Hospital of Rhode Island, one of the nation's leading specialty hospitals for women and newborns. In 2001, after experiencing a random ache in my side, CAT scan results suggested I had ovarian cancer or a burst appendix. As my husband and I walked in the door of Women and Infants, a woman in a business suit walked up and greeted us. She introduced herself as a member of the hospital's management team and asked how she could help us. This woman's job was in administration, but she also volunteered as a member of a team that greeted anyone walking into the hospital to make sure people felt welcome and knew where to go. We were directed to admitting, and a clerk was waiting. Even though I was being admitted as an emergency, my basic paperwork had already been started. In a matter of minutes, I was escorted to a medical floor. The nurse who escorted me to my room described some of the background of the hospital and its mission of honoring the patient. She acclimated me to my room and pointed out that everything had been designed with the patient's needs in mind. Every room in the hospital was a private room with a large bathroom with a curtained door. Initially, I was surprised and uncertain about the curtained door. The nurse said this feature afforded easy access if a patient needed help. Designers thoughtfully provided ample fabric, which afforded privacy in addition to easy access.

As my stay continued, I noticed that housekeeping personnel maintained a specific policy of respect for the patient. If I was sleeping, they would quietly leave the room and return later. When they did work in my room, they acknowledged me with a smile and a greeting. Food service checked to make sure my order was correct and the food satisfactory. One afternoon, my nurse came by and said, "I've got a little time, would you care for a back massage?" As an expert on being sick, I was intrigued and amazed. "Tell me about working here," I asked several people who had some kind of role in my care. "Management cares," I was told. "Management hears us." "When they can't meet our needs, we understand why." Longevity on the job at this hospital was normal. Employees said they could not imagine working anywhere else. Medical professionals have the same basic needs of feeling validated and trusted in their roles just as patients and their caregivers do. When the staff feels recognized and appreciated, they in turn pass that on to the people they are trained to serve. Even though Boston's world-renowned health centers are only one hour away, I continuously encourage women I meet to consider receiving care at Women and Infants in Rhode Island.

LESSON 6: BE OPEN TO HUMOR

I learned the importance of humor the week I entered the seventh grade. Until then, most of my friends did not realize I was a heart patient. Few people suspected that I was living with a chronic, life-threatening health condition. When the seventh grade dawned, my doctor decided gym classes were too risky for me. This meant that I would not get an olive green jumpsuit that served as the gym uniform, and I longed for that jumpsuit more than anything. But there was no swaying school officials or my mother once the doctor said no. Instead, I was assigned the job of library monitor. I would get to shush my peers instead of kicking and running and jumping. I was doomed.

The day the uniforms were handed out, my fellow seventh graders were quick to notice. They asked me, "Hey, why don't *you* get a gym uniform? What's *wrong* with you?" There is nothing more traumatic for a seventh grader than to be singled out as different from the group. I needed to respond on a level my peers could understand.

"You know how your heart goes *thump-thump*?" I started. "Well, my heart goes *thump-pssh, thump-pssh* because I was born with a hole in my heart." As my friends contemplated this, I decided to add a bit of drama. As I stared into my inquisitors' faces, I added, "I could go like *that!*" With the snap of my fingers, I became *walking death!* A more mature, sophisticated mind might find this concept a bit repulsive, but in the mind of a seventh grader, *walking death* was cool. I went from sick dork to cool kid with the snap of a finger.

That day, I learned one of the most valuable lessons of my life: I could not control many of the circumstances that would define my life. I could not prevent challenges, but I could control how I chose to look at those circumstances. I realized that if I looked at life through humorous eyes, I could have some control; otherwise I had none.

Once when I was speaking at a conference, a woman said her husband had suffered a heart attack earlier that year. Because of other health issues, his prognosis was guarded. This man had a strong wit and quick sense of humor. Now, months later, he was beginning to incorporate humor into his changed circumstances, but his humor was difficult for his family to accept. They were still focused on the what-ifs. I suggested that if the woman and her family allowed her husband the opportunity to use humor, they would be giving him a valuable coping tool.

Humor is a powerful tool that bridges relationships, promotes healing, and inspires control. After I developed heart block following my second open-heart surgery, my cardiologist said that my pacemaker would be managed by the office's electrophysiologist. During our first discussion, I noticed a bulletin board behind his desk with many cartoons about medicine and cardiology. I knew before he opened his mouth that we would have a positive relationship. Healthcare professionals who take their professions seriously but themselves lightly will open doors of communication for the benefit of everyone.

LESSON 7: GRANT ME A GOOD DEATH

Systems of care often focus only on recovery. Wellness or effective accommodations of the patient's condition are the only acceptable outcome. People who spend their lives focused on health see death as a failure. Yet every person will die. Systems of care that view death as normal and acceptable create an environment in which the needs of the patient and his loved ones can be met at this very significant time.

Six days before my husband's death, exploratory surgery revealed that cancer was having a field day inside his gut. As the surgeon entered the waiting room, his eyes said it all. Nothing could be done to save my husband's life. At that point, I decided that I would offer what little companionship and comfort I could. If my husband needed only a tissue, I was going to be there to give it to him. I grabbed sleep in increments of 15 minutes in a chemotherapy chair in my husband's room. My love for him translated to a watchful vigilance that unfortunately was often abrupt and unfriendly. Finally, after six days of maintaining a vigil at his bedside with only brief trips home to give the kids a hug and take a shower, I took the nurses' advice and went home to sleep. That night my husband passed away. At no time during those six days was hospice service or palliative care offered or suggested. Instead, the day before my husband's death, an unfamiliar doctor walked into his room and announced that my husband's case would be presented at the hospital's next tumor board meeting. The purpose was to select some regimen of chemotherapy for my husband, even though every oncologist involved in his care had said chemo would have little if any effect. "Oh, and you know, we're not thinking of a cure," the doctor stated matter-of-a-factly as he turned and left the room.

If hospice care had been made available, our family could have spent these last six days together focused on our love. My children would have had the opportunity to say good-bye to their daddy. Physical comfort for my husband would have been a top priority rather than an afterthought when I insisted upon it. My needs would have been addressed. Healthcare systems that view death as a sacred time rather than a failure of science honor the love, compassion, and needs of the people facing this ultimate end.

Although healthcare systems are complex and require constant change, those that view patients as unique individuals and consumers will best be able to meet the needs of everyone involved. When honor and respect become the cornerstones for decisions within a healthcare system, patients, caregivers, and healthcare workers are able to function as team members, united in purpose and focused on the achieving the best possible outcome.

Key Concepts

- Healthcare is experiencing its own breakneck evolution. In order for healthcare systems to function optimally, they need to embrace constant change, not stick to old patterns.
- When healthcare systems embrace individuality and the fact that the patient and his caregivers are consumers rather than objects, then a team relationship can be formed to better respond to the needs of everyone.
- It is crucial that medical professionals see the patient and his support network as complex individuals with unique histories, fears, hopes,

questions, and passions that profoundly affect who they are and how they will respond to care.

- Healthcare systems that have a policy of explaining every procedure and why it is necessary honor a patient's right to know and solicit his understanding and cooperation. The optimum solution is for patients, their supporters, and medical professionals to function as a team. Team players see themselves as united to achieve the best possible outcome for the patient and his caregivers.

- Healthcare systems that listen effectively will be more able to serve the patient's needs. When a patient's needs are met, the needs of the medical professionals are supported and encouraged.

- Healthcare systems that look at their practices and policies as well as physical environments through the eyes of patients will see opportunities for improvement.

- Humor is a powerful tool that bridges relationships, promotes healing, and inspires a sense of control. Healthcare professionals who take their professions seriously but themselves lightly will open doors of communication that will benefit everyone involved.

- Healthcare systems that view death as a sacred time rather than a failure honor love and compassion and the needs of people facing this ultimate end.

NOTES

1. Baker, S. K. 1998. *Managing Patient Expectations: The Art of Finding and Keeping Loyal Patients.* San Francisco: Jossey-Bass, ix.

2. Cleary, P. D. 2003. "A Hospitalization from Hell: A Patient's Perspective on Quality." *Annals of Internal Medicine* 138 (1): 33–39.

3. Baker, 48.

4. *Merriam-Webster's Online Dictionary.* 2001. Springfield, MA: Merriam-Webster. Available at www.m-w.com.

5. Keiffer, E. 1978. "Twin Miracles." *Good Housekeeping,* January: 75, 129.

6. Frank, A. W. 1992. *At the Will of the Body: Reflections on Illness.* Wilmington, MA: Houghton Mifflin, 1.

7. Roizen, M. F., and M. C. Oz. 2006. *You the Smart Patient: An Insider's Handbook for Getting the Best Treatment.* New York: Free Press.

8. Korsch, B. M., and C. Harding. 1997. *The Intelligent Patient's Guide to the Doctor-Patient Relationship.* Oxford: Oxford University Press.

9. Theodosakis, J., and D. T. Feinberg. 2000. *Don't Let Your HMO Kill You.* New York: Routledge.

10. Baker, 169.

CHAPTER 10

Moving Ideas from the Laboratory to the Marketplace: How Scientists and Business Leaders Engage to Take Action

Lynn Johnson Langer

Biotechnology is a relatively young industry that has evolved rapidly since its beginnings in the early 1970s. Since then, it has developed into a multibillion-dollar industry with many commercial products that have contributed to society with new biopharmaceuticals, food, and energy products and processes. Although biotechnological research and development (R&D) have provided numerous benefits to society, many promising discoveries have not reached consumers because of the difficulties involved in bringing new technologies to market. The high costs and resources required in early-stage research, discovery, and development of new biotechnology ideas can be prohibitive for all but the most promising projects. The Tufts Center for Drug Development estimates that it costs more than $800 million to bring a biopharmaceutical product from the research bench to the consumer.[1] However, this number probably includes the amortized costs of multiple failures and hundreds of millions in marketing costs. The biotechnology industry is highly dynamic, and improvements and changes in research methods occur frequently. New technologies used in drug discovery, for example, may completely change how scientists conduct their investigations. These new discoveries must be assessed and put through the development cycle as quickly as possible. Even so, it may take 10 years or more for new discoveries to reach consumers.

For scientific discoveries such as therapeutics to leave the laboratory and be developed into products, scientists and business professionals must collaborate to bring new products through clinical trials and the regulatory process. The concept of collegial collaboration can be different for basic research scientists who may prefer to work in an environment that reduces their involvement with other scientists. Often, by nature, scientists tend to be more introverted. These differences between how scientists and business professionals interact may partially explain the challenges involving commercializing of new products. Many factors contribute to effective commercialization, but relatively little research has been conducted on what scientists must do to successfully move ideas out of the laboratory in ways that engage business leaders to take action. To understand the difficulty in moving ideas from the laboratory, we must first examine the culture in which research typically takes place.

In a preliminary study, the author reviewed almost 300 research studies that yielded 13 articles related to how best to move ideas from the laboratory. Additionally, the author interviewed nine leaders from the biotechnology industry: Five were scientists holding doctorates of philosophy (PhD), one held a master's of science (MS) in biotechnology and a juris doctorate, two held an MS in chemistry, and one was a nonscientist with a business background. Each respondent was asked, "What do scientists do to successfully move ideas from the laboratory and engage business leaders to take action?" Results from the interviews indicated a diversity of factors; however, the consistent, emergent theme was social interaction that permitted effective communication between both scientists and business professionals. This appears to be critical in moving ideas from the laboratory.

Other themes also emerged in the literature and through the interviews: networking, culture, organizational processes, and leadership. These themes have different levels of influence on the process. Many scholars and practitioners agree that communication is the key element required for moving ideas out of the laboratory; however, several factors influence the organization's and the individual's ability to communicate effectively. These factors include the ability and encouragement to network in a culture conducive to open communication, and having formal organizational processes in place permits the flow of ideas out of the laboratory. Finally, these factors are directly affected by the organization's leadership and its ability to set a tone that allows and encourages open communication. This chapter reviews the literature and assesses initial findings from interviews with science and business leaders in the biotechnology industry.

MARKETPLACE OF IDEAS

Researchers and practitioners (e.g., those responsible for commercializing technologies) collaborate very differently when compared to how such exchanges may occur in purely research settings. The concept of collaboration is different for scientists, who often prefer to keep their findings to themselves until they are fully explored. Scientists also tend to prefer to limit their communications to other scientists. An example of this concept came from a discussion with a nonscientist senior executive in a leading biopharmaceutical company. This executive stated, "Frequent communications, networking, and relationships with frequent internal communication is necessary."[2] She continued that it is not just the idea but how well the scientist is able to communicate that idea and how well he or she can network internally. She discussed observing a research scientist at an informal company gathering. The scientist was excitedly explaining a new discovery to a group of scientists and business staff from different departments. The executive explained that the scientist was effective at moving ideas from the laboratory partly because of his ability to share his excitement over what he had discovered with others. Later that day, the executive mentioned the interchange to the company president. The president had also not heard about the idea but was interested to learn more. Had this conversation not been overheard, the idea may not have been developed. This example suggests two things. First, opportunities should be provided to scientists to share what they perceive to be exciting discoveries and, second, both formal and informal methods should exist for circulating these interactions within the organization.

In 1981, Yin and Gwaltney described a theory that is appropriately here, called *social interaction theory*.[3] They argue that the topic of communication between researchers and others in the organization does not need to be specific to the research at hand. Any communication between researchers and practitioners raises one another's consciousness about the other. Yin and Gwaltney state that such communication "produces a 'rich marketplace of ideas'" (21). This kind of workplace communication can have serendipitous effects. Researchers may change the focus of their research based on dialogue with end users. In addition, users may change future projections to reflect ongoing research. In this environment, acceptance of a new technology ultimately occurs (or does not occur) based on the effectiveness of ongoing communications. A better understanding of others' ways of thinking is important in building trust and further increasing communication.

NETWORKING OR BRAGGING: THE CULTURAL DIVIDE

According to Allen, "increased communication between R&D projects and other elements of the laboratory staff were in every case strongly related to project performance" (123).[4] Allen's 1984 book, *Managing the Flow of Technology: Technology Transfer and the Dissemination of Technological Information with the R&D Organization*, was the culmination of a 10-year research project that examined communication and organizational structure in R&D groups of scientists and engineers. Although increased communication is related to project performance, scientists who talk about their work prior to publication may be seen by other scientists as self-promoting when they communicate their ideas outside their own laboratory. One person we interviewed was a nonscientist leader within a successful biotechnology organization. She described the culture of communication among scientists as taking place within discrete groups that function as a so-called discourse community and operating differently from other networks. (A discourse community is a group with stated and unstated conventions and ways of communicating.) First, scientists tend not to be overly communicative on an informal basis. Second, because some scientists see the discussion of one's discoveries as bragging, some scientists may feel inhibited from this informal communication. Based on our current research, we conclude that although some scientists are chastised for self-promotion, this type of communication needs to become a more natural style for scientists as part of their networking. Organizational leaders must continually work to facilitate, change, or create an organizational culture that values open networking and communication. Allen's research confirmed that it is up to the leaders of the organization to provide multiple, different opportunities for scientists to network and share their results with others. She also said there is always a "tension" when scientists are seen as "overly communicative" and that leaders must constantly be aware of potential tensions created within the internal scientific discourse community.

Another interviewee, a scientist, also discussed bragging, noting that although it is unacceptable for scientists to "brag too much or to talk too much" about the potential of one's findings, in business the opposite is true.[2] In a business environment, scientists are not thought of very highly if they do not champion their own ideas. The respondent noted, however, that there is a "continuum of personality types," with scientists typically at one end of the continuum, and the "used-car salesman types" at the other end. Bringing science to commercial success requires people in the middle who are able to understand and bridge this divide. In a 2003 study conducted by BioPlan Associates of life science commercialization, a large majority of business professionals in life science organizations started their careers or completed their education in the sciences.[5] Therefore, although the great majority of life science business professionals are trained in the sciences, shifting a scientist's focus to business may create a divide between the scientists and their business counterparts. Scientists may feel that those who move into business are shifting their focus to less altruistic work and to more financial gain.

Partly because of the cloistered nature of scientists and their research methods, cross-functional interaction does not happen frequently. Some business professionals may see scientists as introverted and disconnected with what needs to be done to effectively commercialize a product. Scientists may see business professionals as too interested in financial aspects, to the detriment of good science. One chief science officer (CSO) interviewed stated, "we [scientists] really are a very altruistic group, because we feel we are doing good."[2] Scientists fundamentally want to help society at large, even if it does not always make good business sense. The scientific officer explained how hard it can be for scientists to "learn the business." He said, "One of the most important things for scientists to learn is how to develop a value proposition." The CSO stated that making the transition from scientist to business requires a fundamental change in thinking. This change can be difficult for scientists who view technical improvements to a process or discovery as obviously valuable. They frequently cannot understand how such new ideas may not make business sense. The CSO recognized this attitude and explained that even when an idea has scientific merit, the company will not proceed with the research if there is not a large enough market. This difference in perception of what intrinsically makes up a good idea can be the source of friction between the scientific and business communities.

KNOWLEDGE TRANSFER AND NETWORKING

The transfer of knowledge across departments can be difficult because knowledge is frequently tacit, not well defined, and difficult to articulate. As organizations grow, it becomes increasingly difficult to share knowledge on an informal basis. Argote and Ingram studied the transfer of knowledge within scientific organizations and found the need to provide multiple means of communication within and between groups.[6] This view was described by one of our interviewees, who stated, "The easiest part is developing the new assay. The hardest part is trying to wrap it up in a bow and throwing it to the development people to get them to do something!"[2] Therefore, to facilitate knowledge transfer, organizations need to provide a variety of ways in which communication can take place.

Moving ideas out of the laboratory, or technology transfer, becomes more difficult as the level of technology increases, because there are fewer target audiences. The simpler the technology, the easier the process involved in transferring that technology to the business development professionals. This concept may help explain why it is difficult to move most scientific ideas involved in biotechnology and biopharmaceuticals from the laboratory because they are almost inevitably complex. A scientist's social network plays an important role in knowledge transfer and provides links between scientists and groups within organizations to new sources of knowledge. This linking facilitates the integration of new technology and is particularly valuable with researchers compared with other organizational groups. Argote and Ingram note that members of a network identify most strongly with members of that group and may have a more difficult time communicating with those outside their own personal network.[6] For science to be successfully transferred from the laboratory, scientists need to identify with the larger organization and not just with other researchers in their group.

Other researchers found similar results. Kivimaki et al. conducted a quantitative study of 492 employees involved in R&D at 32 companies.[7] The authors found that high levels of interaction and communication between departments is an important factor in innovation of ideas. Kivimaki et al. found that "a participative climate and interaction between the personnel in R&D, marketing and production were related to perceived innovative effectiveness" (3). A climate of frequent interaction fosters higher levels of communication, "which, in turn, may result in the cross-fertilization of ideas" (34). Their studies showed that effective internal communication that involves close interpersonal and interdepartmental contacts substantially contributes to successful problem solving, experimentation, and innovation.

One business leader we interviewed from a small biotech organization felt, "Leadership from the top that encourages cross-functional networking and communication is critical. Whether it is a formal Monday staff meeting or a friendly Friday afternoon gathering, effective interdepartmental communications and networking is dependent on the culture of the organization."[2] However it fits, employees need to feel safe and encouraged to participate in open inter- and intradepartmental networking. The level of formality can be dependent on the specific organization.

Studies by Hirst and Mann further suggest that important decisions are frequently made informally through networks.[8] Hirst and Mann suggest that leaders should also be encouraged to build networks and provide multiple opportunities for employees to network. They suggest "in-house research forums and networking events, particularly for peer groups, provide an efficient means of developing leaders' intra-company links and the potential pool of knowledge sharing resources" (156).

Cross-functional teams provide an opportunity to network for scientists and business professionals. However, creating an environment in which cross-functional teams become self-sustaining and a positive influence on the organization and team members can be challenging. Nonaka describes organization knowledge as being created from the continuous incorporation and feedback of tacit to explicit knowledge throughout the organization.[9] As organizations grow from small start-up businesses, much of the organizational knowledge is tacit. As the company grows, more formal processes need to be implemented so that the organization's knowledge becomes explicit. Explicit knowledge becomes possible partly by creating cross-functional teams that serve as the "basic building block for structuring the organization knowledge creation process" (24). According to Nonaka, teams induce a self-organizing process for the entire organization. This process benefits the organization by elevating the knowledge that resides at the group level to the organizational level. Networking can be encouraged by processes put in place to facilitate communication across functional areas.

FORMAL PROCESSES FOR COMMUNICATION

Everett Rogers's book, *The Diffusion of Innovation,* is widely considered a classic. He explains that diffusion is "the process in which an innovation is communicated through certain channels over time among the members of a social system" (5). Rogers describes two terms: homophily, in which individuals communicating are similar to one another, and heterophily, in which those communicating are different.[10] Diffusion of ideas is easier for groups of homophilic individuals. The individuals share traits and trust one another. Because scientists are part of one homophilic group and business professionals are part of another, the two groups are prone to difficulties in communication. An example of this was described by one scientist respondent, who stated, "Scientists tend to be introverts who want to stick with their own. In order for a scientific idea to be noticed, a scientist has to be willing to be wrong."[2] This respondent claimed that PhD scientists are frequently accustomed to being right and said that, "[F]or scientists who are used to being the smartest people in a room, it can be difficult to take the risk of being wrong about a scientific idea for development."[2] When business professionals determine that a technically good idea will not be profitable, scientists are sometimes left at a loss to understand how such a technically superior product might not also be a commercially superior product. Scientists are not accustomed to the iterative process commonly used in business. Scientists, this respondent feels, are more comfortable with following protocols and making small adjustments to make sure things work. They are not trained for the often-fuzzy nature of business.

Rogers states that for an innovation to be accepted and ultimately adopted, the individuals must go through an "innovation-decision process."[10] According to Rogers, this is "the process through which an individual (or other decision-making unit) passes from first knowledge of an innovation, to the formation of an attitude toward the innovation, to a decision to adopt or reject, to implementation and use of the new idea, and to confirmation of this decision" (20). The innovation-decision process is what business leaders use to determine whether they will take action on a new scientific idea. They must decide to adopt, reject, implement, or use the idea. Scientists and business professionals must develop interpersonal communication networks with one another to allow for easier understanding of ideas developed within the network.

The decision to take action on an innovation can require a great deal of time and resources. Knowledge, persuasion, and decision are the stages in which scientists are most likely to effectively motivate business professionals to take action. Knowledge is more than exposure to an idea; rather, the individual understands how the idea will work. Persuasion comes when the person determines whether the idea has merit and a decision is made regarding further development of the idea. As discussed previously, companies with formal processes in place to evaluate new ideas are at an advantage when establishing effective cross-departmental communication processes. Scientists whom the author interviewed from several successful companies noted that their organizations have formal review processes in place for new ideas. In some, weekly meetings are held with people from different functional areas to determine if a new idea has merit. Business professionals and scientists may hold equal authority in these weekly meetings. Several interviewees mentioned that having formal processes in place makes communication between scientists and business professionals easier.

Another scientist turned business leader stated that, in his organization, strategy is formulated with scientists and business professionals from the beginning of a research project. There are weekly update meetings with scientists and business professionals. If a scientist finds something unexpected, he or she would either wait until the weekly meeting or would approach the team leader about the finding. If the scientists report a new finding to the team leader, it is then brought to the attention of the chief science officer, who makes a determination as to whether the finding should be brought to the attention of the chief executive officer (CEO).

Innovators are change agents and must persuade others to ultimately adopt their ideas. Interestingly, according to Rogers, "the most innovative member of a system is very often perceived as a deviant from the social system and is accorded a status of low credibility by the average members of the system. This individual's role in diffusion (especially in persuading others to adopt the innovation) is therefore very limited" (26).[10] Opinion or informal leaders of the group have the most sway in a group's or individual's decision about the innovation. Opinion leaders are generally informal leaders of a group and are not necessarily related to positional authority. Informal leaders become leaders through the trust of the individuals in the group. In organizations in which change and innovation are encouraged, opinion leaders tend to be innovative. If an organization does not encourage change, however, informal leaders are not encouraged to become innovative. Opinion leaders become role models for others who will mirror their innovative (or static, if that turns out to be the case) behavior. It is important, therefore, that scientists network with opinion leaders within the business decision-makers group. A high degree of interaction and communication is required of scientists and business professionals to build enough trust to adopt new ideas in highly uncertain situations.

One former scientist turned business leader stated that, if the idea is at an early stage, the possibility of moving the idea from the laboratory was often dependent on the effectiveness of a previously developed partnership between the scientist and a business leader. Such partnerships might be established within a variety of departments, including marketing, manufacturing, or finance.

To make these partnerships work, however, requires communication skills. Scientists are not always comfortable or capable of communicating with people with different styles and personalities. When there is no relationship, a transfer of knowledge is not likely to occur. The scientist must be capable of influencing the new person or group and must use information as part of his or her communication process. This information might include such things as social systems or personality profiles. Social systems would include the typical social network that the scientist already has in place. Understanding personality profiles such as those described by Myers et al. provides scientists with the tools to adjust their style to meet those with whom they are attempting to engage.[11]

One scientist interviewed is a manager at a highly successful biotechnology organization. This scientist stated that, every week, the company receives proposals for new product ideas from both inside and outside the company. A team meets weekly to review the new ideas. The team consists of a science officer and key business development professionals. The committee changes its composition depending on the kind of products being reviewed. The interviewee stated that this formally scheduled meeting creates an atmosphere of trust and shared language between the scientists and business professionals.

Rogers also describes three types of knowledge associated with innovation:[10]

- Awareness knowledge: Information that an innovation exists.
- How-to knowledge: Information that is necessary to use an innovation properly.
- Principles knowledge: Information dealing with the functioning principles underlying how an innovation works.

Change agents generally focus on awareness knowledge. Rogers argues that change agents would be most successful if they focus on how-to knowledge, because decisions to accept or reject an idea are most often made from how-to knowledge. If business professionals can more clearly understand how end users might value a technical innovation, they may be more likely to take action toward developing these technologies. Again, this process would involve extensive communication between the scientist and the potential business champion. Such processes can be facilitated by regularly scheduled meetings with cross-functional teams.

Finally, Rogers argues that any innovation must be "consistent with the existing values, past experiences, and needs of potential adoptors" (241).[10] The innovation must also be consistent with values of business professionals making the decision to move forward with a new scientific idea. For instance, an interviewee at one highly successful biotechnology organization stated that all new product ideas must be consistent with the mission of the company and must not have any existing competing alternatives. This is also consistent with the values of that organization. Even for ideas that are technically and commercially meritorious, if they are not aligned with the stated values of the organization, they are rejected.

LEADERSHIP

Leadership directly affects the culture of an organization. One industry leader stated that it is up to the leaders within the organization to provide multiple opportunities for scientists to network and share their results with others. Scientific discourse communities function differently from other networks, and, as a result, scientists tend not to be overly communicative on an informal basis. It tends to be the responsibility of organizational leaders to help create an environment in which open communication is not just accepted but expected.

Hirst and Mann reported on a longitudinal study to discover which communication variables most affected team performance.[8] They evaluated 350 employees from 56 teams in 4 organizations. The researchers found that it is more important for the leader to "boundary span" than for members of the team to do so (147). Their study points to the importance of communication in facilitating innovation and performance. Hirst and Mann suggest that although leadership training programs may rightly teach leaders to stimulate debate and act as "devil's advocates," more attention to systemic issues is critical for long-lasting cultural and behavioral change to occur. In other words, leaders must be held accountable, and they must provide evidence of innovations being developed. The authors further suggest that mentoring and training programs are important for leaders to learn how to be most influential and to hone their "championing skills" (156). Leaders need to be encouraged and trained to network both formally and informally. One scientist turned business leader stated that his organization holds weekly meetings to discuss research findings, but that these meetings also serve as networking and team-building opportunities.

Elkins and Keller reviewed literature related to management of research and development activities within organizations.[12] They found two important insights similar to Hirst and Mann. First, Elkins and Keller uncovered a "small number of studies that examined leadership from a strategic perspective and found links between top management actions and R&D project performance" (600). Second, the authors concluded from their literature review research that "the leaders should also boundary span with important constituents outside the project group, such as managers and personnel in marketing, manufacturing, and operating divisions, as well as with customers from outside the firm. This kind of activity to champion the project can be critical to the survival and success of the project" (601). One scientist from a very successful, established biotechnology organization reiterated this idea. She said her organization also holds weekly meetings with leaders from across the organization to keep everyone up-to-date on existing and new projects. The scientist argues that these sorts of formal boundary-spanning opportunities lead to less structured, informal networking across the organization.

Shim and Lee also did a comprehensive examination of influence styles of R&D project leaders.[13] They collected data from 83 ongoing research projects to explore the behaviors of R&D project leaders by looking at social influences. They found that specific styles of influence work better in different organizations, although a mainly tactical approach was most often effective. Scientists would most likely be more effective at tactical styles of influence with other scientists, because of their communication and cultural similarities. The authors also found that, to be effective, project leaders must cross organizational boundaries to garner the necessary support for new ideas. This concept is supported by interviews with a scientist turned chief operating officer, who felt that team leaders are the true champions of new ideas, not the team members themselves.

Many in the biotechnology industry have debated the need for scientist-managers. Some have advocated that more nonscientists must be brought in to improve the overall quality of management. One scientist we interviewed expressed the counter to this argument, that for science to be a commercial success, the CEO or other senior executives should be scientists. After having worked at several biotechnology organizations both large and small, this scientist noted that other companies founded at about the same time were not as successful. The differentiating factor, according to this respondent, was that the less-successful companies were run by business professionals who were not scientists. The CEO of this respondent's current organization is a scientist and as such is able to understand which potential products have the greater likelihood of being successful. The scientist claims that the scientist-CEO has "a lot of respect for basic research" and has created an atmosphere of open dialogue. At other biotech organizations, the business professionals did not have the depth of experience necessary to bring a complicated product to market. This CEO has created a vision for the company that is well articulated and embraced by the employees, and the company mission statement requires that any new product they develop must not be already available elsewhere. Finally, this scientist has been working for a number of years on a product that will soon receive Food and Drug Administration (FDA) approval for marketing. The scientist claims that this success is a result of the company having the right cultural environment and because new products receive strong support from company leadership from the beginning through the development of the product.

One might argue that the system created by the scientist-CEO is what has established this successful product development process. Had the same system been created by a nonscientist, would it have been adopted as readily and maintained as productively? The answer may be more an issue of effective leadership—a leader that is capable of instilling and maintaining a good product development process than of the exclusive need for the leader also to be a scientist. Perhaps being a scientist is primarily required only in building a cohesive discourse community. One may conclude, then, that it is not the scientific background that is creating success but the leader's ability to create an atmosphere conducive to open dialogue.

Tidd et al. studied 94 biotechnology start-up businesses and found that three factors were associated with success: location within a significant concentration of similar firms, quality of scientific staff (measured by citations), and the commercial experience of the founder.[14] The number of alliances made between an organization with other organizations had no significant effect on success, and the number of scientific staff in the top management team had a negative association, suggesting that the scientists are best kept in the laboratory.

Tidd et al. found other studies of biotechnology start-up businesses that confirm that too many scientists in senior management positions can be detrimental to the overall number of products under development.[14] Although a scientist-heavy management team may not have the business acumen necessary for success, a balance of scientists and business professionals may be necessary to ensure sound scientific and strategic decisions. In addition, it may not matter if there is a scientist or business professional at the helm of the organization, provided the intra- and intercommunications between scientists and business professionals are effective.

Other studies confirm the importance of leadership in the transition of ideas from the laboratory. Waldman and Atwater conducted a mixed-methods research study involving surveys and open-ended interviewing techniques to examine the development arm of three R&D organizations.[15] They stress the importance of senior-level leadership in product development. "Leadership exhibited at higher organizational levels is significantly correlated with effectiveness" (233). However, their research showed that project-level leadership was not as critical on project success as was senior-level leadership. Interestingly, their research also found that, although ineffective leadership may be important in the death of a project, effective leadership may not be able to salvage a project. In other words, although leadership is important, other factors—particularly project feasibility and team synergy—may be more critical to the success of a project. Clearly, the leader has an impact on which projects are chosen for development and which are not. The decision to proceed with a project requires an understanding of both business and science. Many leaders within the biotechnology industry are trained in one area and not the other. Education of future leaders in both science and business will be a critical component to success of future biotechnology organizations.

MOVING TO THE MARKETPLACE

Most authors and interview respondents argue that communication is one of the critical elements required to move ideas from the laboratory to the marketplace. However, most scientists are not typically trained in communication skills. One of the most significant insights from this research is that there is a deep-seated cultural bias favoring research over practice. Although scientists are not trained in the necessary communications skills to move ideas from the laboratory, the culture may be subtly inhibiting their ability and their desire to communicate effectively.

Schon offers insight into a theory of practice versus academia that is important in understanding scientists in biotechnology. Biotechnology is based on the application of research discoveries. Schon states:

> [The] concept of "application" leads to a view of professional knowledge as a hierarchy in which "general principles" occupy the highest level and "concrete problem solving" the lowest. . . . The application of basic science yields applied science. Applied science yields diagnostic and problem-solving techniques which are applied in turn to the actual delivery of services. The order of application is also an order of derivation and dependence. Applied science is said to "rest on" the foundation of basic science. And the more basic and general the knowledge, the higher the status of its producer. (24)[16]

This concept may be the foundation of the divide between science and business. The highest status, in the minds of the scientist, belongs to basic research. The lowest status belongs to the application of the science.

Schon later states:

> [T]his division of labor reflected a hierarchy of kinds of knowledge which was also a ladder of status. Those who create new theory were thought to be higher in status than those who apply it, and the schools of "higher learning" were thought to be superior to the "lower." Thus were planted the seed of the Positivist curriculum, typical of professional schools in American universities, and the roots of the now-familiar split between research and practice. (37)

Scientists who start their careers by studying biochemistry and cell biology enter a culture in which hard science carries the highest status. Along with this status comes a culture that does not necessarily prepare scientists for the collaboration necessary to move science out of the laboratory.

For the scientist to effectively bring science out of the laboratory, he or she must engage in reflective collaboration with practitioners. According to Schon:

> Researchers and practitioners enter into modes of collaboration very different from the forms of exchange envisaged under the model of applied science. The practitioner does not function here as a mere user of the researcher's product. He reveals to the reflective researcher the ways of thinking that he brings to his practice, and draws on reflective research as an aid to his own reflection-in-action. Moreover, the reflective researcher cannot maintain distance from, much less superiority to, the experience of practice. . . . [H]e must somehow gain an inside view of the experience of practice. Reflective research requires a partnership of practitioner-researchers and researcher-practitioners. (323)

This concept of collaboration is very different for scientists who typically prefer to keep to themselves or to stay involved with other scientists.

Biotechnology is creating the need for scientists who are more at ease working in applied fields, such as engineers and veterinarians. One scientist interviewee previously worked in a biotechnology organization that specialized in veterinary medicine. She stated that the organization did not seem to have many of the communication issues she finds common in other biotechnology organizations.

She reflected that this could be because veterinarians are trained in business at the same time they are trained in veterinary medicine. It is expected that veterinarians will work in a private practice in which they will use skills in both science and business.

According to a survey by BioPlan Associates,[5] the majority of people involved in product commercialization in biotechnology were originally educated as scientists. Many of these scientists found the constraints of the research laboratory too confining and moved out of the laboratory and into the business environment. Many company founders and leaders were originally trained as PhD-level research scientists. These scientists believed that because they were the "smartest people in the room" (as one interviewee stated), they felt that running a business would not be as difficult as they may have presumed. The skills required of a business leader involve forms of communication that generally have not been culturally accepted or taught to scientists. Successful organizations require high-level understanding of both science and business, and it is unusual for people in general to be naturally talented in the communication modes necessary for effective process flow.

For scientists to effectively move ideas from the laboratory to the marketplace, they must work within a culture that supports this effort. The culture of an organization is directly influenced by the leadership of the organization. The traditional research culture is not conducive to scientists communicating outside of this realm. Organizational leaders play a key role in developing the organization's culture and can either support or inhibit effective communication across boundaries. Organization culture is certainly influenced by factors other than leadership, but the core of company culture comes from its leadership. Therefore, further study is needed to understand the role of the leadership and how it influences cross-boundary communication within the organization.

CONCLUSION AND AREAS OF FUTURE RESEARCH

Little research has been done on the role of the leader in biotechnology organizations or on the leader's impact on the success of an organization in terms of research and development of new ideas. Stacey reminds us that reality is constructed by the individual.[17] Human interaction is nonlinear, and to study the movement of science from the laboratory, it is important to look on many levels, not just at the scientist or the leader, but on the complex process itself. Hirst and Mann state that their "study re-iterates the importance of communication in driving innovation and project performance. . . . [O]ur findings add that perceptions of performance are relative as different factors predict different stakeholders ratings of performance. Thus, there is an urgent research and practical need to understand why stakeholders adopt different perspectives" (157).[8] Stakeholders include not only scientists and business professionals within the organization but also customers and investors. In addition to looking at the organization and its stakeholders, a particular focus of future research should be placed on the behaviors of its leader and what specific impact his or her actions have on the success of moving ideas from the lab.

Scientist-leaders must develop interpersonal communication networks with business professionals to facilitate the processes needed to persuade business professionals to take action. A crucial component of the innovation-exchange process is the exchange of information in highly uncertain situations. A high degree of interaction and communication is required of scientists for their ideas to be developed. Scientists must learn the language of business and the styles of communication of business professionals to move ideas from the laboratory to the marketplace. The innovation must also be consistent with existing values of business professionals making the decision to move forward with a new scientific idea. Additional research is necessary to better understand ways to help leaders develop the skills necessary to maximize the development of the science.

In summary, communication is a critical component in moving ideas from the laboratory to engage business leaders to take action. To understand what happens in organizations in which moving ideas is successful, however, one must consider not only the scientists but also the collective processes that include communication, networking, leadership, and organizational culture. The culture is deeply embedded in scientists, and as one interviewee stated, "[S]cientists who move into business or try to have their science translated into business think they are selling themselves to the devil."[2]

REFERENCES

1. Tufts E-News. 2001. "The Ballooning Price Tag." Available at: http://www.tufts.edu/communications/stories/120401BallooningCosts.htm. Accessed February 20, 2007.

2. Interview by the author with a biotechnology leader. All interviews were conducted in confidentiality, and the names of interviewees are withheld by mutual agreement.

3. Yin, R. K., and M. K. Gwaltney. 1981. "Knowledge Utilization as a Networking Process." *Knowledge: Creation, Diffusion, Utilization* 2: 555–80.

4. Allen, T. J. 1984. *Managing the Flow of Technology: Technology Transfer and the Dissemination of Technological Information with the R&D Organization.* 2nd ed. Cambridge, MA: MIT Press.

5. BioPlan Associates, Inc. 2003. *Commercializing Biotechnology and Life Sciences: A Survey of Education and Training Life Sciences Commercialization.* Rockville, MD: Eric Langer.

6. Argote, L., and P. Ingram. 2000. "Knowledge Transfer: A Basis for Competitive Advantage in Firms." *Organizational Behavior and Human Decision Processes* 82 (1): 150–69.

7. Kivimaki, M., H. Lansisalmi, M. Elovainio, et al. 2000. "Communication as a Determinant of Organizational Innovation." *R&D Management* 30 (1): 33–42.

8. Hirst, G., and L. Mann. 2004. "A Model of R&D Leadership and Team Communication: The Relationship with Project Performance." *R&D Management* 34 (2): 147–60.

9. Nonaka, I. 1995. "A Dynamic Theory of Organizational Knowledge Creation." *Organization Science* 5 (1): 14–37.

10. Rogers, E. 2003. *Diffusion of Innovation.* New York: Simon and Schuster.

11. Myers, I. B., M. H. McCaulley, N. L. Quenk, and A. L. Hammer. 1998. *MBTI Manual (A Guide to the Development and Use of the Myers Briggs Type Indicator)*. 3rd ed. Palo Alto, CA: Consulting Psychologists Press.

12. Elkins, T., and R. T. Keller. 2003. "Leadership in Research and Development Organizations: A Literature Review and Conceptual Framework." *Leadership Quarterly* 14 (4–5): 587–606.

13. Shim, D., and M. Lee. 2001. "Upward Influence Styles of R&D Project Leaders." *IEEE Transactions on Engineering Management* 48 (4): 394.

14. Tidd, J., J. Bessant, and K. Pavitt. 2005. *Managing Innovation, Integrating Technological, Market and Organizational Change*. Chichester, UK: Wiley.

15. Waldman, D. A., and L. E. Atwater. 1994. "The Nature of Effective Leadership and Championing Processes at Different Levels in R&D Hierarchy." *Journal of High Technology Management Research* 5 (2): 233–45.

16. Schon, D. 1983. *The Reflective Practitioner: How Professionals Think in Action*. New York: Basic Books.

17. Stacey, R. D. 2001. *Complex Responsive Processes in Organizations: Learning and Knowledge Creation*. London: Routledge.

CHAPTER 11

The Cost of End-of-Life Care

Kenneth A. Fisher with Lindsay E. Rockwell

Death is a natural process, a nonnegotiable part of the journey called life. Ninety percent of us would prefer to die peacefully at home, surrounded by family and friends, with minimal discomfort.[1] In reality, 75 percent of us will die in some kind of institution, often receiving protracted and costly care, without the comfort and support of loved ones.[2] Hospice, which accepts and honors our mortality, facilitates dying with dignity and grace, manages pain and discomfort, and supports and encourages family members through the process. However, fewer than one in five Americans die in hospice care.[3]

Inappropriate care of the dying is one of the most disturbing problems of the expensive U.S. healthcare system. Part of the blame lies with the Patient Self-Determination Act, which created advanced directives and living wills. Quite simply, it does not work because only a fraction of the population has them, and, even when they do exist, many are not followed. It is also absurd to assume that patients and family members with no medical training can imagine future end-of-life situations and plan appropriately.[4]

Consequently, many physicians treating patients in end-of-life situations, especially if there is no advanced directive, assume the patient wants everything possible done and often propose options, some of which they know represent unrealistic goals. Thus, patients and their families, with no medical expertise, become consumers of medical services in much the same ways they are consumers of refrigerators, handbags, and golf shoes, and the physician becomes a technician following orders. At other times, physicians know there is no chance of recovery, but families or guardians refuse to accept this reality. Physicians and hospitals afraid of legal action continue heroic measures until eventually nature takes its course.

This sense of consumerism has been reinforced by court actions such as in the Baby K case.[5] In this case, the court supported the insistent mother of an infant who never developed the human part of her brain and was kept alive for two-and-a-half years at great cost, with no possibility of the child ever achieving any semblance of human life. Another example is the Terri Schiavo case.[6] Because physicians and medical societies were largely silent during the highly visible national debate of these two cases, there was no significant discussion of the difference between being disabled and the lack of any human activity due to permanent loss of the cerebral cortex.

Another factor in the dismal state of end-of-life care is money. Medicare has made across-the-board reimbursement cuts, forcing hospitals to stay viable by decreasing general floor care and promoting excessive use of intensive care units to allow for greater billing.[7] Every year, thousands of patients languish in intensive care units with no chance of recovery. Many have bedsores, decaying digits, and other deforming maladies.

In addition, fee-for-service payments for physicians and an escalating diagnostic-related groups (DRG) payment system for hospitals mean the more that is done, especially more procedures, the more dollars for the hospital. Although it is true that patients are free to refuse any treatment a doctor might suggest, that does not mean physicians should be offering procedures that may not bring a desired result or consenting to treatment that would be considered medically futile (see table 11.1).

The system is convoluted and extremely complex and open to varied interpretation when it comes to actual billing and payment for services. For instance, with our present DRG payment system, if a patient leaves the hospital for another facility, including out-of-home hospice, the hospital, depending on the particular situation, may be reimbursed a lesser amount for services rendered during the hospital stay.

We need a medical profession that the public can trust to protect them from a painful and financially disastrous end of life, yet the Dartmouth Group has documented that our large teaching hospitals provide excessive nonbeneficial end-of-life care,[8] thereby teaching principles of aggressive end-of-life care to future generations of doctors.

The former president of the Institute of Medicine, Dr. Kenneth I. Shine, said, "Our professional organizations must initiate efforts to help physicians and patients understand that more is not necessarily better," and, "A physician in a continuously healing relationship has a responsibility to see that the patient receives appropriate evidence-based care, but does not receive care that adds no value."[9]

We now spend almost twice as much for healthcare per person than any other industrialized country in the world.[10] If we continue to practice our present style of end-of-life care, the costs to our society will become prohibitive as the baby boom generation reaches age 70 and beyond. Now is the time to begin making meaningful changes before a crisis occurs and the ensuing panic forces unwise decisions and hastily made solutions.

Table 11.1
Diagnostic-Related Group (DRG) Payment System: Hypothetical Case

A 78-year-old woman with long-standing diabetes and coronary artery disease is admitted to the hospital because of severe diarrhea, secondary to antibiotics for lower-leg cellulitis. She develops an acute myocardial infarction (non-ST wave elevation), receives cardiac catheterization with stenting, and develops acute renal failure requiring dialysis and bleeds 8 units of blood from the catheterization site. She requires intensive care for shortness of breath, and after 8 days in the unit she dies. Her total hospital costs amounted to approximately $20,000. If a tracheotomy had been performed, the payment under other procedures would have been about another $100,000.

Medicare DRG
557   Percutaneous cardiovascular procedure with drug-eluting stent with a major cardiovascular diagnosis
         CMS wt.   2.7616   A/LOS 4.1   G/LOS 3.0

Principal diagnosis
41041   Acute myocardial infarction, inferior wall, initial episode of care

Secondary diagnosis
41401   Coronary atherosclerosis of native coronary vessel
9961   Mechanical complication of vascular device/implant/graft
5849   Acute renal failure, unspecified
25080   Diabetes mellitus with specified manifestation, type 2 or unspecified type, not stated as uncontrolled
6826   Cellulitis and abscess of leg, except foot
78791   Diarrhea

Principal procedure
0066   Percutaneous transluminal coronary angioplasty (PTCA) or coronary atherectomy

Other procedures
3723   Combined right and left heart cardiac catheterization
3607   Insertion of drug-eluting coronary artery stent(s)
0041   Procedure on two vessels
0046   Insertion of two vascular stents
3895   Venous catheterization for renal dialysis
3995   Hemodialysis
9903   Transfusion of whole blood
9604   Insertion of endotracheal tube
9672   Continuous mechanical ventilation for 96 consecutive hours or more

I certify that the narrative descriptions of the principal and secondary diagnoses and the major procedures performed are accurate and complete to the best of my knowledge.

_____   _____
Physician's Signature   Date

Source: Adapted from American Hospital Directory. 1983. "Medicare Prospective Payment System." With help from the finance department at Bronson Methodist Hospital, Kalamazoo, MI. Available at: http://www.ahd.com/pps.html.

So, let us ask ourselves some questions that can lead to meaningful solutions:

1. Is it possible that physicians could address patients' wishes for beneficial care at each hospital admission?
2. Might we energize the neurological community to revisit the definition of brain death to include complete and permanent loss of the cerebral cortex even with a functioning brain stem?
3. Will the palliative care community form a speakers bureau to discuss end-of-life care with the elderly?
4. Can we stimulate chiefs of medicine and surgery to encourage hospice for end-of-life patients in critical care units and design a streamlined transition for appropriate patients from the intensive care unit setting directly into palliative care?
5. Can we foster better palliative care skills among our medical professionals?
6. Is it possible that our government might listen carefully to a dialogue regarding these issues and act wisely before a crisis is upon us?

As we seek answers to these questions in this chapter, we will look at the present state of end-of-life care, the historical events that have brought us to this point, and offer some recommendations for meaningful change.

THE PRESENT: WHERE WE STAND NOW

Where We Die and the Cost of Death in the United States

According to the findings of a survey by Time/CNN conducted in 2000, approximately 75 percent of Americans die in a medical institution and one-third of these have spent at least 10 days in an intensive care unit (ICU). When asked, however, 75 percent would prefer to die at home.[11] Medicare expenditures during the last year of life average from $28,000[12] to $38,000.[13] However, Medicare does not pay for all expenses (studies are not yet available since the inception of the Medicare drug benefit). An estimate of total cost (out of pocket and other insurance) is that approximately $50,000 is spent on medical care during the last year of life. This cost has been increasing faster than the rate of inflation.

As the elderly become a greater fraction of our population, we will have three choices:

a. Increase the fraction of gross domestic product (GDP) devoted to end-of-life care.
b. Lower the cost of end-of-life care by providing palliative approaches to end stage disease.
c. A combination of a and b.

Use of Technology Rather than Palliative Care in End-of-Life Situations

Cardiopulmonary Resuscitation

As it now stands, a physician, usually with patient and family discussion, must write a do not resuscitate (DNR) order to avoid cardiopulmonary resuscitation (CPR) in case of an in-hospital cardiac arrest. At Beth Israel hospital in Boston,[14] 294 consecutive patients received cardiopulmonary resuscitation after suffering a cardiac arrest. During the 18-month study, 44 percent responded, but only 14 percent survived to be discharged from the hospital. Ten percent were still alive after approximately one year. No patient with sepsis (with systemic signs of infection) survived. There was a 95 percent mortality for patients who were home-bound, hypotensive, or had a diagnosis of renal failure, pneumonia, or cancer, versus a 34 percent mortality for patients without these comorbidities. In another study,[15] 89 patients with cancer had attempted resuscitation, but none survived to leave the hospital. Thirty-three were revived and had protracted ICU admissions. Only 1 of 73 patients (1.4 percent) with sepsis survived to leave the hospital. Similar findings have been obtained in other reviews.[16,17]

Writing in the *New England Journal of Medicine*, L. J Blackhall observes:

> Too often CPR just happens, without inquiry into the patient's wishes or consideration of its chances of success. Both patient autonomy and physician responsibility are important factors in making decisions regarding CPR. In cases in which CPR has any potential for success, the principle of patient autonomy dictates the patient's right to choose or refuse such treatment. The issue of patient autonomy is irrelevant, however, when CPR has no potential benefit. Here, the physician's duty to provide responsible medical care precludes CPR, either as a routine process in the absence of a decision by a patient or as a response to a patient's misguided request for such treatment in the absence of adequate information. In such cases the physician should not offer CPR. Both physicians and patients must come to terms with the inability of medicine to postpone death indefinitely.[18]

Many hospitals have policies regarding physicians writing DNR orders even against family wishes. Still, there are many barriers to withholding CPR:[19]

1. Covering physicians may be unsure of the patient's or family's wishes and opt for doing CPR.
2. Physicians may be unwilling to address these issues with patients and families they do not know and have not taken care of in the past.
3. Physicians might choose to perform CPR rather than face the possibility of a lawsuit.
4. Families may feel they are deserting their loved one if they authorize a DNR order.
5. The topic may not have been raised with the family and the patient may not be able to make decisions.

6. Many teaching hospitals will not allow house staff to decide if CPR may be bypassed, and thus in off-hours and on weekends CPR takes place. This raises the concern that the act of doing CPR may become the default response to a critically ill patient rather than considering the potential futility of such heroic measures.

The estimated cost in dollars as a result of the present U.S. CPR policy is approximately $26.3 billion (table 11.2). The present policy also fosters patient suffering and the development of physician callousness, along with excessive cost.

It would be impossible to develop precise criteria for CPR so that it would be attempted only in those patients most likely to survive; however, it would be reasonable to change our hospital CPR policy to require orders to do CPR.[20] A decrease in the performance of CPR by 50 percent by eliminating the most futile cases would increase the long-term survival rate to 20 percent. This single step could save the U.S. healthcare system approximately $13 billion per year.

Moving toward a New Policy on CPR

Perhaps it is time to ask, "Under what circumstances might CPR be beneficial and therefore worth attempting?" Approximately 85 percent of patients who

Table 11.2
Estimated Cost of In-Hospital Cardiopulmonary Resuscitation (Codes) per Year

This cost estimation was gleaned from sources footnoted at the bottom of the table.
196 codes per year at one hospital (Beth Israel)[a]   Of these codes, 21 patients were alive a year later (10.5%).[a]
Estimated cost per code: $43,565[b]   This cost includes not only the CPR but all of the care provided following resuscitation.
Approximately 1,512,500 people die in hospitals per year (60.5% of all U.S. deaths).[c]
605,000 of those deaths came after at least one resuscitation.[d]
Multiplying those deaths (605,000) by the estimated cost per code from the Beth Israel study ($43,565) yields the astounding figure of $26.3 billion as the estimated total expense of in-hospital codes per year.

[a] Bedell, S. E., and T. L. Delbanco. 1983. "Survival after Cardiopulmonary Resuscitation in the Hospital." *New England Journal of Medicine* 309: 569–76.

[b] Lee, K. H., D. C. Angus, and N. S. Abramson. 1996. "Cardiopulmonary Resuscitation: What Cost to Cheat Death?" *Critical Care Medicine* 24: 2046–52.

[c] Field, M. J., and C. K. Cassel, eds. 1997. "How People Die: Symptoms of Impending Death." In *Approaching Death, Improving Care at the End of Life*. Washington, D.C.: National Academy Press, 45.

[d] Thel, M. C., and M. D. O'Connor. 1999. "Cardiopulmonary Resuscitation: Historical Perspective to Recent Investigations." *American Heart Journal* 137: 39–48.

receive CPR on general inpatient services do not leave the hospital alive. It may be preferable on general inpatient services to inform all patients, or their surrogates, about CPR and to require a written order to attempt it. Institutions could have a panel of physicians serving as an appropriate-care committee, which would oversee that the withholding of CPR was indicated to be certain that decisions were not made inappropriately.

Intensive Care Units and End-of-Life Issues

Fees for ICUs are significantly more than regular hospital care.[21] Hospitals have been increasing their percentage of ICU beds while decreasing regular care beds.[22] Is this practice in the patient's and the nation's best interest? Consider the following data.

In a recent study[23] to explain why Medicare expenditures during the last year of life have not decreased, in spite of the increasing use of hospice, the authors found that in their sample of inpatients, the cost increased about 60 percent from $58 billion (1985) to $90 billion in 1999. The proportion of patients with one or more intensive care unit admissions increased by approximately 5 percent among those who died, compared to approximately 2 percent among survivors. Patients who died had a 10 percent increase in procedures versus a 3 percent increase among survivors. In 1999, 50 percent of feeding tubes, 60 percent of intubations and tracheotomies (tracheotomies greatly increase payment in the present DRG system), and 75 percent of CPRs were in hospitalized patients who died during that hospitalization. Although the proportion of Medicare patients dying in a hospital decreased from 44 percent to 39 percent, those admitted to the ICU during their terminal admission increased from 38 percent to 40 percent, and the proportion of patients having an intensive care procedure increased from 18 percent to 30 percent. One-fifth of these patients received mechanical ventilation, although death was imminent. Per capita hospital expenditures, ICU admissions, and intensive care procedures were higher among patients who died.

In another study,[24] 552,157 deaths in 1999 were reviewed from six states; 38 percent were in-hospital and 22 percent were after ICU admissions. It was projected that, nationwide, approximately 540,000 people die after ICU admission each year in the United States. The average length of stay was approximately 13 days, with a cost of about $24,500 per patient. It is estimated that 20 percent of Americans who die in the hospital do so in the ICU.

With critically ill patients, is it feasible to determine that death is days, weeks, or, at most, months away? To a seasoned physician who has developed judgment after careful examination and discussion, in our opinion, it is possible to make this judgment in 85 percent to 90 percent of cases. In the remaining 10 percent to 15 percent, in time, usually in a week or two, this judgment becomes more obvious in all but a very few cases. In prior discussions with 15 ICU physicians from all over the United States, when asked, "About how many of your ICU patients should be in hospice?" The answer was approximately one-third. When physicians in training are asked about this problem, by far the most common response is, "We just do everything for everybody; we do not make judgment decisions."

Another study[25] tested the hypothesis that patients dying in the hospital had informed discussions regarding palliative care before being admitted to the ICU. This was a chart review study from a teaching hospital. There were 252 hospital deaths during the study; 165 patients (65 percent) died in the ICU. There was no statistically significant difference between general floor and ICU patients with known terminal disease. The house staff referred more of these dying patients to the ICU than seasoned physicians. None of the terminal patients transferred to the ICU had discussions about palliative or end-of-life care as an option. Of those who died in the general wards, 25 percent had such a discussion. Patients who were treated in the ICU had more invasive tests performed and were less likely to have adequate pain control or be given the option of hospice. Of the dying patients transferred to the ICU, the cost was about $33,000 versus $8,500 for those treated on the general wards. Patients who died in the ICU did not live longer than general ward patients, had inadequate pain relief, and were not offered the alternative of palliative care.

In a study[26] conducted to determine whether six end-of-life care domains were documented in the charts of ICU patients, documentation was found infrequently as to:

1. Patient- and family-centered decision making (more about this in the next section).
2. Communication.
3. Continuity of care.
4. Emotional support.
5. Symptom management and comfort care.
6. Spiritual support.

Palliative Care Consultation

Patients and families could benefit from active palliative care and ethics consultation in the ICU. A prospective randomized controlled study in seven U.S. hospitals tested the premise that ethics consultation in the ICU in patients who were terminally ill would improve care and shorten ICU stay.[27] Five hundred fifty-one patients were identified for whom conflict arose between the physicians and patient and/or family regarding the discontinuation of aggressive care. Two hundred seventy-eight of these patients and/or families were offered ethics consultations, and the remaining 273 were given usual care. Mortality was not significantly different in either group; however, the group receiving ethics consultations had fewer ICU and hospital days. All parties reported that the ethics consultations were beneficial.

When physicians come to the conclusion that there is no chance of survival, many families are unable to deal with this reality. Some hospitals have active ethics committees and do their best to settle these issues. The American Medical Association (AMA) has an accepted protocol that balances the families' needs with physician professionalism,[28] but it is frequently not used (figure 11.1).

Many hospitals have suffered legal setbacks in dealing with these issues, as in the Baby K case.[29] Many physicians go along with the family because they feel the hospital will not support them and that the hassle of a lawsuit is not worth the effort. Some hospitals misinterpret the Patient Self-Determination Act, thinking what the patient or the family wants is what must be done. Medical societies have not yet developed procedures to support physicians in these conflicts.

Toward a Different ICU Approach

In 1995, a study looked at the relationship between resource use and two-year outcome in 402 ICU patients.[30] As a result of a patient's lack of response to medical intervention, they coined the term *potentially ineffective care* (PIC) and assessed its cost. They concluded that patients who received PIC constituted 13 percent of the patients and used 32 percent of resources devoted to critical care at an academic teaching hospital. They recommend that ICUs should assess ineffective care based on outcome, resources used, and a patient's response to treatment over time. Medicine is not an exact science, of course; judgment is needed in interpreting the facts for every individual case.

Figure 11.1 Fair Process for Considering Futility Cases

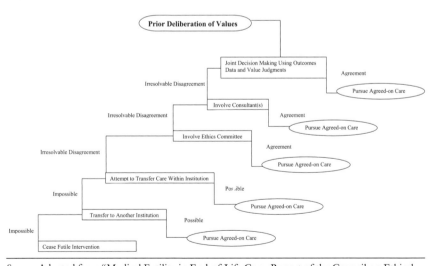

Source: Adapted from "Medical Futility in End-of-Life Care; Report of the Council on Ethical and Judicial Affairs." *Journal of the American Medical Association* 281 (10): 937–41. Copyright © 1999 American Medical Association. All Rights Reserved. Used with permission.

The authors published a follow-up article in 1997.[31] Their impression was that the worst outcome for ICU patients is not death but rather an extended dying process in which suffering has been prolonged by ineffectual care. They found that PIC was delivered in 4.8 percent of all Medicare patients admitted to the ICU and that these patients consumed 21.6 percent of all ICU resources for the period of study (all California patients in the year 1994).

In 2001, total healthcare costs in the United States reached $1.4 trillion, 14 percent of the GDP, double the per capita healthcare spending of most other Western nations.[32] According to the World Health Organization (WHO), however, the United States ranked 37 out of 191 in disease-adjusted life expectancy.[33] They studied data from 1999 and found that the cost for inpatient Medicare service was $90 billion, one-quarter of which was spent on those who died. Approximately $9 billion was spent in the last month of life, and 40 percent of these patients were admitted to ICUs during their terminal illness.[34]

Medical judgment is required to appropriately use these technologies. We must teach our younger doctors these lessons and provide high-quality, humane, and realistic care to our patients. We and our medical societies must also educate the public about medical reality, so that patients and families have more realistic expectations about end-of-life care.

Other studies have also concluded that it is appropriate to treat acute illness rather than terminal illness in ICU settings.[35] Consequently, physicians must develop better judgment and acuity as to which patients will benefit from being in the ICU environment. Such understanding is gleaned from years of treating patients. It is from these insights that clinical wisdom grows. Seasoned physicians are an important resource for teaching new doctors how to evaluate and decide what may constitute appropriate care.

Variability in End-of-Life Care in the United States and Its Effect on Physician Training

Cost comparisons of regional variations in cost for the last six months of care for three diagnoses—colon cancer, heart attack, and hip fracture—revealed that residents of high-spending regions received 60 percent more care but did not have better quality of life or better outcomes. The highest spending areas were in more heavily populated cities with large tertiary care facilities.[36] These hospitals are where most of the training for young physicians takes place, and the study brings home the importance of reexamining the training of doctors regarding appropriate end-of-life care choices.

Kenneth I. Shine, MD, a cardiologist and past president of the Institute of Medicine, adds weight to these findings in his editorial in the *Annals of Internal Medicine.*[37] He points out that:

- The greater the availability of hospital resources and physicians (specialists and subspecialists), the more they will be used, whether they provide any benefit to the patient.

- Medical societies should begin to teach their members and the public that, in end-of-life situations, appropriate care is not more technological care but, rather, palliative care.
- Care that adds no value should be avoided and could save about one-third of our total healthcare costs.
- Physicians should lead in this effort to provide appropriate care because the government and insurance carriers are not equipped to perform this task.
- Physicians must engage and educate the public, explaining to them that this is about better care, not rationing.

We need large tertiary care referral hospitals that are also the site of high-quality physician training. These hospitals are frequently called places of last resort, where the most difficult cases are sent for resolution. These institutions also need senior physicians with proven judgment who can help decide which patients are candidates for curative care and which are candidates for thoughtful, compassionate palliative care. Fisher and colleagues' research demonstrates that this kind of thinking is *not* taking place at our tertiary centers[38] but, rather, is a mentality that drives the wheels of referrals forward, enabling the use of every known modality to keep the patient alive in spite of an underlying awareness that such efforts are of little value.

Judgment Needed in End-of-Life Situations

Dialysis

It is not uncommon for octogenarians to be placed on chronic hemodialysis. Chronic dialysis now accounts for about 5 percent of the entire Medicare budget and is growing faster than the increase in Medicare itself.

Is it possible to select which patients will benefit from dialysis? In a study of patients with end-stage renal failure, it was found that those patients recommended for palliative care had a lower Karnofsky score (i.e., more functionally impaired), were older, and diabetic.[39] In these patients, dialysis did not prolong life but was associated with poorer palliative care. This finding is supported by another study, which found that a modified Karnofsky score of <70 was associated with early mortality.[40]

Prominent ethicist A. H. Moss wrote: "Deciding not to offer dialysis is a fundamental responsibility of nephrologists. If nephrologists fail to make these decisions, patients, their families, other patients, dialysis staff, society and nephrologists can be harmed."[41]

The United States Congress funded chronic dialysis in 1972 and mandated that nephrologists screen candidates for appropriateness. The Institute of Medicine has sought, and the dialysis community has responded with, guidelines for determining when the burdens of dialysis outweigh the benefits.[42] However, there is no oversight by the organized nephrology community helping to enforce these guidelines.

Cancer Care

A study of 1996 data revealed that 22 percent of Medicare patients start a new chemotherapy regimen in the last month of life; within two weeks of death, the total is 18.5 percent.[43] This was regardless of whether the cancer was considered responsive or unresponsive to chemotherapy. The study concluded: "More people are now starting chemotherapy regimens closer to death with unintended consequences of delayed hospice referral, escalating costs" and suboptimal quality of life.

Long-Term Acute Care

Long-term acute care is a new category of care for patients deemed no longer to require acute hospital services but in need of extended medical and nursing care. Patients needing this level of care are considered to be too ill for discharge to a nursing facility, an acute care rehabilitation hospital, or their homes. Long-term acute care facilities have an average length of stay greater than 25 days and have been increasing in number and Medicare expenditures over the last few years. It is expected that Medicare will spend $2.96 billion for these facilities in 2006. The 2006 payment by Medicare is $37,975 per patient, with outlier (a statistical term for patients having a protracted hospitalization) payments beginning at an additional $11,544.[44]

For the appropriate patient, there is the opportunity for excellent care, but for the patient and/or family with unrealistic expectations, long-term acute care can provide a setting for a protracted death with great emotional cost to the family and great financial cost to society. Appropriate-care committees would also be helpful in this setting. Many patients in long-term acute care require prolonged mechanical ventilation (recently defined as 21 days or more for at least 6 hours per day[45]), and the majority do not survive.[46] In this group of patients, those older than 74 years of age and those 64 years and older not functionally independent had a 95 percent (84 percent to 99 percent) one-year mortality.[47] Thus the need to be careful when selecting patients for long-term acute care to those who have a reasonable chance of recovery.

Impact of Aggressive Nonbeneficial End-of-Life Care

The Public

A survey of family members and significant others of 1,578 deceased patients was conducted to determine the quality of physical and emotional support to the patient, whether decision making was shared, if the dying person was treated with respect, if the families' emotional needs were met, and whether care was coordinated.[48] Most patients (67 percent) died in an institution, whereas 16 percent died in hospice care. Those dying at home with hospice were felt to have received excellent care more frequently than those dying in other situations, such as hospitals or nursing homes.

Medical School

Options for palliative care are not currently covered extensively in the training of new physicians in end-of-life care. Using the palliative education assessment tool for medical education (PEAT),[49] New York medical schools had enhanced the palliative care content in their curricula. A curriculum for teaching palliative care to medical students has been developed[50] and should become a part of every prospective doctor's training.

Resident Physicians

A review of the literature from 1966 to February 2005 found that residents were unprepared to handle patient end-of-life decisions and misinterpreted DNR orders and the concept of nonbeneficial care.[51] The residents found that the end-of-life decision-making process did not reflect in practice what had been taught in their formal curriculum.

Practicing Physicians

A 2004 survey of 1,236 physicians from different specialties investigated their perceived adequacy of training in 10 competencies in the care of patients with chronic illness, geriatric syndromes, chronic pain, nutrition, developmental milestones, end-of-life care, psychological issues, patient education, assessment of caregiver needs, coordination of services, and interdisciplinary teamwork. Most physicians thought their training in these areas was inadequate.[52]

In another study,[53] the three greatest barriers to appropriate end of life care were:

1. Physicians' reluctance to make referrals to hospice.
2. Physicians' lack of understanding about the availability and usefulness of hospice.
3. The association of hospice with death.

HISTORICAL PERSPECTIVE

After World War II, the United States embarked on a medical research program unparalleled in human history. The National Institutes of Health, pharmaceutical companies, foundations, and citizens (through organizations like the March of Dimes) funded this work. It was, and still is, primarily focused on the mechanisms of disease and their treatments. Many of the problems we have today with end-stage chronic illness are a result of the success of these programs' ability to prolong life.[54]

With the advent of Medicare and Medicaid in 1964, a fee-for-service payment schedule was adopted. Payment for procedures was reimbursed at a higher rate than areas such as critical thinking, time speaking to patients, and preventive care. In the 1980s, hospitals started to be reimbursed using diagnostic-related groups (table 11.1), but physician reimbursement remained fee for service. As Medicare and Medicaid budgets have grown, politicians have chosen to make across-the-board cuts instead of dealing with high-cost issues involving end-of-life care.

Medicare has also decreased funding for graduate medical education. The Balanced Budget Act of 1997 had a planned decrease of indirect medical education reimbursement (IME) funding from 7.7 percent to 5.5 percent of an intern/resident-to-bed ratio. Although some funding has been restored, hospitals are still receiving less than they did in 1996. Subspecialty training direct medical education reimbursement (DME) is now at a lower amount than in 1996.[55] These cuts have led academic medical centers to increase the volume of patient care to prevent deficits, given their high fixed costs. It has also resulted in less time for teaching and personal supervision and more reliance on tests and technology.

This trend results in inefficient, expensive care and patient dissatisfaction. Many people have criticized medical education for emphasizing scientific knowledge instead of biologic understanding, clinical reasoning, history taking, physical exam skills, and the development of character, compassion, and integrity. There is a new "harsh commercial atmosphere," with students hearing about throughput, market share, units of service, and the bottom line, which overwhelms concentrating on prevention and relief of suffering, caring, and compassion.[56] To appropriately train physicians, teachers need time and resources to teach students how to integrate evidence-based medicine with individual patients.

The Patient Self-Determination Act and Advanced Directives

Since World War II, a large research effort has led to advances that have radically transformed our understanding of the nature of life and death. It takes wisdom and time to learn how to apply these advances in a proper and humane manner. We have learned how to postpone death. In some cases, this ability is marvelous; in others, it is inappropriate. Experience and judgment are required to know when to pursue the marvelous and avoid the inappropriate. We as a society have not yet reached that level of wisdom. An attempt was made in 1990 when Congress passed the Patient Self-Determination Act (PSDA), but it has led to profound, unintended negative consequences.

Here is an example of the misinterpretation of the absence of an advanced directive and the subsequent involvement of the courts.[57] It points out the need for workable systems and procedures for handling these situations in the best interest of the patient.

In the following case, the absence of a known advanced directive led to an unfortunate outcome for a 97-year-old woman. The woman had a recent heart attack, failing kidneys, and progressive loss of mental activity. She was being sustained by a feeding tube. Frequent spillage of gastric contents into her lungs required a breathing tube down her windpipe, and a ventilator helped sustain her breathing. Because of infections, she was also treated with a series of potent anti-infectious agents.

Her attending physician in the intensive care unit of a smaller community hospital asked the probate court to allow her full code status to be changed, her breathing tube removed, and measures instituted to make her comfortable. The doctor noted that it was a struggle for the hospital staff to walk in the room. The patient pushed away staff, writing, "I want tubes out, and I want to die, help me."

The newspaper reported that the patient was not married, had no children, and had outlived all of her friends. Her care was directed by a court-appointed guardian. The judge refused the petition, saying a ruling by a previous state attorney general, now governor, that, "Only adults of sound mind may execute a Do Not Resuscitate order, and may do so only on their own behalf. The legislature has not authorized a guardian to sign a DNR order on behalf of his or her ward."

The judge in this case felt that the doctor was overstepping his bounds in making the request.[58] He stated that a physician should not advocate to the court for the removal of apparatus being used to keep his or her patient alive and that the physician's role should be to advise the family or guardian and, at most, offer an opinion.

After approximately one month at the smaller hospital, her guardian had her transferred to a larger referral hospital, insisting that every possible measure be done regardless of her overall condition. At the referral hospital, she was transferred to the intensive care unit the day after admission, was again intubated (breathing tube down her throat), placed on a respirator, and given various antibiotics. Because the court ruled that everything should be done to save her life, the hospital staff felt they were unable to follow her wishes to die.

She was discharged from the referral hospital to her nursing home but was returned to the larger hospital after only three hours. She was severely malnourished and had developed antibiotic-resistant bacteria in her respiratory and urinary tracts. She had severe dementia, fluid retention, and renal failure and was referred to another chronic care facility at the request of the guardian approximately one-and-a-half months after admission to the smaller hospital.

After one month in the new facility (two-and-a-half months after initial admission), she had no awareness of her surroundings, still needed mechanical ventilation, and required a feeding tube and multiple antibiotics. The new physician caring for her also felt this was abuse of a dying woman but that his hands were tied because of the court's actions.

Although both medicine and law deal with judgment, medicine must consider not only the physical manifestations and potential consequences of a disease process but also the personal context in which illness occurs. Judges do not examine patients; they are trained to interpret legal precedent, not to integrate the multiple factors that go into a medical decision.

The Meaning of Advanced Directives

The meaning of advanced directives and patient autonomy, for patients, physicians, and the United States, has been misinterpreted. The current understanding, by many physicians and hospitals, unless an advanced directive is present limiting care, is that all possible therapies, regardless of their merit or beneficence, must be undertaken. Families are baffled that their loved ones are being treated in this manner. The patient undergoes a needlessly protracted death, the family is in turmoil, the medical staff is demoralized, and as a consequence the U.S. health-care system has less funds devoted to caring for the under- and uninsured, medical education, and primary care.

Genesis of the Patient Self-Determination Act

In 1968, in response to the need to define a more humane definition of death and to help procure organs for transplantation, an ad hoc committee of the Harvard Medical School developed guidelines to define brain death. These guidelines have been accepted worldwide as standard medical care. The committee based its recommendations on the premise that with the loss of total brain activity coma was irreversible and further care futile.[59] Now almost forty years later, it is time to revisit this issue. Much has been learned in this area; acquired evidence from the fields of neurology, biology, and physiology point to the location of self, or personhood, as being in the cerebral cortex rather than in the total brain. Loss of the cerebral cortex should be defined as death, the absence of life. The total brain death definition left open the possibility of loss of the more sensitive cerebral cortex but maintenance of the brain stem and respiration, leading to what we now call a persistent vegetative state, as in the Terry Schiavo case.

In April 1975, Karen Ann Quinlan, at age 21, had a transient episode of lack of oxygen supply to her cerebral cortex, causing permanent loss of function. Her brain stem, however, was still functional, and thus she did not meet the criteria of brain death. Technology kept Quinlan's bodily functions intact (i.e., blood pressure, digestion, urine output, etc.), although with the loss of her cerebral cortex the person Karen Ann Quinlan was gone. Quinlan's physician, the local prosecutor, and the New Jersey attorney general opposed Quinlan's father, who wanted to continue medically administered nutrition and water but discontinue artificial respiration. The New Jersey trial court denied the father's appointment as legal guardian and ruled that the attending physician and prevailing medical standards should prevail. The New Jersey Supreme Court reversed the trial court and appointed Quinlan's father as guardian. She was weaned from the respirator but was given nutrition and water. Her body slowly deteriorated and ceased to exist 10 years later.

Another widely publicized case occurred in 1983. Nancy Cruzan, at age 25, was thrown from her car and experienced inadequate oxygen to her brain, resulting in permanent nonfunction of her cerebral cortex. She was resuscitated and had only brain stem activity.

Because the cerebral cortex is the thinking, feeling, speaking, and motion-controlling part of the brain, without a cerebral cortex one may see what looks like a person, but what we call *human* is absent. This is not a disability; the person is gone.

As with Karen Quinlan, the roots of society's and medicine's conflict regarding the definition of death were revisited as Nancy Cruzan's bodily functions were maintained though she ceased to exist as a person. Cruzan's parents, knowing their child would not wish to be slowly decaying when in fact she no longer had awareness or any other human trait, sought to have her feeding tube and other support measures stopped. Because she was in a state hospital and, in part, because medical societies had not yet (even to this day) organized to teach the public about lack of cerebral function and personhood, the case was appealed to the Missouri Supreme Court asking to remove her support systems. This court agreed that a person had the right to refuse treatment but did not feel Cruzan had made her wishes "clear and convincing."[60] The court decided that this was not a case of right to die but the right of others to take her life.

The court's finding that at issue was the right of others to take her life was flawed. She in fact had no life to take. The U.S. Supreme Court in 1990 heard the case and did codify the right of a competent individual to refuse any life-prolonging treatment. In the case of incompetent people, a state could insist on clear proof of a person's preference.[61] This decision was made on legal grounds and with little attention to medical knowledge. The Supreme Court sent the case back to the Missouri Supreme Court, which in 1990 did allow the support services to be removed. Cruzan's body quickly ceased to exist. The dissenting Supreme Court opinion of Associate Justice John Paul Stevens quotes Judge Charles B. Blackmar of the Missouri court, who said, "The Missouri policy was illegitimate because it treats life as a theoretical abstraction, severed from and indeed opposed to, the person of Nancy Cruzan."

In response to these two cases, with input from a presidential commission, the U.S. Congress on November 5, 1990, as a part of the Omnibus Budget Reconciliation Act, passed the Patient Self-Determination Act (PSDA) to go into effect on December 1, 1991. This act stated that patients have the right under state law to create advanced directives stipulating what they wish done in an end-of-life situation. Although many medical ethicists state that medical judgment must be used and physicians should not offer nonbeneficial care, other well-known physicians argue that we must err on the side of patient or family choice if a patient's wishes are unknown.[62]

This concept is further reinforced by the decision in the Baby K (1993) case in which first the trial court[63] and then the U.S. Court of Appeals ruled that a baby born with only a brain stem should have mechanical respiration applied in the emergency room if needed.[64] The court made this decision based on the Emergency Medical Treatment and Active Labor Act,[65] a decision made in spite of the medical knowledge that such an infant can never become a person and cannot survive. Paraphrasing a review of the Baby K case, to avoid medicine being a commodity and becoming unbearably expensive or having the government set arbitrary standards, physicians must set standards for medical practice and follow them.[66] Unfortunately, organized medicine has not yet addressed this problem.

Revisiting the Definitions of Life and Death

Many of the arguments in the Quinlan and Cruzan cases dealt with the questions of what is life and what is death. It may be time to revise these definitions.

The current legal definition of *brain death* is "total and irreversible cessation of all brain function, including the brain stem." The cerebral cortex is the thinking, feeling, speaking, and motion-controlling part of the brain. Without the cerebral cortex, one may see what looks like a person, but what we call *human* is gone, even if the brain stem is still functioning.

The cerebral cortex is the most complex of human organs, with neurons making billions of interconnections and developing as we age. The variations and numbers of those interconnections are what make us different: our personalities, memories, and intelligence, everything that makes us human, unique. Once these neurons and their person-specific interconnections are lost, there is no possibility of their return. Even if at some time in the future we could inject new neurons that were from a stem cell line identical to ourselves and these young neurons started to grow and make new connections, who and what would we be? Would we be the same person? We would have no memory or experience; we would be newborns in the body of an older individual. Our personhood would be completely different because our connections would be different.

When families visit these patients, the sheets are usually pulled up to the neck. What are unseen are the decubiti (skin breakdown); dying fingers and toes; swollen, lifeless limbs; and body discoloration. Is it fair to that individual who has no chance of recovery to put his or her body through such degradation?

If the standard of human life were to be addressed by legislators, maybe these tragedies could be avoided. Hopefully, in the future, our medical societies will embrace the opportunity to grapple with difficult issues and help society develop a more rational approach, based on scientific information.

Problems with the Patient Self-Determination Act

In May 1991, in anticipation of the PSDA becoming effective that December, Kevin O'Rourke, OP, JCD, STM, the director of the Center for Health Care Ethics, Saint Louis University, University Medical Center, Saint Louis, Missouri, wrote that the PSDA used a sledgehammer approach to a delicate situation. "Potentially, the most serious ethical issues resulting from PSDA is the implied assumption that physicians are simply to carry out the wishes of the proxy."[67] Physicians must listen to the patient or proxy to learn as clearly as possible what the patient does and does not want, but they ultimately must do what is medically appropriate for the patient. Patient wishes must be interpreted in light of medical knowledge.

Other authors have found serious problems with the PSDA as well.[68] The PSDA has not significantly increased the use of written advanced-care documents, nor has it increased discussion between physicians and patients regarding end-of-life issues.[69]

After a few years, the PSDA contributed to the illusion that death is an option and that life can be prolonged indefinitely.[70] The choice paradigm (patient autonomy) presents options that are not real, such as the option of not dying of a terminal illness and that patients and families who have a positive end-of-life experience choose to accept death as the final stage of life.

When used with judgment, lifesaving measures engender and restore faith in medical prowess and offer second chances to patients and families. They also exemplify the reason that medical training attracts bright, well-meaning students: to make a difference in patients' lives.

If, however, the same measures are employed in a situation with little or no chance of recovery, then the potential to cause harm rather than do good is great. The consequences to patients, families, colleagues, and physicians are innumerable. The PSDA, in its attempt to provide for patient autonomy, oversimplified the complex dynamics of the dying process. It needs to be revisited.

A possible amendment, for example, might replace specific medical terms, such as the use of drugs or a ventilator, with the requirement that physicians document with each hospital admission that a conversation has taken place explaining to family members and patients that individually tailored beneficial care based on sound medical principles will be offered. The patient, however, has the right to refuse any aspect of that care.

Part of the intent of the PSDA was to encourage communication by the medical providers with the patient and family in the midst of challenging emotional circumstances. Conversations about death and dying occur rarely. A so-called appropriate death in the context of our medical culture, intensive care units, oncology units, and fluorescent-laden medical wards is impossible without continuous guidance and support from physicians, nurses, discharge planners, and hospital support staff. Each member plays a pivotal role in the experience of dying. Each must be embraced as we consider reconfiguration of responsibilities and open lines of communication. The role of medical societies in such a paradigm shift could be one of leadership, exemplifying clarity while also fostering the rekindling of honesty and compassion in the patient-physician relationship.

Facilities have to inform patients of their rights under state law to make decisions about their medical care, including the right to refuse care and to formulate an advanced directive.[71] There is a significant difference between refusing or limiting care and directing care.

RECOMMENDATIONS FOR CHANGE

What Remains to Be Done to Decrease the Cost of Dying

Change the Policy of CPR by Default

The protocol for CPR should be changed. It should be ordered if indicated, with the default position being no resuscitation. The present policy of performing CPR on all in-hospital patients unless a DNR order is in place originated in the mid-1960s before the advent of Medicare.[72] Although the hospital population is now different, with many frail and end-of-life patients, this policy is still in place. This action alone could decrease by half the number of resuscitations attempted in the United States, thereby alleviating patient and family suffering and saving approximately $13 billion per year.

Establish Appropriate-Care Committees

Appropriate-care committees made up of experienced physicians at the hospital, state, and national level should be created to help individual doctors and families decide that the dying process has begun and palliative, not curative, care is now appropriate. Presently, it is estimated that more than 500,000 Americans die in intensive care units yearly, experiencing extended suffering at tremendous cost, both emotional and financial.[73] Congress, through Medicare and Medicaid, could create and fund a system of appropriate-care committees to ensure a standard of medical care and amend the PSDA to include, "care that is beneficial according to the best available medical evidence, adapted to the individual."

Amend the Definition of Brain Death

Another step is to revisit the Harvard Medical School committee definition of end-of-life to include loss of the cerebral cortex, even with a functioning brain stem. In the United States, there are now tens of thousands of patients in a long-term persistent vegetative state with no blood flow to the cerebral cortex.[74]

Extend the Reach of Palliative Care

Good palliative care does not shorten life but does help the patient die with dignity and as symptom free as possible.[75,76] Hospice and palliative care options in the United States are available to all. Engage the Association of Professors of Medicine and Surgery, the American Hospital Association, and the American Academy of Hospice and Palliative Medicine to create programs to educate the public about care options, encourage more training and funding for graduate medical training in palliative care, and promote the inclusion of palliative care teams in hospitals, including rounds in ICUs.

Although the challenges are substantial, an improved approach to end-of-life care will result in improved quality of care, less suffering for patients and families, and substantial savings that can be invested in research and improved processes of care.

NOTES

1. Field, M. J., and C. K. Cassel, eds. 1997. "How People Die: Symptoms of Impending Death." In *Approaching Death, Improving Care at the End of Life*. Washington, D.C.: National Academy Press.

2. Barnato, A. E., M. E. McClellan, C. R. Kagay, and A. M. Garber. 2004. "Trends in Inpatient Treatment Intensity among Medicare Beneficiaries at the End-of-Life." *Health Services Research* 39: 363–75.

3. Field, M. J., and C. K. Cassel, eds. 1997. *A Profile of Death in America, In Approaching Death, Improving Care at the End-of-Life*. Washington, D.C.: National Academy Press, 40–41.

4. Drought, T. S., and B. A. Koenig. 2002. "'Choice' in End-of-Life Decision Making: Researching Fact or Fiction." *Gerontologist* 42 (3): 114–25.

5. Annas, G. J. 1994. "Asking the Courts to Settle Standard of Emergency Care—The Case of Baby K." *New England Journal of Medicine* 330: 1542–45.

6. "Terri Schiavo." n.d. *Wikipedia.* Available at: http://en.wikipedia.org/wiki/Terri_Schiavo. Accessed November 15, 2006.

7. Barnato, McClellan, Kagay, and Garber, 363–75.

8. Fisher, E. S., D. E. Wennberg, T. A. Stukel, et al. 2003. "The Implications of Regional Variations in Medicare Spending, Parts I and II." *Annals of Internal Medicine* 139: 273–98.

9. Shine, K. I. 2003. "Geographical Variation in Medicare Spending." *Annals of Internal Medicine* 138: 347–48.

10. Reinhardt, U. E., P. S. Hussey, and G. F. Anderson. 2004. "U.S. Health Spending in an International Context. Why Is U.S. Spending So High, and Can We Afford It." *Health Affairs* 23: 10–25.

11. Cloud, J. 2000. "A Kinder, Gentler Death." *Time.* Available at: http://www.time.com/time/printout/0,8816,997968,00.html. Accessed November 12, 2006.

12. Emanuel, E. J., A. Ash, W. Yu, et al. 2002. "Managed Care, Hospice Use, Site of Death, and Medical Expenditures in the Last Year of Life." *Archives of Internal Medicine* 162: 1722–28.

13. Hoover, D. R., S. Crystal, R. Kumar, et al. 2002. "Medical Expenditures during the Last Year of Life: Findings from the 1992–1996 Medicare Current Beneficiary Survey." *Health Services Research* 37: 1625–42.

14. Bedell, S. E., T. L. Delbanco, E. F. Cook, and F. H. Epstein. 1983. "Survival after Cardiopulmonary Resuscitation in the Hospital." *New England Journal of Medicine* 309: 569–76.

15. Taffet, G. E., T. A. Teasdale, and R. J. Luchi. 1988. "In-Hospital Cardiopulmonary Resuscitation." *Journal of the American Medical Association* 260: 2069–72.

16. McGrath, R. B. 1987. "In-House Cardiopulmonary Resuscitation—After a Quarter of a Century." *Annals of Emergency Medicine* 16: 1365–68.

17. Thel, M. C., and M. D. O'Connor. 1999. "Cardiopulmonary Resuscitation: Historical Perspective to Recent Investigations." *American Heart Journal* 137: 39–48.

18. Blackhall, L. J. 1987. "Must We Always Use CPR?" *New England Journal of Medicine* 317: 1281–85.

19. Murphy, D. J., and T. E. Finucane. 1993. "New Do Not Resuscitate Policies: A First Step in Cost Control." *Archives of Internal Medicine* 153: 1641–48.

20. Alpers, A., and B. Lo. 1995. "When Is CPR Futile?" *Journal of the American Medical Association* 273: 156–58.

21. Frezza, E. E., D. M. Squillario, and T. J. Smith. 1998. "The Ethical Challenge and the Futile Treatment in the Older Population Admitted to the Intensive Care Unit." *American Journal of Medical Quality* 13: 121–26.

22. Halpern, N. A., S. M. Pastores, H. T. Thaler, and R. J. Greenstein. 2006. "Changes in Critical Care Beds and Occupancy in the United States 1985–2000: Differences Attributable to Hospital Size." *Critical Care Medicine* 34: 2105–12.

23. Barnato, McClellan, Kagay, and Garber, 363–75.

24. Angus, D. C., A. E. Barnato, W. T. Linde-Zwirble, et al. 2004. "Use of Intensive Care at End-of-Life in the United States: An Epidemiologic Study." *Critical Care Medicine* 32: 638–43.

25. Rady, M. Y., and D. Johnson. 2004. "Admission to Intensive Care Unit at the End-of-Life: Is It an Informed Decision?" *Palliative Medicine* 18: 705–11.

26. Clarke, E. B., J. M. Luce, J. R. Curtis, et al. 2004. "A Content Analysis of Forms, Guidelines and Other Materials Documenting End-of-Life Care in the Intensive Care Units." *Journal of Critical Care* 19: 108–17.

27. Schneiderman, L. J., T. Gilmer, H. D. Teetzel, et al. 2003. "Effects of Ethics Consultations on Nonbeneficial Life-Sustaining Treatments in the Intensive Care Setting: A Randomized Controlled Trial." *Journal of the American Medical Association* 290: 1166–77.

28. "Medical Futility in End-of-Life Care: Report of the Council on Ethical and Judicial Affairs." 1999. *Journal of the American Medical Association* 281: 937–41.

29. Barnato, McClellan, Kagay, and Garber, 363–75.

30. Esserman, L., J. Belkora, and L. Lenert. 1995. "Potentially Ineffective Care: A New Outcome to Assess the Limits of Critical Care." *Journal of the American Medical Association* 274: 1544–51.

31. Cher, D. J., and L. A. Lenert. 1997. "Method of Medicare Reimbursement and the Rate of Potentially Ineffective Care of Critically Ill Patients." *Journal of the American Medical Association* 278: 1001–7.

32. Reinhardt, U. E., P. S. Hussey, and G. F. Anderson. 2004. "U.S. Health Spending in an International Context. Why Is U.S. Spending So High, and Can We Afford It." *Health Affairs* 23: 10–25.

33. World Health Organization. 2000. "World Health Organization Assesses the World's Health Systems." Press release, June 21. Available at: http://www.who.int/inf-pr-2000/en/pr2000-44html. Accessed November 17, 2006.

34. Barnato, McClellan, Kagay, and Garber, 363–75.

35. Esserman, Belkora, and Lenert, 1544–51.

36. Fisher, Wennberg, Stuckel, et al., 273–98.

37. Shine, K. I. 2003. "Geographical Variation in Medicare Spending." *Annals of Internal Medicine* 138: 347–48.

38. Fisher, Wennberg, Stuckel, et al., 273–98.

39. Smith, C., M. Da Silva-Gane, S. Chandna, et al. 2003. "Choosing Not to Dialyze: Evaluation of Planned Non-Dialytic Management in a Cohort of Patients with End-Stage Renal Failure." *Nephron: Clinical Practice* 95: C40–C46.

40. Ifudu, O., H. R. Paul, P. Homel, and E. A. Friedman. 1998. "Predictive Value of Functional Status for Mortality in Patients on Maintenance Hemodialysis." *American Journal of Nephrology* 18: 109–16.

41. Moss, A. H. 2003. "Controversies in Nephrology: Too Many Patients Who Are Too Sick to Benefit, Start Chronic Dialysis, Nephrologists Need to Learn to 'Just Say No.'" *American Journal of Kidney Diseases* 41: 723–27.

42. Renal Physicians Association and American Society of Nephrology. 1999. *Clinical Practice Guideline on Shared Decision-Making in the Appropriate Initiation of and Withdrawal from Dialysis.* Clinical Practice Guideline No. 2. Washington, D.C.

43. Matsuyama, R., S. Reddy, and T. J. Smith. 2006. "Why Do Patients Choose Chemotherapy Near the End-of-Life? A Review of the Perspective of Those Facing Death from Cancer." *Journal of Clinical Oncology* 24: 3490–96.

44. U.S. Department of Health and Human Services, Centers for Medicare and Medicaid Services. 2005. "Medicare Proposes Payment Changes for Long-Term Care Hospitals for Rate Year 2006." Press release, January 28. Available at: http://www.cms.hhs.gov/apps/media/press/release.asp?Counter=1339. Accessed September 2006.

45. MacIntyre, N. R., S. K. Epstein, S. Carson, et al. 2005. "Management of Patients Requiring Prolonged Mechanical Ventilation: Report of NAMDRC Consensus Conference." *Chest* 128: 3937–54.

46. Carson, S. S. 2006. "Outcomes of Prolonged Mechanical Ventilation." *Current Opinion in Critical Care* 12: 405–11.

47. Carson, S. S., P. B. Bach, L. Brzozowski, and A. Leff. 1999. "Outcomes after Long-Term Acute Care, Analysis of 133 Mechanically Ventilated Patients." *American Journal of Respiratory and Critical Care Medicine* 160: 1788–89.

48. Teno, J. M., B. R. Clarridge, V. Casey, et al. 2004. "Family Perspective on End-of-Life Care at the Last Place of Care." *Journal of the American Medical Association* 291: 88–93.

49. Wood, E. B., S. A. Meekin, J. J. Fins, and A. R. Fleischman. 2002. "Enhancing Palliative Care Education in Medical School Curricula: Implementation of Palliative Education Assessment Tool." *Academic Medicine* 77: 285–91.

50. Quill, T. E., E. Dannefer, K. Markakis, R. Epstein, et al. 2003. "An Integrative Biopsychological Approach to Palliative Care Training of Medical Students." *Journal of Palliative Medicine* 6: 365–80.

51. Gorman, T. E., S. P. Ahern, J. Wiseman, and Y. Skrobic. 2005. "Residents End-of-Life Decision Making with Adult Hospitalized Patients: A Review of the Literature." *Academic Medicine* 80: 622–33.

52. Darer, J. D., W. Hwang, H. H. Pharm, E. B. Bass, and G. Anderson. 2004. "More Training Needed in Chronic Care: A Survey of U.S. Physicians." *Academic Medicine* 79: 541–48.

53. Feeg, V. D., and H. Elebiary. 2005. "Exploratory Study on End-of-Life Issues: Barriers to Palliative Care and Advanced Directives." *American Journal of Hospice and Palliative Care* 22: 119–24.

54. Lynn, J. 2004. *Sick to Death and Not Going to Take It Anymore*. Berkeley and Los Angeles: University of California Press.

55. Rich, E. C., M. Liebow, M. Srinivasan, et al. 2002. "Medicare Financing of Graduate Medical Education: Intractable Problems, Elusive Solutions." *Journal of General Internal Medicine* 17: 283–92.

56. Cooke, M., D. M. Irby, W. Sullivan, and K. M. Ludmerer. 2006. "American Medical Education 100 Years after the Flexner Report." *New England Journal of Medicine* 355: 1339–44.

57. Agar J. 2006. "Judge Rules Lawton Women's Life Must Be Preserved." *Kalamazoo Gazette*, April 25, 2006.

58. *American Medical News,* June 12, 2006.

59. Doig, C. J., and E. Burgess. 2003. "Brain Death: Resolving Inconsistencies in the Ethical Declaration of Death." *Canadian Journal of Anesthesia* 50: 725–31.

60. *Cruzan v. Harmon,* 760 S.W. 2d 408, 427 (Mo. 1989) (en banc).

61. *Cruzan v. Director, DMH*, 497 U.S. 261 (1990) at 284.

62. Quill, T. E. 2005. "Terri Schiavo, a Tragedy Compounded." *New England Journal of Medicine* 352: 1630–33.

63. *In the Matter of Baby K*. 832 F. Supp. 1022 (E.D. Va. 1993).

64. *In the Matter of Baby K*. 16F. 3d 590 (4th Circ. 1994).

65. Emergency Medical Treatment and Labor Act, P.L. 99-272, 42 U.S.C. Sec. 1395 dd (1985)(renamed in 1989).

66. Annas, G. J. 1994. "Asking the Courts to Settle Standard of Emergency Care—The Case of Baby K." *New England Journal of Medicine* 330: 1542–45.

67. O'Rourke, K. n.d. "Ethical Issues in Health Care." Available at: http://www.op.org/domcentral/study/kor/index.htm. Accessed December 3, 2006.

68. Emmanuel, E. J., D. S. Weinburg, R. Gonin R, et al. 1993. "How Well Is the Patient Self-Determination Act Working: An Early Assessment." *American Journal of Medicine* 95: 619–28.

69. Teno, J., J. Lynn, N. Wenger, et al. 1997. "Advance Directives for Seriously Ill Hospitalized Patients: Effectiveness with the Patient Self Determination Act and the SUPPORT Intervention. SUPPORT Investigators Study to Understand Prognoses and Preferences for Outcomes and Risk of Treatment." *Journal of the American Geriatrics Society* 45: 500–507.

70. Drought, T. S., and B. A. Koenig. 2002. "'Choice' in End-of-Life Decision Making: Researching Fact or Fiction." *Gerontologist* 42 (3): 114–25.

71. Thomas, K. R. 2005. "The 'Right to Die': Constitutional and Statutory Analysis." Congressional Research Service, order code 97-244A.

72. "National Academy of Sciences-National Research Council Endorse CPR for all In-hospital Patients." 1966. *Journal of the American Medical Association* 198: 372–79.

73. Drought, T. S., and B. A. Koenig. 2002. "'Choice' in End-of-Life Decision Making: Researching Fact or Fiction." *Gerontologist* 42 (3): 114–25.

74. "Persistent Vegetative State." n.d. *Wikipedia.* Available at: http://en.wikipedia.org/wiki/Persistent_vegetative_state.

75. Sykes, N., and A. Thorns. 2003. "Sedative Use in the Last Week of Life and the Implications for End-of-Life Decision-Making." *Archives of Internal Medicine* 163: 341–44.

76. Vitetta, L., D. Kenner, and A. Sali. 2005. "Sedation and Analgesia Prescribing Patterns in Terminally Ill Patients at End-of-Life." *American Journal of Hospice and Palliative Care* 22: 465–73.

About the Editors and Contributors

KENNETH H. COHN, MD, MBA, FACS, is a board-certified general surgeon. He obtained his medical degree from Columbia College of Physicians Medical School, completed his residency at the Harvard-Deaconess Surgical Service, and performed fellowships in endocrine and oncological surgery at the Karolinska Hospital and at Memorial Sloan-Kettering Cancer Center, respectively. He was assistant professor of surgery at the State University of New York Health Science Center at Brooklyn and later moved to Dartmouth-Hitchcock Medical Center as associate professor of surgery and chief of surgical oncology at the Veterans Administration Hospital at White River Junction. With the change in the medical economic climate, Dr. Cohn entered the MBA program of the Tuck School at Dartmouth and graduated in June 1998. He worked initially as a consultant at Health Advances, assisting six firms to commercialize new products. Since joining the Cambridge Management Group, he has led change-management initiatives for physicians at affiliated hospitals within the Yale New Haven, Banner Colorado, Cottage Santa Barbara, and Sutter Sacramento health systems. He remains clinically active, covering surgical practices in New Hampshire and Vermont. Dr. Cohn has written forty articles published in peer-reviewed medical journals and two books, *Better Communication for Better Care: Mastering Physician-Administration Collaboration* and *Collaborate for Success! Breakthrough Strategies for Engaging Physicians, Nurses, and Hospital Executives*. His Web site is http://www.healthcarecollaboration.com.

DOUGLAS E. HOUGH, PhD, is associate professor and chair, The Business of Health, at the Carey Business School of Johns Hopkins University. He is responsible for eight programs, including the innovative Hopkins Business of Medicine, a four-course graduate certificate program and an MBA program with concentration in medical services management, designed for experienced physicians (offered in partnership with the Johns Hopkins University School of Medicine). Dr. Hough has more than twenty-five years of experience in industry and academia. He has been a research economist at the American Medical Association, a manager in the healthcare consulting division of Coopers and Lybrand, and a partner in two health-care strategy consulting firms. His research interests are in identifying the optimal size and structure of a physician practice and in determining the impact of changing physician demographics on the structure of medical practices. His consulting interests focus on methods of strengthening hospital-physician relations (e.g., the development of integrated delivery systems, physician-hospital initiatives, and management service organizations) as well as the organization and strategic direction of physician practices. Dr. Hough is a frequent speaker and author on healthcare issues related to physicians. His research has been published in such professional journals as the *Journal of the American Medical Association,* the *Journal of Human Resources,* and the *Journal of Medical Practice Management.* Dr. Hough earned his MS and PhD in economics from the University of Wisconsin. He received his BS in economics from the Massachusetts Institute of Technology. He is a member of Academy Health, the American Economic Association, the International Health Economics Association, and the Medical Group Management Association.

STUART H. ALTMAN, PhD, is dean of the Heller School for Social Policy and Management and Sol C. Chaikin Professor of National Health Policy at Brandeis University. He has an MA and PhD in economics from the University of California, Los Angeles, and he taught at Brown University and the Graduate School of Public Policy at the University of California, Berkeley. Dr. Altman is an economist whose research interests are primarily in the area of federal and state health policy. In June 2004, he was awarded the AcademyHealth Distinguished Investigator Award, and in 2003, 2004, and 2005, *Modern Healthcare* named him among the 100 Most Powerful People in Healthcare. From 2000 to 2002 he was cochair for the Legislative Health Care Task Force for the Commonwealth of Massachusetts. In 1997, he was appointed by President Bill Clinton to the National Bipartisan Commission on the Future of Medicare. Dr. Altman was dean of the Florence Heller Graduate School from 1977 until July 1993 and interim president of Brandeis University from 1990 to 1991. He served as the chairman of the congressionally legislated Prospective Payment Assessment Commission for 12 years. Dr. Altman is a member of the Institute of Medicine of the National Academy of Sciences and its Committee on the Future of Emergency Care in the United States; a member of the Board of Tufts-New England Medical Center in Boston, Massachusetts; and cochairman of the Advisory Board to the Schneider Institute for Health Policy at the Heller School. In addition, Dr. Altman has served on the board of the Robert Wood Johnson Clinical Scholars Program and on the governing council of the Institute of Medicine. He is the chair of the Robert Wood Johnson Foundation–sponsored Council on Health Care Economics and Policy.

He is also chair of the Health Industry Forum, which brings together diverse group leaders from across the healthcare field to develop solutions for critical problems facing the healthcare system. Between 1971 and 1976, Dr. Altman was deputy assistant secretary for Planning and Evaluation/Health at the Department of Health, Education, and Welfare.

JACK BARKER, PhD, is an Airbus pilot and aviation safety instructor at United Airlines. He develops and teaches Crew Resource Management (CRM) courses to pilots, flight attendants, and ground personnel. Prior to joining United Airlines, Dr. Barker spent 17 years on active duty in the United States Air Force. During his military career, he served as an aircraft maintenance officer, piloted several different aircraft, and taught as a professor of psychology at the United States Air Force Academy. As a professor, he was involved with NASA-sponsored high-performance team research and organizational development consulting. He is the chief executive officer of Mach One Leadership, Inc. Mach One adapts the aviation safety model to other organizations that use high-performance teams. He has successfully adapted aviation safety tools for the past five years in various healthcare settings, including helping the American College of Surgeons develop and implement crew resource management programs. Dr. Barker has a BS in human factors engineering from the United States Air Force Academy and a PhD in cognitive psychology from Florida State University.

ANIRBAN BASU serves as chairman and chief executive officer (CEO) for Sage Policy Group, Inc., an economic research firm. Prior to founding Sage, Mr. Basu was chairman and CEO at Optimal Solutions Group, a company he cofounded. Prior to that, Mr. Basu oversaw the Regional Economic Studies Institute at Towson University. His clients included Fortune 500 companies such as BGE, the St. Paul Companies, and BP as well as numerous government agencies and associations. Mr. Basu has conducted numerous economic and fiscal impact analyses and has conducted seminars on the economy. His forecasts are used by numerous businesses as well as Maryland's Office of the Comptroller. Mr. Basu is a faculty member at the Johns Hopkins University, where he teaches micro-, macro-, and international economics. Frequently quoted in the media, including the *Washington Post* and *Baltimore Sun,* he is host of the *Morning Economic Report,* a radio spot that is heard weekdays on WYPR, Baltimore's National Public Radio station. Mr. Basu is on the boards of Union Memorial Hospital and Chesapeake Habitat for Humanity, among others. He is currently president of the Baltimore Economic Society and chairman of the Baltimore County Economic Advisory Committee. Mr. Basu received a bachelor of science in foreign service from Georgetown University, a master in public policy from the John F. Kennedy School of Government at Harvard University, a master of arts in mathematical economics from the University of Maryland, and a Juris Doctor from the University of Maryland School of Law. He is currently a candidate for a doctor of philosophy in health policy from the University of Maryland, Baltimore County.

IAN BATSTONE is a research analyst with Sage Policy Group, Inc. He is completing his BS degree at Johns Hopkins University. Prior to entering the undergraduate program, he enlisted in the U.S. Air Force. He joined Sage in 2007.

PHIL BUTTELL, JD, MHSA, is the vice president for business development at Creighton University Medical Center. Previously, he was chief operating officer at Centennial Medical Center (CMC) in Frisco, Texas, a subsidiary of Tenet Healthcare. He had been with Tenet since June 2002 and joined CMC soon after the hospital opened in June 2004. In addition to the management of day-to-day hospital operations, Mr. Buttell also consults in the development of new medical facilities and the transformation and implementation of advanced technologies.

BARRY P. CHAIKEN, MD, MPH, FHIMSS, is associate chief medical officer in the healthcare practice at BearingPoint, Inc., an international professional-services consulting firm. He has lectured extensively on medical quality, patient safety, and the use of information technology in healthcare, and he writes a regular column on healthcare quality and information technology for *Patient Safety and Quality Healthcare*. Dr. Chaiken serves on the board of directors of the Health Information Management Systems Society (HIMSS). He also sits on the editorial boards of the *Journal of Patient Safety* and *Patient Safety and Quality Healthcare* and is conference chairperson of the Digital Healthcare Conference held each spring at the Fluno Center, University of Wisconsin, Madison. He holds an appointment as adjunct assistant professor in the Department of Public Health and Family Medicine at Tufts University School of Medicine. Dr. Chaiken is board certified in general preventive medicine and public health as well as healthcare quality management; he has delivered more than fifty continuing medical education (CME) lectures and authored more than sixty original articles. Dr. Chaiken received his MD from the State University of New York Downstate Medical Center in New York City and his masters in public health from the Harvard School of Public Health.

DEBI CROES, MBA, a principal of the Croes•Oliva Group, is a nationally recognized expert in the field of medical group management. Prior to founding the Croes•Oliva Group with partner Jayne Oliva, Ms. Croes was director of provider relations at Maxicare, director of practice management services at a Boston-area healthcare organization, and director of a nonprofit health agency in western Massachusetts. She also managed her own $4 million billing service. Her twenty-plus years of experience with top academic medical centers and integrated delivery systems nourish a profound insight. She is an expert in reconfiguring operations and developing strategies that boost profitability and protects her commitments to teaching and research. Armed with deep understanding of the forces at work in today's healthcare marketplace, she finds effective ways to deal with the unique pressures medical organizations face. A sought-after consultant and writer, Ms. Croes is also a respected, motivating speaker and teacher. She regularly addresses the Medical Group Management Association and its subgroup, the Academic Practice Association, as well as the Healthcare Financial Management

Association's Annual National Institute (ANI). She has taught a graduate-level physician practice management course, and her articles and commentary have appeared in *American Medical News,* the *Medical Group Management Journal, Group Practice Journal,* and the *Boston Globe.* Ms. Croes earned an MBA from Simmons College Graduate School of Management in Boston and her BA from Boston University.

JENNIFER DALEY, MD, FACP, is the chief medical officer of Tenet Healthcare in Dallas, Texas. She is responsible for the development and implementation of the Commitment to Quality, a system-wide initiative that promotes evidence-based clinical practice, patient safety, standards-based quality assessment in high-volume and high-cost clinical product lines, clinical resource management including care coordination and utilization management, and physician excellence. The author of more than 140 original contributions, book chapters, and clinical reports, she was the recipient of a Senior Career Development Award in Health Services Research from the Department of Veterans Affairs from 1990 to 1996. She is also an adjunct associate professor of community and family medicine at Dartmouth Medical School in Hanover, New Hampshire.

MICHAEL T. DOONAN, PhD, is an assistant professor at the Heller Graduate School at Brandeis University, the executive director of the Massachusetts Health Policy Forum, and director of the Council for Health Care Economics and Policy. Dr. Doonan has in-depth knowledge of the Massachusetts healthcare system, with particular expertise in federalism and federal-state relations. His PhD from Brandeis is in both political science and health services research. His research and publications focus on issues related to access to healthcare, Medicaid, SCHIP, federal-state relations, prescription drugs, public health, and the economics of health system change. Dr. Doonan worked as program specialist for the Centers for Medicare and Medicaid Services (CMS) in the area of Medicaid managed care and state healthcare reform. He served as a member of President Bill Clinton's Health Care Taskforce, working primarily on the Low-Income and Working Families work group, and as a member of the Taskforce Speakers Bureau. He also worked as a fellow for the U.S. Senate Finance Committee as it considered national reform in 1994. He began his career as a legislative aide for Senator John Kerry, where he worked on health and environmental issues. He has a master's degree in public administration from the George Washington University and an undergraduate degree in political science from St. Anselm College.

KENNETH A. FISHER, MD, is a nephrology consultant for the Borgess and Bronson Hospitals in Kalamazoo, Michigan. For more than thirty years he has served in a variety of clinical, teaching, and research positions, including chief resident in medicine at Mount Sinai Hospital, assistant professor of medicine at the University of Chicago Pritzker School, director of internal medicine at Michigan State University, and director of the fellowship program at Henry Ford Hospital. He was also professor of medicine at the Chicago Medical School and at Michigan

State University School of Medicine. He has written dozens of scientific and policy articles in such publications as *Clinical Nephrology, American Journal of Physiology, American Journal of Medicine,* and *American Journal of Obstetrics and Gynecology.* Dr. Fisher is coauthor of the forthcoming *In Defiance of Death: Exposing the Real Costs of End of Life Care* (Praeger, 2008).

RUDY WILSON GALDONIK is a professional speaker and author of *Take Heart!* a compilation of humorous essays that look at life through menopausal eyes. Ms. Galdonik is a three-dimensional expert on being sick: She has been the patient, the caregiver of a patient, and a former hospital human resources manager. She understands the challenges, emotions, and issues of being sick. She understands the pressures endured by caregivers and the problems and challenges of doctors, hospitals, and medical personnel. Her passion is to couple this expertise with humor to encourage people to take charge of their health. Ms. Galdonik has served as cochair of the American Heart Association Rhode Island Chapter's Women and Heart Disease Committee. In 2003, Rudy received the American Heart Association's Heart of the Year Award. She has served on the national board of directors of the Adult Congenital Heart Association and is an advocate for WomenHeart. org, the National Coalition for Women with Heart Disease. She is a member of the Association for Applied and Therapeutic Humor.

JONATHAN GERTLER, MD, MBA, joined Leerink Swann as managing director and head, BioPharma Investment Banking in 2007. He had been managing director in investment banking at Cowen and Company after serving for many years as head of life science investment banking at Adams Harkness. Before he began his investment banking career in 2001, Dr. Gertler was director of the Surgical Intensive Care Unit at Yale New Haven Hospital (1986–87), and chief of vascular surgery at SUNY-HSCB in New York (1988–92). From 1992 to 2001, he was one of five vascular surgeons at the Massachusetts General Hospital in Boston and associate professor of surgery at Harvard University. Additionally, Dr. Gertler was associate director of the clinical and research vascular laboratories at the Massachusetts General Hospital. He is the author or coauthor of more than one hundred articles, abstracts, and chapters centered on clinical vascular surgery, vascular biology, and life science entrepreneurship. Dr. Gertler retains appointments at both the Massachusetts Institute of Technology and Harvard Medical School, where he is on the advisory board of the Biomedical Enterprise Program. Dr Gertler is a frequent lecturer on the financing of life science technologies as well as growth strategies for public and private biotechnology and medical technology companies and investors. From 1998 until 2001, in addition to his surgical and academic responsibilities, Dr. Gertler was a venture partner for Schroder Ventures Life Science Fund, one of the world's largest dedicated life sciences and healthcare private equity funds and was also the founding inventor and president of Cardiovascular Technologies. Dr. Gertler holds a BA from Wesleyan University, an MD from Columbia University College of Physicians and Surgeons, and an MBA in health policy and management from Boston University.

ROBERT HENDLER, MD, is vice president of clinical quality and chief medical officer of the Texas Region for Tenet Healthcare. He has been involved in quality initiatives, physician relations, technology assessment, and hospital/corporate operations since 1998. Prior to that, he was in active practice as a gastroenterologist for 20 years and was assistant clinical professor at University of Texas Southwestern Medical School for 15 years. As a vice president, he serves as a corporate medical consultant to other Tenet departments. As chief medical officer for Texas, he is responsible for promoting high-quality medical care through interactions with hospital medical staff, hospital administrative leadership, other regional leadership, and hospital staff in support of clinical quality initiatives throughout the Texas region. His research interests include relational coordination, high reliability, and quantification of healthcare processes.

DAVID I. KOVEL is chief operating officer and chief information officer at Sage Growth Partners. Over his career, he has served in leadership roles in a variety of healthcare delivery, service, and technology organizations, and he is recognized for his expertise in business process innovation, IT management, systems integration, data warehousing, and strategic architecture design. Mr. Kovel, a cofounder of Sage, is responsible for enterprise operating, transaction, and information systems. Prior to his role with Sage, Mr. Kovel was chief information officer for Lighthouse Risk Solutions; director of health services for IWIF, one of the largest workers' compensation insurers in the United States; lead data warehouse architect at Kaiser Permanente; and chief information officer for Ascendia Healthcare, Inc. Mr. Kovel is a member of the information technology faculty at the Johns Hopkins University. He is a member of the Healthcare Information and Management Systems Society, the Medical Group Management Association, and the Data Warehouse Institute. He received his bachelor of science in biochemistry from the University of Maryland, Baltimore County, and a master of information systems, also from the University of Maryland, Baltimore County.

LYNN JOHNSON LANGER is senior associate program chair for Advanced Biotechnology Studies at Johns Hopkins University. She develops curriculum and is responsible for the master of science in bioscience regulatory affairs, the joint degrees MS/MBA in biotechnology, the certificate in biotechnology enterprise, and the regulatory affairs and enterprise concentrations in the MS in biotechnology. She has published more than fifty articles, mainly in business areas of biotechnology, and has taught a variety of graduate courses in biotechnology and business. Prior to working and teaching at Johns Hopkins, she worked in senior marketing and management positions at several biotechnology organizations.

GREG MADONNA is a 777 pilot for a major U.S. airline and the founder and former practice leader of Mach One Leadership, Inc., which provides leadership and error management training to teams in high-risk industries. Mr. Madonna is an accomplished and sought-after teacher and public speaker, having delivered keynote addresses and instructed at Harvard Medical School, Royal Caribbean

Cruise Lines, the University of Miami, and the American College of Surgeons. His students have seen 50 percent reductions in human errors.

R. DONALD MCDANIEL Jr. is president and chief executive officer of Sage Growth Partners, LLC. He has played a leadership role in a variety of healthcare, insurance delivery, service, and technology organizations. Prior to his role with Sage Growth Partners, he was chief executive and general manager of Lighthouse Risk Solutions, a business unit of IWIF. Additionally, he has served as president, Integrated Solutions Group, Ascendia Healthcare Management, and vice president, Business Strategy, for Bon Secours Baltimore Health System. Prior to that, he was vice president, Managed Care Operations, for Liberty Medical Center in Baltimore, Maryland, and founder and partner of the Healthcare Consulting Group, a management and technology consulting firm. Mr. McDaniel served as chairperson of MedBank of Maryland, Inc., and is currently a director of Goodwill of the Chesapeake, Inc., and an advisory board member of Cura Management Technologies, LLC, a health technology and business process outsourcing firm. He is an advisory board member at the University of Baltimore's Merrick School of Business and a member of the faculty at Johns Hopkins University's Business of Medicine Program, where he teaches health economics.

JAYNE OLIVA, MBA, is founder and principal of the Croes•Oliva Group, a medical practice-management consulting firm that helps clients boost performance in the areas of profitability, productivity, patient access, and practice operations. Her work has been showcased in *Health and Hospital Networks, The Wall Street Journal,* and numerous other national and local publications. Ms. Oliva uses her twenty-plus years of experience to help senior administrators, physician leaders, and practice managers achieve performance improvements previously thought unattainable. In addition to her consulting work, she writes and teaches graduate-level practice management courses. Recent articles have appeared in *The Physician Executive* and *Group Practice Journal.* She frequently addresses hospital associations and physician organizations, including the Academic Practice Assembly, American College of Healthcare Executives, Connecticut Hospital Association, Governance Institute, Healthcare Financial Management Association, and Massachusetts Medical Society. Prior to founding the Croes•Oliva Group with partner Debi Croes, Ms. Oliva was vice president of a Boston-area hospital system, where she started a division of physician-practice support. At the Research and Educational Trust of the American Hospital Association, she was responsible for identifying and informing hospital leaders of emerging health trends and strategies. Ms. Oliva received her MBA from Northwestern University's Kellogg Graduate School of Management in Chicago and her BS from Boston University.

LINDSAY E. ROCKWELL, DO, is a hematologist/oncologist in private practice in Northampton, Massachusetts. She received her training in internal medicine and hematology/oncology through Tufts University's Baystate Medical Center in Springfield, Massachusetts. She received her doctorate in medicine from the

University of New England College of Osteopathic Medicine. She has been published in the *Journal of Clinical Oncology,* is actively involved in teaching and breast cancer research, and has a special interest in palliative care and end-of-life issues. Dr. Rockwell is coauthor of the forthcoming *In Defiance of Death: Exposing the Real Costs of End of Life Care* (Praeger, 2008).

KAREN RUBIN, MD, is medical director of the Division of Pediatric Diabetes and Endocrinology at Connecticut Children's Medical Center (CCMC), Connecticut's only freestanding children's hospital. CCMC is the home of the Department of Pediatrics at the University of Connecticut School of Medicine and the pediatric residency training program. Dr. Rubin is professor of pediatrics with a joint appointment as professor of ob-gyn, Division of Reproductive Endocrinology, at the University of Connecticut School of Medicine. Dr. Rubin's pediatric endocrine practice provides multidisciplinary team care to nearly 800 children and adolescents with type 1 diabetes. Dr. Rubin's clinical focus has been on the development of innovative models of care in the pediatric ambulatory care setting, including the outpatient management of diabetes and the transition of adolescents with complex chronic conditions from pediatric to adult care. She has spoken nationally on the topics of outpatient diabetes management and on transition from pediatric to adult care. She has authored papers that have appeared in the *Journal of Pediatric Endocrinology and Metabolism* and the *Journal of Pediatrics.* Recognition of her contributions to improving chronic disease care include the Humanitarian Award, Juvenile Diabetes and Research Foundation, 2003; Best Doctor, Hartford, 2005; and honoree, Women in History at the University of Connecticut Health Center, 2007.

CARL W. TAYLOR, JD, is the assistant dean of the University of South Alabama College of Medicine and director of the Center for Strategic Health Innovation. Under his direction, the Center for Strategic Health Innovation has won two innovator of the year awards for its work in patient-centric e-health strategies. He has received commendations from the U.S. Senate and the governor of Louisiana for deployment of software tools, advice, and training to support Hurricane Katrina relief. Mr. Taylor leads the team that created the Advanced Incident Management System and operates the Advanced Regional Response Training Center, a facility dedicated to training healthcare professionals to assume leadership roles in disaster response. A frequent speaker and e-health consultant, he also serves on the Health and Human Services Gulf Coast IT Task Force and cochairs its clinical adoption work group.

Index